Radical Pedagogy

Psychoanalysis, Education, and Social Transformation

Series Editors:

jan jagodzinski, University of Alberta
Mark Bracher, Kent State University

The purpose of this series is to develop and disseminate psychoanalytic knowledge that can help educators in their pursuit of three core functions of education:

1) facilitating student learning,
2) fostering students' personal development, and
3) promoting prosocial attitudes, habits, and behaviors in students (i.e., those opposed to violence, substance abuse, racism, sexism, homophobia, etc.).

Psychoanalysis can help educators realize these aims of education by providing them with important insights into:

1) the emotional and cognitive capacities that are necessary for students to be able to learn, develop, and engage in prosocial behavior,
2) the motivations that drive such learning, development, and behaviors, and
3) the motivations that produce antisocial behaviors as well as resistance to learning and development.

Such understanding can enable educators to develop pedagogical strategies and techniques to help students overcome psychological impediments to learning and development, either by identifying and removing the impediments or by helping students develop the ability to overcome them. Moreover, by offering an understanding of the motivations that cause some of our most severe social problems—including crime, violence, substance abuse, prejudice, and inequality—together with knowledge of how such motivations can be altered, books in this series will contribute to the reduction and prevention of such problems, a task that education is increasingly being called upon to assume.

Other books by Mark Bracher:

Being Form'd: Thinking through Blake's Milton
Lacan, Discourse, and Social Change: A Psychoanalytic Cultural Criticism
The Writing Cure: Psychoanalysis, Composition, and the Aims of Education

RADICAL PEDAGOGY

IDENTITY, GENERATIVITY, AND SOCIAL TRANSFORMATION

MARK BRACHER

RADICAL PEDAGOGY
© Mark Bracher, 2006.

First published in 2006 by
PALGRAVE MACMILLAN™
175 Fifth Avenue, New York, N.Y. 10010 and
Houndmills, Basingstoke, Hampshire, England RG21 6XS
Companies and representatives throughout the world.

PALGRAVE MACMILLAN is the global academic imprint of the Palgrave Macmillan division of St. Martin's Press, LLC and of Palgrave Macmillan Ltd. Macmillan® is a registered trademark in the United States, United Kingdom and other countries. Palgrave is a registered trademark in the European Union and other countries.

ISBN-13: 978–1–4039–7562–1
ISBN-10: 1–4039–7562–0

Library of Congress Cataloging-in-Publication Data

Bracher, Mark
    Radical pedagogy : identity, generativity, and social transformation / Mark Bracher.
        p. cm.—(Psychoanalysis, education, and social transformation)
    Includes bibliographical references and index.
        ISBN 1–4039–7562–0 (alk. paper)
        1. Critical pedagogy. 2. Identity (Psychology)—Social aspects.
    3. Education—Social aspects. I. Title. II. Series.

LC196.B73 2006
370.11′5—dc22   2006040867

A catalogue record for this book is available from the British Library.

Design by Newgen Imaging Systems (P) Ltd., Chennai, India.

First edition: October 2006

Transferred to Digital Printing 2007

In memory of my parents,
Gladys Bauer Bracher
(1919–2004)
and
Frederick Luther Bracher
(1917–1987)
Whose generativity inspires this book's pursuit
of identity, generativity, and social justice.

Part Four
Promoting Students'
Identity Development

ACKNOWLEDGMENTS

This book owes its existence to jan jagodzinski, whose invitations to contribute to his book *Pedagogical Desire* and to present a series of lectures and workshops at the University of Alberta in the spring of 2001 provided both stimulus and venue for the development of many of the ideas presented here, and whose creation of the series this volume inaugurates enabled their publication. Lynn Worsham, the award-winning editor of *JAC*, played an important role in encouraging the development of key portions of the book's literary pedagogy. Marshall Alcorn and Jeff Berman have provided invaluable encouragement and assistance over the years for this book and beyond. Thanks are also due to the Division of Research and Graduate Studies at Kent State University for providing various forms of support to facilitate the writing and publication of this book.

For permission to reprint previously published material I thank the following:

Greenwood Press, for "Identity and Desire in the Classroom." In *Pedagogical Desire: Authority, Seduction, Transference, and the Question of Authorial Ethics*, ed. jan jagodzinski. Westport, CT: Bergin & Garvey, 2002. 93–121.

The Ohio State University Press, for "Editor's Column: Psychoanalysis and Education." *JPCS: Journal for the Psychoanalysis of Culture & Society* 4, 2 (1999): 175–192.

College Literature, for "Transference, Desire, and the Ethics of Literary Pedagogy." *College Literature* 26, 3 (Fall 1999): 127–146.

JAC, for "Healing Trauma, Preventing Violence: A Radical Agenda for Literary Study." *JAC* 24, 3 (2004): 515–561.

PREFACE

The fundamental aim of education should be to support and develop students' identities, those configurations of self that provide us with vitality, agency, and meaning and give us a sense of ourselves as a force that matters in the world. Identity development has always been a function of education, but until recently it was often more of an implicit aim or an afterthought than the primary goal of educators. Recently, however, education theorists have increasingly been calling for identity development to be the central purpose of education. Chickering and Reisser state the case as follows in *Education and Identity*:

> In earlier eras, the principal task of education was "socialization," and the problem of individuals was to learn the attitudes, actions, and skills necessary for a satisfying and productive fit with "society." The symphony had a clearly stated theme and rhythm. The types and positions of the instruments were settled. To contribute, one had merely to choose a standard instrument, learn to play it, and practice the part. In the global society of the twenty-first century, where change is the only certainty, not socialization but identity formation becomes the central and continuing task of education. (Chickering and Reisser 208)

Chickering and Reisser advocate this focus on identity development largely because it will better allow students to effectively assume diverse roles in an unstable world. But there are also three other compelling reasons to make identity development the central goal of education, though these are not yet fully appreciated by educators because current understanding of identity is not well developed. The first is that a strong identity is a valuable and even essential basis for the development of intelligence and the capacity and motivation to learn. Second, identity development is crucial for personal well-being. And third, the increasing role of education as a means of solving social problems such as crime, violence, prejudice, and substance abuse mandates a focus on identity problems, which are key causes of these social problems.

refers, in reductive fashion, to certain high-profile group memberships such as race, class, gender, and sexual orientation. My first task is thus to sketch out a more comprehensive model of identity that will allow us to grasp how it motivates learning and resistance to learning and how it is also a key cause underlying many social problems. Drawing on a diverse body of work in psychoanalysis, cognitive science, and social psychology, this model of identity explains how identity maintenance is the ultimate motive for all behavior and identifies three interacting but distinct types of experience and memory—those of words, affects, and images—that constitute the substance of identity by producing one's sense of oneself.

Part two explains how teachers' identity needs motivate certain prominent pedagogical practices that do more to threaten the identities of many students than to support them and help them develop. In part three, acknowledging that we teachers therefore operate under an imperative that is at once ethical, practical, and self-enhancing to own and assume responsibility for the ways in which our identity needs drive and direct our teaching practices, I argue that an ongoing process of self-analysis can help us more fully recognize and more effectively enact the fundamental need that Erik Erikson found at the core of every identity: the need to teach, which means the need to help others develop their identities and the capacity to maintain them through prosocial action. And in the book's final part I provide an account of some basic pedagogical practices for promoting students' identity development, focusing primarily on literary study.

As the book's title indicates, the pedagogy proposed here is radical, in several senses. It is radical first in the etymological sense, in that it addresses the root causes of learning, intelligence, resistance to learning, and social problems. Such an approach, focusing on the roots of these phenomena, is also radical in the sense of unconventional, since root-cause interventions, particularly regarding social problems, have been marginalized for several decades now by political conservatives who want to maintain the status quo. Third, viewing identity development as a primary means of preventing violence in all its forms is also radical in the sense of unconventional in that identity development and violence prevention are not usually seen as legitimate aims of either education in general or literary study in particular, or as functions to which they can feasibly aspire. The basic argument of this book is that there is no more legitimate aim or feasible function for education than the development of students' identities, if the fundamental purposes of education are indeed to promote learning and understanding, foster intelligence, enhance our students' capacities for success and fulfillment, and contribute significantly to the general welfare.

PART ONE

IDENTITY, LEARNING PROBLEMS, AND SOCIAL PROBLEMS

CHAPTER 1

IDENTITY, MOTIVATION, AND RECOGNITION

Identity as the Prime Mover of Human Behavior

The first thing educators need to understand about identity is its importance as a motivating force. As the ground-breaking work of Heinz Lichtenstein and Norman Holland demonstrates, maintaining one's identity is the most basic human need and thus the ultimate motive underlying all human behavior, more fundamental than even homeostasis and the pleasure principle (Lichtenstein 59, 91, 98–99, 103, 115; Holland 75ff.). The Freudian drives—libido and aggression—are not ultimate motivating forces but manifestations of the effort to maintain identity, as are the superego and the repetition compulsion (Lichtenstein 24, 103, 116–117, 267, 274–278, 287). The sexual drive, Lichtenstein states, is not an end in itself but rather a means "to achieve an ecstatic climax of the sense of being" (41; see also 116, 270), and even the strongest of drives, including hunger, are less powerful motivators than identity, which "is absolutely compelling" (Lichtenstein 116). As James Gilligan puts it, "People will sacrifice anything to prevent the death and disintegration of their individual or group identity" (Gilligan, *Violence* 97).

Such claims, originally advanced on the basis of clinical observation, are now being substantiated by a growing body of experimental evidence supporting the conclusion that as the most basic motive the identity principle can be found at the root of all human behaviors, including political action (Hoover 8) and social problems such as "the alienation of our youth, the despair of the black minority, [and] the threat of violence that hangs over our world today" (Lichtenstein 278). One group of studies concerns the self-verification hypothesis, the idea that people's behavior is motivated by a continuous need to verify their identity—that is, to receive feedback demonstrating that they are the type of person they believe themselves to be—even if that identity is negative. Among various studies supporting this hypothesis are several showing that people with a low opinion of themselves prefer and

actually seek out negative feedback about themselves and also prefer being with people who will provide them with such feedback (see Swann et al.). Perhaps the most significant empirical demonstrations of the identity-maintenance motive come from studies in self-affirmation theory, developed by Claude Steele. This theory posits that a global "self-affirmation system" is activated whenever the self encounters any sort of threatening experience or information and that this system then directs either cognition or behavior in such a way as to restore the security of the self. In a series of experiments, Steele has studied the various ways people respond when their identities are either threatened or affirmed. He found that when people experience a threat to their identity, they will take various steps, depending on the means available, to reestablish its integrity. In one study, subjects were told that as members of their community they were either 1) uncooperative with community projects, 2) bad drivers, or 3) cooperative with community projects. Two days later these subjects, together with a fourth group that had not been previously contacted, were asked to assist in planning for a food co-op in their community by listing everything in their kitchens. Subjects whose identities had been impugned (threatened) in the initial contact as either uncooperative or bad drivers showed a rate of cooperation twice that of subjects whose identities had been reinforced by being told they were cooperative. Steele concludes from this and similar experiments that when our identity is threatened, we will make use of whatever means are available to reestablish its integrity. In some cases this may involve addressing the threat or repairing the threatened area of our identity, but in many cases the affirmation is of an aspect of identity unaffected by the threat, such as when subjects who were told they were bad drivers responded not by demonstrating their driving skills but by being more cooperative (Steele 374–375).

Another prominent body of empirical work demonstrating the fundamental nature and wide-ranging effects of the identity-maintenance motive is the one associated with terror management theory (TMT), developed by Pyszczynski, Greenberg, and Solomon. The guiding hypothesis of TMT is that "the most basic of all human motives is an instinctive desire for continued life, and that all more specific motives are ultimately rooted in this basic evolutionary adaptation" (Pyszczynski et al. 1). According to TMT, "the self-preservation instinct—the goal of staying alive—is the superordinate goal toward which all behavior is oriented," including the pursuit of meaning and value, which "is just as surely linked to self-preservation as are hunting and food gathering" (Pyszczynski et al. 5). TMT assumes that self-preservation means avoiding death and hypothesizes that the threat of death will motivate people to invest in various symbolic forms of immortality, such as their cultural worldview and group identity. These hypotheses are confirmed by a series of experiments showing that reminding people of death leads them

to greater conformity with the standards of their culture, to more positive assessments of others who share or praise their cultural values, and to more negative assessments of outgroup members and of people who criticize or violate their values (Pyszczynski et al. 4). While Pyszczynski and his colleagues argue that fear of death is the primary motive, they acknowledge that their findings just as easily support the view being advanced here, that identity maintenance is primary: "It could certainly be argued that people fear death because death implies the dissolution of self, that fear of biological death is rooted in a fear of the loss of one's identity" (Pyszczynski et al. 12). And there is one compelling fact that would seem to tip the balance in favor of our view: the fact that people will sacrifice their lives in order to defend or restore their identity. As Marshall Alcorn points out, people are often more willing to risk biological death than ideological death, the death of their identity or sense of self (Alcorn, *Changing* 14, 18).

Identity and Learning

As the prime motivator of human behavior, identity affects learning in three general ways. That learning, like all other behavior, is motivated by the effort to maintain and enhance identity means, first, that for learning to occur, either the process or the anticipated result of learning must provide support for identity in some way. Such support can be in the form of either recognition or the opportunity to enact certain identity contents. When one enacts and/or is recognized as possessing these identity contents—the nature of which will be discussed shortly—one experiences identity, the sense of oneself as a force that matters in the world.

The need to maintain identity can also interfere with learning, in two ways. First, the motivation to learn can be lacking when students are able to get all the identity support they need from sources other than education with less effort or with fewer threats to identity. Such learning-undermining effects of identity can be seen in the cases of students whose athletic prowess, physical attractiveness, social fluency, and/or family wealth provides them with all the recognition and opportunities for identity enactment that they need in order to sustain a strong sense of self, with the result that they lack motivation to learn and so take little interest in the subject matter of their courses.

Second and even more problematic is the fact that even when students do experience learning as providing some identity support, they often experience it as more threatening than supportive of their identities and thus resist learning, often with great vigor and effectiveness. As we will see, learning can threaten students' identities in numerous ways, most of which are invisible to educators and students alike.

Identity Vulnerability at the Root
of Social Problems

The fundamental need to maintain one's identity is also a root cause of some of our most serious social problems, including crime, violence, terrorism, prejudice, substance abuse, and more. Research on each of these problems points to identity as the prime motivator of the behavior that constitutes the problem in each instance. Each problematic behavior, that is, functions in one or more ways to enact, defend, and/or elicit recognition for some aspect of the perpetrator's identity.

In addition to motivating the respective behaviors constituting each of these social problems, identity needs are also responsible for the ineffective and even counterproductive social practices, policies, and institutions through which our society attempts to combat these problems. That is, policies such as our War on Crime, War on Drugs, and War on Terrorism function primarily to bolster the identities of us "good, law-abiding citizens" by demonizing the perpetrators and thus establishing them as suitable receptacles for the externalization of our own aggressive and even murderous impulses that our identities are too fragile or constricted to incorporate. This need for identity-protecting scapegoats is so great that it motivates punitive social attitudes and policies regarding not only violent offenders but also individuals and groups who are themselves the victims of misfortune and injustice, such as the poor, the homeless, the unemployed, the uninsured, and racial, ethnic, religious, and sexual minorities.

The Nature of Identity

To enhance learning and reduce our most serious social problems, it is thus crucial that educators, policymakers, and the general public come to understand more fully the nature of identity and its needs and the way these needs motivate both learning and the failure to learn and also contribute to our social problems. What, then, is identity, and how does it affect learning and social behaviors? In most disciplines that concern themselves with identity—including education, psychology, sociology, and the humanities—it is usually equated with a person's membership in certain key social groups, such as race, ethnicity, gender, sexual orientation, social class, nationality, and perhaps age and religion. I mean something different by identity, however. In my usage, which follows that of Erikson and Lichtenstein, the term means, minimally, one's sense of oneself and, more comprehensively, the sense of oneself as a force that matters in the world.

Having a sense of oneself as a force that matters in the world involves the experience of several distinct qualities, including continuity, consistency, agency, distinction, belonging, and meaning. Each of these qualities has been

taken by certain psychologists to be the prime motivator of human behavior, and with good reason: each can, when an individual experiences it as deficient, become the focal point of the individual's behavior. However, unless all the other qualities are experienced as well, achieving just one or several of them is inadequate to sustain a person. Rather than being separate motives, each of these qualities is in fact a crucial feature of identity, and when we appear to seek one of these qualities as an end in itself, what we are actually doing, as Claude Steele's work suggests (376), is attempting to enact an essential aspect of our identity. Continuity, for example, is the sense of oneself as an enduring force that persists, or has a certain permanence. Consistency is essential to identity because in its absence, a person is more than one thing and hence not anything at all. Distinction is crucial for identity because it is one's sense of delimitation or separation from otherness that establishes one's boundaries and thus defines one. Connection with others is also necessary, because one's sense of self is a function of one's experienced effects on otherness: without at least a rudimentary effect on otherness, there is no evidence that the self exists. The same is true of agency, which is experienced when we receive feedback from the world demonstrating that we have had an effect on it. Meaning is the experience of significance that one receives from the multiple dimensions of interrelationship with otherness enacted by the other features of identity.

The key question for educators, then, is what is necessary in order to have an adequate sense of oneself, and how does the attempt to produce and maintain such a sense manifest itself in human behavior, particularly in education and in social problems?

Recognition as a Basic Human Need

The most fundamental identity need is the need for recognition, the need to have one's being appreciated and validated, or at least acknowledged, taken into account, by others: "Fundamentally, elementally, and basically, one wants to be recognized" (Tingle 110). As the philosopher Charles Taylor states, "our identity requires recognition by others" (45). As a prerequisite for identity, recognition functions as a fundamental and universal motivator in its own right, a fact recognized by philosophers such as Adam Smith, Rousseau, and Hegel, among others (see Todorov 10–26). The attainment of recognition, according to Smith, is "the most ardent desire of human nature" (qtd. in Todorov 15), and Todorov concludes that "there is no price we are not prepared to pay to obtain it. . . . The need to be acknowledged is not just one human motivation among others; it is the truth behind all other needs" (15–16). Even wealth and material possessions "are not an end in themselves but a way for us to be assured of the recognition of others" (16). The absence of recognition is, correspondingly, "the worst evil that could befall us" (15).

Because the need for recognition is so fundamental, people often devote considerable energy to eliciting and controlling recognition from others. This effort is such a prominent dimension of human behavior that an entire subfield of social psychology is devoted to it, under the names of impression management and self-presentation. Research in this field has found that when people's identity is threatened, they often go out of their way to elicit positive responses from others, such that "self-presentational motives underlie and pervade nearly every corner of interpersonal life" (Leary xiii). This effort takes the form of various strategies of self-presentation, most of which are employed, for example, by most candidates for public office. One common strategy is self-description. Not only in campaign speeches but also in situations such as first dates, job interviews, and conversations with strangers on an airplane, people often state quite explicitly their characteristics, attitudes, social roles, backgrounds, and future plans (Leary 17–18). The expression of attitudes can be particularly significant in influencing others' opinions of us, particularly when those attitudes involve socially contentious issues such as abortion, affirmative action, or gay marriage. Attitudes can be expressed not only explicitly but also tacitly, through facial expressions and body language (Leary 20). A basic reason for such self-description and expression is to elicit recognition and hence validation from others.

Motivating and Interfering with Learning

These efforts can both motivate and interfere with both learning and teaching. It is not unusual for learning, especially among younger students, to derive from the effort to present oneself as smart, knowledgeable, or good and thus impress one's teacher and/or one's classmates. Most teachers, similarly, are at least partially motivated by their desire to impress their students, their peers, their supervisors, and/or their own teachers, as we will see in chapter 6.

Self-presentation and impression-management efforts can also interfere with both teaching and learning, such as when they produce self-disclosures or expressions of attitude that are tangential or total non sequiturs to the topic or process of learning. One way to avoid such interferences and at the same time support students' identities and thus enable their learning is to provide opportunities for them to engage in self-description and expression of attitudes as part of the learning process. These opportunities can be made available in class discussions, in small-group discussions, in individual conferences, and in writing assignments. Whenever their expression of attitudes, opinions, and other personal qualities is met with attention and respect, students experience identity support and are more receptive to new (and hence potentially identity-threatening) knowledge and understanding and also experience less need to pursue recognition in ways that interfere with rather than support the learning process.

Self-serving attributions of causes and responsibility for events and conditions also function to manage the impressions that others—including the internalized others that constitute our superegos—have of us. Thus if we fail at a task or fall short of certain standards, we often try to give the impression that the shortcoming was caused by factors beyond our control—for example, we explain that we were late for a meeting because of unusually heavy traffic rather than poor time management on our part. Similarly, when things go well for us, we may take various steps to create the impression that the success was due primarily not to chance or special treatment but to our virtuous character or hard work (Leary 21). In education, such self-serving attribution often impedes the acquisition of knowledge and understanding concerning one's various identity groups and any social, cultural, political, historical, or economic events in which one of them is implicated. For example, when their own group engages in violence, people see the action as justified by some form of provocation by the other party, but when their group is the victim of violence, people perceive themselves to be innocent of all provocation and attribute all the blame to the other party, which is seen as the aggressor. In such instances self-serving attributions produce egregious misunderstandings of people and events, which often lead in turn to enthusiasm for unjustified and self-destructive group actions—a result that can, unfortunately, be observed in much U. S. foreign and domestic policy, including our various wars on drugs, crime, and terrorism.

We also use various nonverbal behaviors to produce impressions. The expression of emotion, for instance, is often amplified, muted, totally suppressed, or even totally contrived in order to give the impression that we are kind, sensitive, daring, or tough. Personal appearance—clothing, hairstyle, body shape and weight—are variously selected, regulated, or disguised in order to produce a favorable impression. Similarly, posture, gesture, movement, gaze, and vocal tone are often carefully managed to make the desired impact. We also use personal possessions (houses, cars), social relations (connections with famous or powerful individuals, or associations with successful sports teams), and other behaviors (eating, athletic activity, risk-taking, teamwork) to elicit the sort of recognition we desire (see Leary 25–36).

Each form of recognition can either support or interfere with learning. When students seek recognition as being "a good student" or "intelligent" and such recognition is not received, they may feel depressed, anxious, or angry and as a result be less effective in their learning, or pursue noneducational means of achieving recognition. The motivational force of recognition is also frequently undercut by other sources—such as peers, family, and ethnic culture—providing recognition for attributes (such as anti-intellectualism) that oppose educational activities such as knowing, learning, reading, writing, and reflecting. In fact, such recognition is the strongest form available for many students, especially in high school, as is evident in the prestige accorded to students (especially girls) who are physically attractive and to students (especially boys) with athletic prowess. The pursuit of such recognition obviously can interfere in multiple ways with learning. We need only consider the amount of time some students spend maintaining their appearance (hair, complexion, muscle tone, clothes), developing and performing their athletic abilities, and/or attending athletic events to realize what a serious competitor recognition of bodily attributes is to recognition of psychological qualities, cognitive abilities, and educational achievement.

One particularly powerful form of recognition is involuntary attraction to a person's charm, charisma, sex appeal, or animal magnetism. This is the form of recognition being offered, for example, in ads for perfume or cologne that promise to drive the other wild with passion. Some students and teachers pursue such recognition, as is made evident when they dress or behave in sexually provocative ways. While this recognition may in some instances support education by sparking greater mutual interest between students or between teachers and students, its pursuit can also be quite disruptive to both teachers and students, both socially and psychologically.

An even greater impediment to learning comes in the form of recognition for what Erikson called negative identity, a sense of self based on antisocial values, attitudes, and behaviors. People resort to negative identities when they are unable to elicit adequate recognition for benign qualities, in which case they may turn to aggression in order to elicit involuntary recognition of malignant qualities. Such is often the dynamic behind the various forms of aggression that students manifest. Recognition in the form of disapprobation positions one as what Lacanian psychoanalytic theory refers to as the object *a*, a factor that is excluded from the social-symbolic order in general, or from a specific system (such as the education system, a knowledge system, the economic system, or the system of morality or propriety). Such negative identities can be observed in students who seek to be recognized as one who resists, transgresses, undermines, or disrupts the classroom, disciplinary paradigms, professional protocols, or the social order in general. A well-known instance is the "trenchcoat mafia" of Columbine High School, a group that was composed of students who were excluded from the dominant system ruled by jocks and preppies.

From a certain perspective, such negative qualities and disruptive forces can be seen as positive: elements that, though excluded by the system, are nonetheless extremely valuable for the system, or elements that might constitute the core around which a new system could be constructed. Thus a contrary student may desire to be recognized by his peers as a vital force that enlivens the classroom and rescues learning and thinking from a moribund system. While such forms of recognition can be an impediment to education, they can also provide motivation to learn in cases where the system itself does not, or motivation to acquire knowledge that the system ignores or excludes.

Besides the direct, voluntary, and explicit recognition from other people, there is also indirect, tacit, and/or involuntary recognition, including recognition from the Real itself rather than from a person. Such recognition is sometimes preferred to direct, voluntary, explicit recognition because one realizes that the latter can be faked or unwarranted. Thus teachers who suspect that praise from a student is insincere may desire instead or in addition the tacit and involuntary recognition of being a "good teacher" that is provided by the reality of the student's learning and growth. And most teachers would prefer the tacit recognition of their worth in the form of respectable salaries and benefits to the express praise of politicians and taxpayers who often refuse to pay teachers what they are worth even while occasionally paying lip service to their indispensability. Similarly, in addition to or instead of the teacher's explicit praise, students desire the tacit, indirect recognition of being a "good student" or being "intelligent" that is provided by the teacher's respect and trust, by good grades, or by the reality of enhanced knowledge, skills, performance, or well being.

Social Problems

The need for recognition is also a prime motivator behind various social problems, such as crime, violence, substance abuse, and teen pregnancy. As Erich Fromm explains, crime can be an excellent means of recognition, or "narcissistic gratification":

> [An important motive] in crime causation and development is the gratification of narcissistic needs. The particular strength of such needs is . . . rooted in individual development. With the proletarian, however, often the problem is not the particular strength of these needs, but rather a form of narcissistic "malnutrition." It is quite clear that the propertied person—in addition to the possibilities of gratification that can be purchased directly, such as beautiful clothes, good food, beautiful houses, etc.—has far greater opportunities for narcissistic gratification than does the propertyless one. . . . A member of the subordinate class experiences a repetition of the narcissistic humiliation that he received as a child. Crime offers far-reaching gratifications—being named in the news, appearing in court, the attention of so many people who otherwise would not care about him. (138–139)

UCLA sociologist Jack Katz found the need for recognition to be a significant motive in the criminal activity of many of the criminals he interviewed.

One youthful shoplifter declared, "What kept running through my mind was this idea of a self-centeredness. I felt like everyone was watching me, following me and like the whole store was at a stand still just concentrating on my next move" (Katz 72).

Much interpersonal and intergroup violence is also motivated by the need for recognition as a means of identity support, as John Burton explains:

> Empirical evidence suggests that a paramount need being satisfied by the violent is the need for recognition as an individual or group. Individuals in society have always employed whatever means are currently available to them to attain recognition and identity. These means include the now widespread frustration responses of young people who have no ordinary means of attaining a role in society. Typical responses include leaving home and school, joining street gangs, and enacting roles of violence at community and ethnic levels that attract attention and provide some individual recognition. Membership of a street gang and carrying a gun, where one is available, as in the United States, is a practical solution to a lack of personal identity. . . . Specific problems, such as family violence, aggressive street gangs, ethnic conflict, secession movements and others, are merely symptoms of this underlying condition. . . . Denial by society of personal recognition and identity leads, at all social levels, to alternative behaviours ranging from participation in street gangs, to dictatorial leadership, to terrorism. . . . [P]roblems of violence can be traced to the pursuit of human needs of recognition and identity. (Burton 10, 19–20, 31)

One of the attractions of substance abuse for some users is its provision of recognition, the reactions of others that affirm one's identity:

> Apart from just meeting others, the user can become part of the subculture, part of a local group of young people. There is the comforting feeling of belonging. . . . The user's identity is affected by being part of the subculture. Belonging to any group is likely to have an effect on its members and a person's identity is largely determined through personal interaction, through the reactions of others. (Lockley 48–49)

The need for recognition is also a powerful motivation for a young girl to become pregnant. A pregnant girl and a girl with a baby elicit much more frequent, sincere, and intense attention from family, friends, and even strangers than does a girl without a baby who is not pregnant. "I like it when people notice I'm having a baby," one pregnant teenager told an interviewer. "It gives me a good feeling inside and makes me feel important" (qtd. in Musick 109). Reporter Leon Dash concluded from his interviews with teen mothers that "while the better students strove for a diploma, the poorer students achieved their form of recognition with a baby" (10).

Enacting Identity Elements

Recognition can by itself provide identity support: being praised or acknowledged for no particular qualities can be quite sustaining, as proponents of unconditional love have insisted. But when recognition is arbitrary or without justification, it often loses its sustaining quality and hence its motivating force. This is a danger to which the emphasis on bolstering students' self-esteem can easily succumb. Enactment of one's identity, in contrast to recognition in the normal sense, provides tacit but objective and hence irrefutable evidence of one's identity—that is, of the sense of oneself as a force that matters in the world. In addition, when one enacts or embodies a particular quality such as intelligence or honesty that one takes to be part of one's identity, such an enactment or embodiment helps to sustain one's identity whether anyone else is aware of it or not. The reason is that whenever one enacts an identity-bearing quality, one receives a silent but potentially powerful recognition from the generalized other that one has internalized (an internalization that Freud named the superego).

The question, then, is what exactly gets enacted, how is it enacted, and what are the implications for education and for social transformation? What get enacted are the elements of identity, which are of three basic types: affects, images, and words. Recent work in neurology and cognitive psychology, as well as longstanding tenets of Lacanian psychoanalytic theory, indicate that identity is produced by the continual reiteration of specific self-states in three different registers, which I will refer to as the affective-physiological, the imagistic, and the linguistic orders. The neurologist Antonio Damasio has argued that our sense of self is based on a proto-self composed of rapid pulse-like (unconscious) neurological mappings of our organism's condition, including the current state of our viscera, our skeletal musculature, and our skin. On the basis of this physiological experience, a core self is constituted by re-representing in imagistic form these body aspects in relation to the (internal and external) objects that give rise to their state at each particular moment. This continuous representation of our body is what accounts for our sense of sameness and continuity of self that is sustained through great changes that we undergo both across our life span and sometimes even moment to moment: because our body's basic design and its central systems and organs endure throughout life, the representations of these systems that constitute our core identity or sense of self remain the same as well (Damasio 22–23, 125–153). Our extended identity, or full sense of self, is established as some of these physiological and imagistic experiences are given verbal form and then inscribed as memories in three interlinked registers (physiological, imagistic, and verbal).[1]

The psychoanalytically oriented cognitive psychologist Wilma Bucci has arrived at similar conclusions. Drawing on various branches of cognitive science, Bucci too identifies three fundamental registers of experience and memory, registers that she conceives of as codes. The most basic order of experience and memory is a function of subsymbolic codes, which produce experiences such as tastes, odors, visceral sensations, and affects. Such experiences occur along a continuum rather than in discrete elements or categories and are processed simultaneously in multiple parallel channels, rather than sequentially, along a hierarchical chain of command, as is the case with the other two codes. In the subsymbolic register, our sense of self resides primarily in the realm of affects, which as Bucci observes "are particularly well suited to contribute to the continuing sense of a core self" (150), since an individual's experiences and expressions of core affects are relatively unchanging throughout life.

The second register of experience and memory is a function of imagistic codes. In this register, the "continua and flows" of affective-physiological experience are "chunked" into discrete perceptual categories that we experience as images (Bucci 111, 118, 181). Stable, prototypic images of both our external and our internal worlds must be formed, Bucci observes, in order for us to have a relatively stable and continuous sense of our own bodies (121), or body ego. In the imagistic register, then, identity is the sense of oneself as "a single, coherent, bounded physical entity" (Stern 82) that results from repeated experiences and memories of prototypic images of one's bodily form and agency, and of the specific spaces, places, and objects in relation to which this form and agency are optimally enacted.

The third register of experience and memory is composed of linguistic or verbal codes. Bucci notes that verbal codes are also indispensable to our sense of self. In particular, language constitutes the optimal mode for both organizing and directing the self, and for communicating with others (142, 217).

In the field of psychoanalysis, the three registers of identity are prominently identified in Lacanian theory as the Real, the Imaginary, and the Symbolic, which have certain affinities, respectively, to the id, ego, and ego ideal of Freudian theory (see Samuels). Although many Lacanians are reluctant to use the word identity and prefer to emphasize intrapsychic disruption and difference and ignore continuity and sameness, Lacan's accounts of the activities of these three registers point clearly to the homeostatic, repetitive function of each: the drives of the Real, the unified body image of the Imaginary, and the master signifiers and ossified knowledge systems of the Symbolic order all function, both individually and conjointly (in the form of what Lacan called a "Borromean knot"), to continuously reiterate the momentary states of the individual subject and to thus produce a fundamental sense of sameness and continuity through time that is unmistakable to both the individuals themselves and to others who know them.

If identity, or one's sense of self, is thus a function of the continual (re)activation of certain states in three different registers of the mind/brain, and if identity maintenance is the fundamental motivation underlying all behavior, then it follows that the fundamental motive is to enact one's identity-bearing states in each register. How, then, does this process manifest itself in behavior? What do these different states look like, and where can we see them being enacted in learning, resistance to learning, and other problematic behaviours?

of one's own religion, for instance, may produce knowledge of internal contradictions in one's belief system, of conflicts between the beliefs and one's experience or knowledge of reality, or of contradictions between the religion's central values and some of its basic practices. Similarly, study of one's favorite music, movies, television programs, or video games may lead to the knowledge that one's own enjoyments and impulses engaged by the entertainment are antithetical to some of the core values or ideal attributes constituting one's identity. For example, students who experience themselves as intelligent, perceptive, knowledgeable, savvy, or streetwise will have their claim to these signifiers undermined by knowledge of how their favorite movies or television shows manipulate their desires, enjoyments, and aversions in ways that hoodwink them. And students who experience themselves as fair, just, egalitarian, kind, loving, gentle, or peaceful may be deprived of these identity-bearing signifiers by knowledge of how their favorite cultural pleasures are implicated in perpetrating aggression or injustice. As a result, students often resist such knowledge, or, if they do take it in, they may hold it in isolation rather than integrating it and altering their cognitive maps of self and world.

Sometimes the threat to students' identity-bearing signifiers comes not from the content of learning but rather from the process of learning. Some students feel that the effort required to learn threatens to deprive them of signifiers such as "smart," "intelligent," or "brilliant." Students who view themselves as inherently superior or fortunate may feel their identity threatened if they have to exert themselves in order to learn. Klein describes the case of "an intelligent 17-year-old boy" who studied only at the last minute before exams and thus performed below his potential. The reason for such behavior, Klein reports, was that the boy "felt that almost anyone could get good marks if he studied hard. . . . He insisted that if he had only studied a little he would surely have gotten all *As*. He felt contempt for the pupils who studied regularly and got high grades. They were only dullards who worked hard, he said scornfully" (371).

Other students may avoid effort because their identity-bearing signifiers would be severely compromised by *failure* of the effort, which would demonstrate that they were not really "intelligent," "brilliant," or "superior." Students employ various strategies to defend against such a result, and virtually all of them impede learning. Often students defend against the identity-eroding effects of poor academic performance by rationalizing it and thus preventing their identity from being implicated by their performance. One type of rationalization criticizes the validity of the test, thus denying that it fairly or accurately evaluates their academic identity. As Hoyle and his colleagues note, "We regularly see this phenomenon in college classrooms when students receive exam grades. Students who receive a high grade think that the test was a fair and valid measure of their knowledge; those who do poorly find innumerable problems with the exam" (Hoyle et al. 104).

Another form of rationalization, the sour-grapes response, is more insidious, for it can lead to the renunciation of learning as an important component of identity. The sour grapes defense involves denying not the validity of an exam but rather the importance of a good grade. As Hoyle and his colleagues observe, "If we convince ourselves that the outcome we failed to attain was not really important or desirable to us, then we will not feel as bad about ourselves for failing to get it" (Hoyle et al. 103). Students also engage in "preemptive sour-grapes rationalization," or "defensive pessimism," which involves anticipating a negative outcome so that however bad the reality is, it will not be worse than one's expectations: "If the student can convince himself that he does not really aspire to an A, his self-esteem will be less affected if he receives a C" (Hoyle et al. 111).

In addition to leading students actually to care less about academic achievement and thus reduce their effort to learn, threats to their identity-bearing signifiers can initiate another defense that undermines learning even further—namely, the divestiture of those identity-bearing signifiers that are being threatened. That is, students whose academic performance is not strong enough to garner adequate recognition for identity-bearing signifiers such as "smart" or "a good student" may divest themselves of these academically essential identity contents, ceasing to identify themselves as, and hence to care about being, "smart," "a good student," and so on. This defense often goes hand-in-hand with compensatory self-affirmation, which involves investing more heavily in other (in this case nonacademic) identity contents for which enactment and recognition are more secure (see Hoyle et al. 106). Thus, "the student who fails a test may think about what a successful athlete she is" (Hoyle et al. 106) and eventually come to gain adequate identity support from being an athlete, thus rendering learning and academic achievement unnecessary.

Another defense of identity-bearing signifiers that undermines learning is self-serving attribution, which involves deflecting responsibility from oneself for events that negatively implicate one's identity. Hoyle and associates note that students often claim credit for good test grades but deny responsibility for bad ones. "When asked *why* they performed as they did, participants [in an experiment] who thought they did poorly are inclined to point to factors that absolve them of responsibility for the failure" (Hoyle et al. 102). In some cases, students who anticipate a possible poor performance engage in "preemptive self-serving attributions," or "self-handicapping":

> Even before knowing how they performed on a test (or even before taking the test, for that matter), students who are worried about their grade may think

about all of the things that are working against them: There is too much material on the test, the professor's tests are always unfair, I haven't felt well for several days, I had two other tests this week, and so on. . . . People seem particularly inclined to dredge up these excuses prior to a possible threat to their self-esteem. Should the dreaded failure occur, they are already armed with an arsenal of self-serving explanations. (Hoyle et al. 108)

Some students not only invoke but actually create obstacles to optimal performance in order to preserve their identity-bearing signifiers ("smart," "intelligent," "brilliant") by providing themselves with objective and irrefutable external causes for their failure (see Hoyle et al. 109). Examples include procrastination, overcommitment, and poor time management, whereby students arrange things so that they must rush to write a paper the night before it is due or are unable to find adequate time to study for a test, such that any degree of failure can be attributed to lack of time rather than to the fact that they are not "intelligent" or "smart." The detrimental consequences of such defenses for learning are obvious.

Sometimes, when students cannot rationalize their poor performance or shield their identity-bearing signifiers from being undermined by it, they seek to maintain their hold on these signifiers through downward social comparison or relationship management, both of which can further undermine learning. Downward social comparison is a tactic whereby people support their identity by comparing themselves to others who are inferior to them in a significant way. Students frequently use this method, comparing their academic performances, achievements, and prowess to those of others who are equal or inferior to them.[1] In doing so, they lower the standards for being "smart" or "brilliant" and thus potentially undermine their motivation to work hard to achieve all that they are capable of. In addition, downward social comparison can lead to relationship management, which can involve either excluding from one's circle of friends individuals who surpass one's own level of achievement, or, alternatively, abandoning one's own pursuit of excellence in order to maintain relationships with friends who would otherwise abandon one in pursuit of their own downward comparisons (Hoyle et al. 112–113). The latter strategy can be observed in those intelligent minority students, who, for fear of being perceived by their peers as race traitors, reduce their efforts and levels of accomplishment.

Social Problems

The behavior constituting various social problems, including crime, violence, substance abuse, prejudice, and teen pregnancy, is also motivated by the need to defend and enact one's identity-bearing signifiers. Researchers have observed that the crimes tend to enact the perpetrator's gender identity, with men committing more crimes of aggression and transgression and women committing more low-level property crimes, such as theft of cosmetic items or of things for their children (Radosh 65–67; Katz 71). Katz found that much of the crime committed by men functioned to enact not only the identity-bearing signifier "man" but also other, hypermasculine signifiers such as "bad-ass" and "hardman" (88ff., 227). Katz's research revealed that individuals who make a career of robbery do so in order to enact the identity of a "hardman" (196), which is a "formally evil identity" (Katz 227) and an excellent example of Erikson's "negative identity." "Being a hardman," Katz concludes, "is not simply lived as a dispensable tool; rather, it is an organizing theme in the lives of those who stick with stickup" (227). Such career robbers "find local audiences who enthusiastically celebrate the hardman's identity. . . . [A]ll eye movements are either toward or away from him. For everyone his identity becomes what the moment is about" (Katz 231–234).

Violent men are even more frequently motivated by the need to enact and defend their identity as a "man." James Gilligan, a Harvard psychiatrist and former head of mental health for the Massachusetts state prison system, found that virtually all the violent behavior of violent criminals is motivated by the need to establish and maintain their identity as a man, which they experience as having been threatened or destroyed either by external circumstances or by their own inner, "unmasculine" qualities. Gilligan found, for example, that one man's brutal murder and mutilation of a former high school classmate after she gave him a ride in her car was motivated by the man's desperate effort to reclaim his identity as a "man," an identity that his own lack of a car and his consequent dependence on a woman with a car had stripped him of. Gilligan explains that "mechanical expertise with cars was important to him, as it is to many teenage males, as a means of proving his adequacy as a man. . . . He committed his crime when he was without a car," a situation that made him feel less a man and that aggravated his chronic sense of his inadequacy as a "man" (*Violence* 63). Another murderer that Gilligan studied had committed his crime in an effort to deny his passive, dependent qualities, which manifested themselves in the wish to live with his mother and have her take care of him. Committing the murder allowed him to behave "in a way that was active, independent, powerful, and aggressive, . . . [thus wiping] out the opposite image of himself as passive, dependent, impotent, and needing love and care"—that is, as not a "man" (*Violence* 82).

A similar dynamic underlies much prejudice and group hatred. Misogynistic and homophobic men, for example, use their antipathy, and sometimes violence, toward women and gay men as a means of demonstrating to themselves and others that they are "men" and thus overriding their own "feminine" and homoerotic impulses and characteristics.

Substance abuse is also frequently motivated by the need to support one's identity-bearing signifiers. Being an "addict" constitutes a linguistic identity, and for some addicts, Lockley believes, "the identity as a junkie might be a positive term, and this might well be the case for those who are either trying to find some identity or have a very low opinion of themselves (49; see also Zinberg 151).

Teen pregnancy, too, is often motivated by the need to acquire and maintain an identity through enacting powerful identity-bearing signifiers. In this case the signifiers are "woman" and "mother." As Dash observes, having a baby "is one way of announcing: I *am* a woman" (Dash 9). Having a baby also gives an identity-depleted girl the powerful identity-bearing signifier "mother":

> At the developmental crossroads of adolescence, when everything in her life seems up in the air, in an environment that offers no chance to explore other options, no other models or avenues out, motherhood promises a path to personhood, a path to her own place in the world. Having a baby means the adolescent no longer need wonder who she is: she knows—she is a mother. (Musick 70)

For some girls, Musick concludes, motherhood is "the only identity imaginable" (Musick 140).

Identity-Bearing Knowledge and Beliefs

Resistance to Learning

The enactment, expansion, and defense of one's identity-bearing knowledge and belief systems also constitute a major impetus for both learning and resistance to learning. When students encounter information that supports or enhances their identity, they welcome it and often pursue it with greater energy and commitment than they do more neutral knowledge. Conversely, when students encounter knowledge that threatens their beliefs—such as evidence supporting the theory of evolution rather than the biblical story of creation, or accounts of the atrocities committed by Columbus or of the evils of capitalism or American foreign policy—they often vigorously resist such knowledge in order to preserve their identity-bearing beliefs. As Marshall Alcorn observes,

> [S]ome modes of discourse . . . function to constitute the subject's sense of identity. . . . Something within a subject operates to preserve and maintain a characteristic identity. This mechanism . . . prompts subjects to actively challenge rather than passively internalize the discourse they are given. . . . In some cases, student responses to oppositional political discourse can be quite

extreme. They perceive such discourse . . . as an act of political terrorism; . . . they are assassinated as subjects by a discourse that purports to be educational. What is at stake for them in such discourse is simply survival. . . .[M]any subjects would prefer to be biologically dead than to exist as different subjects of discourse. (*Changing* 16–18)

The new knowledge students encounter thus inevitably either supports or threatens their identity. Indeed, as Nick Tingle points out, the very act of reading does so: "When one reads, one's thoughts are modified. These modifications may act psychologically in one of two basic ways. They may affirm the reader in his or her sense of who he or she is and thus prove narcissistically stabilizing, or they may seem not to affirm the self of the reader and thus be experienced as destabilizing" (85–86). For university students, some degree of identity destabilization is thus almost inevitable, especially in classes where critical thinking is required:

Ideas, thoughts, beliefs, and the massive realm of common sense all may act for individuals as stabilizing selfobjects, as things taken as existing in the world, that affirm and give substance to a particular psychological configuration of self. Questioning these objects can and frequently does destabilize the self. This destabilization is central to the developmental move enjoined by the university: to question, to doubt, to look critically at all that one thought one knew and took for granted. (Tingle 9)

A major problem for educators is thus how to help students protect their threatened identities in ways other than resisting the identity-threatening knowledge. For as Deborah Britzman observes, defense against threatening new knowledge can produce not only a failure to learn but in some cases even a "hatred in having to learn" (115). Studies by self-affirmation theorists substantiate this observation, demonstrating that beliefs that are components of one's identity are defended by resisting any information or arguments that threaten to disconfirm them (Cohen et al. 1161). Thus students who support capital punishment often persist in believing that the death penalty deters crime even though studies have shown that it does not (Cohen et al. 1151), and those who oppose gays in the military are more resistant to contrary messages the more central this attitude is to their identity (Zuwerink and Devine 941). Psychologists have concluded that "evidence that challenges the validity of such cherished beliefs presents a self-threat insofar as giving up that belief would entail losing a source of esteem or identity. To neutralize that threat, people are apt to evaluate evidence defensively" (Cohen et al. 1151). Such defensiveness clearly interferes with learning (Cohen et al. 1161).

Studies done by terror management theorists (TMT) lead to similar conclusions. TMT studies have found that people whose identities are threatened by reminders of their mortality experience increased need to maintain the identity-bearing beliefs constituting their worldview, and that this need in turn produces more positive evaluations of people and ideas that support these beliefs and more negative assessments of people and ideas that threaten these beliefs (Pyszczynski, Greenberg, and Solomon 836). The implications for education are clear: any ideas, teachers, or authors that challenge or fail to support students' core beliefs about religion, society, politics, morality, or human nature will be resisted by students whose identities are insecure. For some students, the mere encounter with difference can be enough to threaten their identity-bearing beliefs and worldviews, as Schimel and his colleagues point out: "the mere existence of differences between oneself and others calls into question the absolute validity and correctness of one's own beliefs, values, and lifestyle. Because such threats challenge an individual's faith in his or her worldview, he or she is likely to respond to those with divergent worldviews with disdain and hostility" (Schimel et al. 906). The same logic applies to students' encounters with such differences in the study of history, literature, art, music, and the various social sciences: whatever diverges from the core beliefs constituting their worldview threatens their identity and thus will trigger resistance unless they have sufficient identity security to sustain themselves in the face of the belief-threatening information.

The defense against belief-threatening information can take many different forms, and all of them undermine learning. The simplest form is avoidance, which can manifest itself as a resistance to understanding, coming into contact with, or even hearing about the threatening information. Lack of interest and boredom can also be indications of defensive avoidance of the topic because of the threat it poses to one's identity. As Zuwerink and Devine note, tuning out an opposing message can be an effective form of resisting its threat (932).

Another mode of resistance is simply to deny the validity of identity-threatening knowledge (Zuwerink and Devine 932). This tactic is sometimes used in conjunction with the uncritical acceptance of arguments that support one's beliefs (Cohen et al. 1151). An example of this mode of defense can be found in students who deny evidence in support of evolution and continue to uncritically embrace the belief in divine creation, or who ignore the social causes of poverty and crime and continue to place blame for these conditions solely on poor people and criminals. Often such denial is assisted by ad hominem attacks on the source or purveyor of the threatening information (Cohen et al. 1151) and/or denial of the validity of the methodology by which the information was produced (see Kunda 490), as when students (and others) reject evolution on the grounds that it was invented by atheists who relied on evidence of the senses and ignored faith.

There are also more sophisticated and reality-oriented modes of defense, modes that do not simply avoid or deny the validity of the threatening information but instead offer what they believe to be rational counterarguments. But though such arguments may assume the form of logic, they involve the logical fallacy of special pleading, which considers only information and arguments supporting one's belief while leaving out of account everything that contradicts the belief. Such special pleading is itself enabled by all sorts of specific (and largely unconscious) cognitive processes, as Ziva Kunda explains:

> People motivated to arrive at a particular conclusion attempt to be rational and to construct a justification of their desired conclusion that would persuade a dispassionate observer. They draw the desired conclusion only if they can muster up the evidence necessary to support it. . . . In other words, they maintain an "illusion of objectivity". . . . To this end, they search memory for those beliefs and rules that could support their desired conclusion. They may also creatively combine accessed knowledge to construct new beliefs that could logically support the desired conclusion. It is the process of memory search and belief construction that is biased by directional goals. . . . The objectivity of this justification construction process is illusory because people do not realize that the process is biased by their goals, that they are accessing only a subset of their relevant knowledge, that they would probably access different beliefs and rules in the presence of different directional goal, and that they might even be capable of justifying opposite conclusions on different occasions. . . . [Self-affirmation] motives may have an effect on any or all stages of the hypothesis-testing sequence—that is, on the generation and evaluation of hypotheses, of inference rules, and of evidence. (Kunda 483)

The defense of identity-bearing beliefs can thus not only prevent students from acquiring specific types of knowledge, it can also engage them in various cognitive distortions that can become habitual and thus produce a more general impairment of thinking, learning, and even intelligence.

Social Problems

Enacting and defending one's systems of knowledge and belief can also motivate behaviors constituting social problems. Some drug users get identity support from possessing and performing specialized knowledge of how to procure, conceal, and use drugs. Lockley reports, for example, that among heroin users "injecting is a skill and status that is given in the subculture to those who learn to inject themselves with a degree of expertise" as well as to those possessing "knowledge about the whole injecting way of life" (Lockley 52–53). Similarly, the possession and performance of knowledge of how to care for a baby can be a significant source of identity for teen mothers.

Prejudice and group hatred also function to enact one's identity-bearing worldviews, as well as to defend them by attacking people with different worldviews, which constitute a threat to one's own identity-bearing beliefs (see Pyszczynski, Greenberg, and Solomon 16; Schimel et al. 922). Some of the most prominent instances of identity-bearing knowledge motivating social problems can be found in the group hatred that many "law-abiding citizens" have for criminals, drug addicts, and terrorists, a hatred that produces the counterproductive wars on crime, drugs, and terrorism. In all these cases of group hatred, prejudice constitutes an identity-supporting belief in the superiority of one's own group, and it is validated, enacted, and defended through the punishment or elimination (through exclusion, incarceration, or death) of the putatively inferior other.

Identity-Bearing Scripts and Narratives

Maintaining one's identity-bearing scripts and narratives is also an important (though largely unconscious) concern for most people. In the first place, as Joan Atwood observes, the enactment of master signifiers (such as "the good mother" and "the good husband") is directed by scripts: "Human beings expect their lives to follow certain scripts, and they make efforts to follow these scripts. Human beings try to make their experiences congruent with these scripts, sometimes even reinterpreting their reality so as to make it fit them better." More generally, "scripts provide us with a general idea of how we are supposed to behave and what is supposed to happen" (Atwood xvi). "Scripts are the 'blueprints for behavior,' that specify the whos, whats, whens, and whys of behavior." To maintain clear, unambiguous instructions for enacting one's identity-bearing signifiers, "competing constructions, even the awareness of them, must be kept at the periphery of each individual's life and identity." Consequently, "these alternative or shadow constructions tend to be denigrated or denied" (Atwood 12–13).

Jerzy Trzebinski has found that individuals have "self-narratives" that motivate and direct behavior. Self-narratives are representations of actions and events that are personally important, that involve an important role for the individual, and that delineate the individual's identity in a particular area of life (Trzebinski 74). For any individual, the characters, motives, relationships, conflicts, and beginnings and endings of the stories are relatively unique and persistent. Like the transference phenomena of psychoanalytic treatment, these narratives are produced by unconscious self-narrative schemas (SNS) that direct the individual's attention, expectations, assumptions, and interpretations in the given domain and thus predispose the individual to find particular kinds of people having specific kinds of intentions, and to expect particular kinds of issues and conflicts, leading to particular resolutions and conclusions (75–76). Trzebinski emphasizes that self narratives are important motivational forces: In order to maintain meaning, or identity, individuals have to enact an SNS for the given domain (77). Thus the SNS

> not only directs the individual's interpretations of on-going and foreseen events, but also pushes him or her toward specific aspirations, decisions and actions. By particular moves within the events an individual elaborates, fulfils, and closes important episodes in the developing self-narrative. Personal decisions and actions are inspired by, and take strength from self-narratives. . . . Establishing self-narratives, maintaining them, and receiving social support for them [thus] provides a motivational basis for individual decisions and actions. (77–78)

The importance of narratives for identity can be seen by the responses when the minutes of a meeting, a news report, a movie, or a history book gets someone's (individual or collective) story wrong. Concern for one's individual history is also quite pronounced in the effort made by presidents and other public figures to influence how they are portrayed in history.

Interference with Learning

Such self-narratives influence learning in powerful ways. Most fundamentally, students' educational achievements depend significantly on the position accorded to education in their life scripts. A life script in which education is a prominent goal, or a necessary means to achieving an important goal, will motivate one toward educational achievement, while a life script in which school or academic work is positioned as an impediment or an irrelevancy with regard to the full realization of one's identity will promote under-achievement and even failure in education. Trzebinski found that students who passed a university entrance exam had generated more elaborate self-narratives concerning the exam and the university than had students who failed the exam, and that it was the effects of these self-narratives, rather than the students' high school grades or the relative importance of the exam for them, that determined their success. The self-narratives produced this success, Trzebinski concludes, because they motivated action and reduced distraction: since the self-narratives of the successful students had articulated their identities in terms of taking exams, passing them, and going to the university, these students more frequently imagined taking exams and being a university student, and these imaginings produced effective focus and action in the form of preparing for the exam (79).

Narratives are threatening when they contradict an important identity content, be it a signifier, a belief, or another narrative. For example, some students are threatened by, and therefore resist, noncreationist accounts of the origin of the cosmos and of the human species because such narratives challenge their narrative of creation, deny their belief in a providential deity, and threaten to reduce the signifier "human" to the same status as "animal." Similarly, historical narratives telling of Columbus's brutal enslavement, torture, and slaughter of indigenous people, spelling out the U.S. government's treacherous and barbaric actions against Native Americans, detailing the nature and magnitude of slavery in America, or documenting wartime atrocities committed by American governments and troops are routinely resisted and suppressed not only by students but also by teachers and scholars, because such stories threaten narratives bearing important components of their (group) identity.

Social Problems

Identity-bearing narratives also produce social problems. One example is identity-depleted individuals who make a name for themselves in history by enacting scripts of violence. A notable instance is that of the Columbine killers, Eric Harris and Dylan Klebold, who fantasized that the massacre they were planning would make them famous and the subject of a Hollywood movie. Other social problems result from the promotion of narratives that support one's identity by misrepresenting events. The most significant of such narratives are those that deny the degree to which villains—terrorists, murderers, rapists, addicts, and other criminals—are themselves victims of their childhood and contemporary circumstances and thus cannot legitimately be demonized as the sole or even primary cause of their own terrible actions. The identity-supporting narratives that "law-abiding citizens" tell about child molesters, murderers, and terrorists focus on these perpetrators' planning of or disposition toward their terrible actions, their execution of the actions, and the aftermath, and they downplay and often totally exclude the molestation suffered by the molester and the physical abuse or neglect suffered by the murderer when they were children, or the various forms of violence that the United States has perpetrated on Middle Eastern nations and Islamic peoples, as detailed by writers such as Ted Honderich. The media, the government, the courts, and even education all collude in presenting egregiously truncated, self-serving narratives of these individuals or groups and their actions, suppressing all the ways in which "innocent bystanders" actually bear some responsibility for the perpetrators' actions, so that these "good citizens" can maintain their sense of themselves as morally pure and innocent in contrast to the damnable perpetrators.

CHAPTER 3
AFFECTIVE AND IMAGISTIC IDENTITY

Affective-Physiological Identity Contents

The affective-physiological register sustains one's sense of self through the body's adequate physiological functioning, including the processing of sensory information, and through the periodic repetition of what infant researcher Daniel Stern has called "vitality affects," which derive from "the many 'forms of feeling' inextricably involved with all the vital processes of life, such as breathing, getting hungry, falling asleep and emerging out of sleep, or feeling the coming and going of emotions and thoughts" (Stern 54). Such vital processes are occurring continually even from before birth—"we are never without their presence," Stern says (54)—and they manifest themselves in specific affect states, or what Stern calls activation contours, such as a rush, lassitude, hypervigilance, acute need, and so on.

Because of differences in endowment and in developmental experiences, different people have different vitality affects at the core of their identities. Some people feel most alive when they are in a state of tension brought on by pressure or even danger. Others feel the greatest vitality when they are immersed in a supportive, stable, highly predictable environment that eliminates virtually all affective-physiological tension. For some people, a state of anger or rage is identity-supporting: they have become so habituated to such a state that it has become a key component of their affective-physiological homeostasis, such that they feel the greatest vitality when they are in such a state. For them, physical violence can be a powerful means of maintaining or restoring their identity-bearing affective-physiological states. No matter what one's identity-supporting vitality affects may be, every individual is constantly operating in such a way as to reproduce those affective-physiological states and their activation contours.

Interference with Learning

Identity-bearing affective-physiological states affect learning in a number of ways. Generally speaking, if the subject matter or the process of learning elicits an identity-bearing affect, learning will be facilitated, while if either the content or process of learning blocks such affects—or worse, evokes an identity-threatening affective-physiological state—learning will be impeded. But some affective-physiological states, such as a calm alertness, are inherently conducive to learning, while others—such as anger, sadness, and hyper-arousal—make it difficult if not impossible to learn. This means that individuals whose identities incorporate and are supported by the former states will have an easier time learning than individuals whose identities include the latter states. We can see the importance of affective-physiological identity contents most easily when they interfere with learning. When physiological processes are not functioning well, as in extreme fatigue or illness, or due to injury, people feel out of sorts, not themselves, and in such circumstances, learning can be quite difficult. The same is true when people experience extreme affective states that have not been incorporated into their sense of self, as is often the case with sadness, rage, terror, anxiety, shame, or depression. In such instances, people engage in specific tactics to restore their identity-bearing affective-physiological states. Such tactics can be grouped into five general types.

Most obvious, perhaps, is the consumption of substances that alter one's mood or affective-physiological state through producing chemical changes in the body and brain. Prominent examples include drinking coffee, tea, alcohol, and soft drinks (many loaded with sugar and/or caffeine), smoking tobacco, consuming spicy foods, eating chocolate, and snorting, smoking, swallowing, eating, or injecting recreational and prescription drugs. Some of the resultant affective-physiological states facilitate learning while others undermine it. All teachers have observed drowsy students who are simply unable to attend to class discussions or even to stay awake without their cup of coffee. And teachers are also familiar with students whose energy level or state of excitement is too high for them to participate effectively in class. Such students are often treated with Ritalin.

A second means of producing vitality affects is sensory stimulation. All five senses produce vitality affects. An obvious example is sexual arousal, which can be produced by the sense of touch, as well as by certain smells, as demonstrated by the heavy investment in perfumes, and various sounds, particularly of the human voice. Visual images of the human body are often even more effective in producing sexual arousal. But apart from sexual arousal, sensory stimuli also produce a sense of well-being through inducing other vitality affects. Visual images of certain landscapes can produce awe (anxious excitement) in the face of the sublime, lassitude in the presence of the picturesque, and enthusiasm in our contact with the beautiful, and our attention to the colors, shapes, and textures of our dwelling spaces and clothing demonstrates the power of such stimuli to affect our affective-physiological states. Certain tastes and smells can also produce powerful

affective reactions, as Proust documented and as the cultivation of various culinary pleasures and fumiary experiences (now formalized as aroma therapy) demonstrates. Relaxation tapes featuring sounds of birds, a mountain stream, or the ocean bear witness to the power of sound to produce similar results, and also passivity, indolence, or quiescence, as do the healing power of the human touch and the sense of well-being produced by massage. In contrast, harsh sounds and unpleasant tactile sensations, as well as unpleasantly warm temperatures, can elicit aggressive affective-physiological states.

Learning can be both enabled and impeded by the affective-physiological states produced by various sensory stimuli. Some students frequent parks or pastoral areas of college campuses because the sights, sounds, and smells of nature facilitate their studying by reducing their level of affective-physiological arousal. Other students, in contrast, study more effectively in cafeterias, coffee shops, or sidewalk cafes because the sights, sounds, and smells of crowds, pedestrian hustle and bustle, or city traffic increase their affective-physiological arousal to an optimal level. Various types of sensory stimuli can interfere with learning by producing too much or too little affective-physiological arousal. Upton Sinclair, for instance, found that as a young man studying art he was too excited by nude paintings and statues to concentrate and therefore changed his major. For other students, such arousal may be optimal for engaging their interest in art.

A third common strategy for inducing particular affects is to engage in certain types of physical activity, some of which trigger the release of drug-like substances into the brain or bloodstream. Having sex, engaging in endorphin-releasing exercise, subjecting one's body to severe stress or even danger (as in adrenaline-activating extreme sports), or enacting more calming movements and postures (as in yoga and other Eastern bodily disciplines) all induce particular affective-physiological states that carry people's core sense of self. Like the consumption of certain external substances and the experience of certain sensations, such activities can also contribute to both learning and its failure. Students whose optimum sense of self resides in a hyperaroused rather than quiescent state may experience a kind of depersonalization when forced to sit still in class for extended periods of time, while other students may be affectively overwhelmed by sustained intense physical exertion. The former may be able to concentrate on their studies most effectively after tension-reducing activities such as exercise or sex, while members of the latter group may respond to these same activities by falling asleep.

A fourth, related strategy for producing identity-bearing affective states involves seeking out or producing certain kinds of situations or interpersonal relationships. An obvious example is participation in certain types of games. Zero-sum games that involve competition, aggression, and physical contact are more likely to evoke vitality affects of hypervigilance and anger than are activities of cooperation and mutual benefit. The interpersonal and social relations of learning activate affective-physiological states that can either threaten to overwhelm the self or that are antithetical to a core identity component. Some students perform optimally in stressful, anxiety-producing situations such as pop-quizzes, high-stakes exams, and highly competitive and even aggressive classroom debates, while others become affectively flooded and unable to perform under such conditions. Students whose identities exclude the affective-physiological states associated with aggression and competition—historically, many girls—will be threatened by the affective-physiological states that competitive classes, programs, and institutions evoke in them. Others, especially boys, whose identities are often constructed on precisely these states, may be threatened or merely unengaged by the states of hypoarousal and lassitude produced by more relaxed, cooperative, and noncompetitive learning situations. Students often regulate their affective states either by seeking out or provoking certain kinds of situations in classrooms, such as competition and conflict or cooperation and harmony, or by avoiding such situations because they threaten or fail to support their particular identity-bearing affective-physiological states.

A fifth fundamental means by which we maintain our affective-physiological identity is through various kinds of cultural stimulation and experience. Rituals and ceremonies function to regulate affect, often by incorporating one or more of the first four strategies, including the ingesting of mood-altering substances (food, drink, drugs), engaging in certain physical activities (e.g., marching, dancing, kneeling, speaking, singing, and shouting), and enacting particular structures of relationships among the participants (e.g., dominance, subordination, equality, mutuality). Moods are also altered by visual sensations provided by culture (e.g., through painting, sculpture, architecture, landscape architecture, and the staging of spectacles) as well as by culturally contrived smells and tastes, the importance of which can be seen in the interest, effort, time, and money we devote not merely to eating but also to finding or producing foods and beverages that smell and taste good to us. Perhaps the most common cultural activities for mood regulation are listening to music—which can induce, reinforce, or moderate virtually any affective state, depending on the type of music involved—and consuming narratives (most obviously in the form of watching television and movies), which also function to support a wide range of affective-physiological states, by allowing us to simulate encounters with affect-producing people, objects, and situations.

Students frequently avail themselves of such opportunities to regulate their affective-physiological states by withdrawing to their televisions, computers, or iPods. Education in the fields of art, music, dance, literature, theater, film, and television can function to support this mode of identity-maintenance by eliciting students' identity-bearing affective-physiological states, and whenever it does so, learning is facilitated. But education in these fields probably just as frequently, if not more often, prevents the experience of students' identity-bearing affective states and even challenges their legitimacy. Much cultural criticism, for example, either explicitly or implicitly challenges the validity or the defensibility of the pleasures students get from their music, their favorite movies and television shows, their sports spectatorship, and so on, and in doing so, it may threaten students' identities to such an extent that they must reject the knowledge and understanding of the cultural criticism. Anyone who has taught popular culture is familiar with the resistance some students have to the very idea that popular culture "means" anything at all. In insisting that it's "just entertainment," these students are often defending their identity-bearing affective states against what they correctly perceive as an assault.

The affective-physiological identity components may thus be just as important—or even more important—in both learning and the failure to learn as the linguistic identity components that education engages more directly. The importance of educators' attending to the affective-physiological register of identity is even greater in light of the fact that postmodernity has made the alteration of one's affective-physiological state much easier than it was in previous times. Moreover, it is now also easier to find acceptance and recognition for a wider range of affective-physiological states than has often been the case historically. Because of these two facts, people are often tempted to seek identity support in this register at the expense of the other two registers. Thus students who find optimal affective-physiological identity support by drinking, doing drugs, partying, having sex, or exercising may have less need for identity support in the linguistic register, which may lead, in turn, to reduced investment in learning and in linguistic identity in general.

Social Problems

Many of the behaviors that constitute social problems are motivated in part by their ability to produce certain identity-bearing affective-physiological states or to regulate or prevent certain identity-threatening states. Substance abuse is an obvious instance, since the most powerful effect and prime motive for using is usually precisely the alteration of one's affective-physiological state. Edward Khantzian finds that much illegal drug use is an effort to prevent or control various identity-threatening affects such as depression, anxiety, loneliness, shame, and rage (88–89). "An addict's main motivation for drug dependence," Khantzian states, "is to use the effects of drugs to relieve or change feelings that are experienced as painful or unbearable" (226).

Khantzian finds that users of stimulants such as cocaine are often seeking greater arousal, either to avoid states of listlessness, inner emptiness, or depression or to achieve an identity-bearing state of hyperarousal (191–192). Sedative-hypnotic substances such as alcohol, in contrast, are used to allow the experience of affective states that one normally experiences as too threatening to one's identity (Khantzian 194). And opiates, including heroin, are often taken for the purpose of avoiding identity-threatening affective states such as aggression and rage (Khantzian 193). Some drug users also achieve an identity-bearing affective-physiological state as a result of the risk and excitement that result from procuring, holding, and using illegal substances (see Lockley 19, 23) and/or as a result of the social interactions involved.

Other forms of criminal activity produce similar identity-bearing affective-physiological states. In fact, the danger of criminal activity in and of itself functions quite literally to inject a stimulant—adrenaline—into the individual's bloodstream. One young shoplifter interviewed by Katz declared, "Every time I would drop something into my bag, my heart would be pounding and I could feel this tremendous excitement, a sort of 'rush' go through me." Another stated, "The experience was almost orgasmic for me. There was a build-up of tension as I contemplated the danger of a forbidden act, then a rush of excitement at the moment of committing the crime, and finally a delicious sense of release" (Katz 71).

Violence can also produce identity-bearing affective-physiological states. A person whose core, affective-physiological identity comprises anger or intense excitement can get a quick identity fix when needed by turning to violence in the same way as (and for the same basic reason that) a drug addict turns to drugs. Many men have affective-physiological identities that exclude virtually all intense affects except anger and triumph, and the anger that both produces and is reinforced by violent behavior may be the fullest experience they have of their affective-physiological core. Thus when they begin to feel the identity-depleted states of shame, sadness, anxiety, or depression, they often either seek out or produce violent situations or manipulate their perceptions of the situation they are in so as to turn these feelings into the identity-supporting affect of rage, which in turn predisposes them to violent behavior. Such an affective-physiological state of intense aliveness can also be evoked by the dangers that are encountered in a violent lifestyle. In such cases, not only the act of violence but also its planning and its aftermath produce a state of hyperarousal that is experienced not as anxiety (the signal of a threatened identity) but as a state in which they have never felt more alive.

War and terrorism function in much the same way for many of their participants, producing an identity-sustaining affective-physiological arousal to which some individuals actually become physiologically addicted. Veteran war correspondent Chris Hedges reports that for some, "the adrenaline-driven rushes" of battle (159) make war "the ultimate drug experience. . . . In times of peace, drugs are war's pale substitute. But drugs, in the end, cannot compare with the awful power and rush of battle" (162–163). Hedges recalls his own addiction to the fear-induced affective-physiological high after narrowly escaping from a deadly crossfire early in his career: "My heart was racing. Adrenaline coursed through my bloodstream. . . . I was hooked" (42).

Nonviolent forms of prejudice and group hatred can also support people's affective-physiological identities, in two basic ways. On the one hand, they can function like violence to produce a state of elevated excitement and arousal. But they can also help to protect people from identity-threatening affective-physiological states—such as aggressive and libidinal feelings of unusual strength or form—by providing a subaltern group onto which these threatening states can be projected or externalized and thus avoided in oneself.

Fortunately, there are ways to alter both one's investment in and one's mode of enacting one's identity-bearing affective states. As Stern notes, extremely diverse types of experience can function to produce the same vitality affect (57–58). A rush, for example, can be produced through a surge of anger or joy, a rapid sequence of powerful thoughts, an eruption of intense light or sound, or taking drugs (55). This means that there are often benign, prosocial, learning-enhancing ways of achieving much the same affective-physiological states as those produced by drinking, partying, and other problematic behaviors, and in such cases the problematic behaviors can be reduced by making these alternative means more available, much as methadone can be used to wean addicts from heroin. Examples of such activities might include not only socially sanctioned and controlled violent behaviors such as those of contact sports, but also other athletic pursuits, such as extreme sports (hang gliding, sky diving, rock climbing, mountain biking, motocross, acrobatic skiing, snowboarding, skateboarding, etc.), and, at a further remove from violent behavior, watching action-thriller movies and, finally, reading books describing and narrating such activities. Education can often play a significant role in offering more benign alternatives to the violent and antisocial means of affective-physiological arousal.

Imagistic-Perceptual Identity Contents

The need to maintain one's imagistic sense of self can also contribute to learning problems and social problems. The motivating force of maintaining the identity-bearing images of one's bodily form and movement is evident from the myriad ways in which people constantly monitor and adjust their bodily shape and impact and also the visual and material environments that variously enable and constrain their enactment of their imagistic identity. The most obvious of such interventions involve alterations of one's bodily form, the most radical of which invade the body and either implant material to enlarge or reshape certain bodily parts or remove fat, cartilage, muscle, or bone in order to alter the shape or reduce the size of certain parts of the body. The time, expense, and pain involved in such procedures, undergone by hundreds of thousands of Americans each year, are all indicators of the motivating force of establishing and maintaining one's imagistic identity. Even more common are the daily efforts of millions of Americans to alter their bodily shape through body building, body sculpting, and dieting—activities that have each spawned multibillion-dollar industries. And then there are the ubiquitous and supposedly insignificant practices of altering or maintaining the appearance rather than the actual shape of one's body, such as looking in the mirror, grooming oneself (hair, teeth, nails, skin), applying makeup, buying clothes (of the most flattering styles, patterns, and colors), and selecting the clothes to wear each time one gets dressed. Such activities, too, demonstrate the substantial investment we have in maintaining a particular body image, which entails concern for and alteration of our weight, height, strength, agility, and coordination, as well as our bodily shape. Perhaps the most accessible indicator of the motivating force of maintaining one's imagistic identity is the fact that when an aspect of our body image fails to conform to our prototype—as in a "bad hair day"—we feel out of sorts, not completely ourselves. This motivating force is directly experienced in the form of the emotions of pride and shame that we feel as a consequence of our body image.

Interference with Learning

Students from elementary school onward are caught up in the concern of establishing and maintaining an ideal body image. This concern interferes with education in several ways. On the one hand, it can produce anxiety and thus reduce the time and energy students can devote to learning. On the other hand, success in enacting an ideal body image can be so supportive of identity that it reduces the need to find identity support through academic achievement, a principle that seems to be borne out by the fact that relatively few individuals who attain the highest academic levels could be mistaken for models or movie stars. To the extent, conversely, that students' efforts fall seriously short of attaining their ideal body image, they may be motivated to invest more in academic identity components in order to compensate. But failing to embody one's ideal image can also lead to investment in destructive identity components, including those that entail violence and other social problems. This violence can be psychological as well as physical and is often directed toward the body images of others, as when students who are overweight or fall short of bodily ideals in other ways are socially excluded and sometimes even ridiculed and taunted. Such students serve as convenient receptacles for the projected bodily deficiencies and the accompanying anxieties of their tormenters.

In addition to our appearance, conforming to our prototypes of bodily agency and efficacy is also crucial for us. This identity component is experienced not only in feats of unusual skill, grace, or strength such as those performed by sports heroes and other virtuosi, but also in taken-for-granted actions such as standing, walking, and manipulating objects with one's hands, the importance of which is evident from the sense of triumph they bring to the toddler or to anyone who has been deprived of them, and from the sense of frustration that occurs when one is unable to perform them. Again, the motivating force of this aspect of identity is evident from the time and money people invest in it. Children, and also some adults, will spend hours working on their jump shot, backhand, curve ball, or putting stroke, and many people spend thousands of dollars on equipment, training, and facilities that allow them to optimize their sense of agency in sports. Here, too, the fact that we experience pride and disappointment or even shame in our bodily agency constitutes direct evidence of its implication in identity and its motivating force. Success in enacting bodily agency can reduce the need to invest in and enact academic identity contents, as can be seen in the star athletes who feel no shame in academic failure. Conversely, athletic failure can in some instances result in greater investment in academic identity elements, as can athletic success for students who would otherwise have too much of their identity riding on academic performance to risk failure (as in some of the defenses of identity-bearing signifiers, beliefs, and narratives we considered in the previous chapter).

The motivating force of body image and agency is also manifested in our pursuit of prosthetic enhancements of our bodies. Someone who feels small and powerless inside his or her body can feel big and strong driving a motor vehicle, operating a machine, or wielding a powerful tool or weapon. One reason for the fierce devotion that many Americans have to cars and guns is the enhanced sense of bodily agency that such possessions provide. Such prostheses are also present in many academic activities, especially research in the physical sciences, and the sublimated bodily agency such researchers experience may be one important reason why some of them pursue such research.

We also enact and enhance our bodily identity through surrogate images and agents of various sorts. Indeed, motor vehicles often function as surrogates as well as prostheses for their owners, as do houses: one's car and one's house are one's externalized body. So too are one's more extended and collectively owned abodes, such as neighborhood, home town, state, and nation. Spectatorship is a particularly significant form of surrogacy, providing a surrogate performance of certain fundamental elements of one's imagistic identity, such as bodily agency, efficacy, and coherence. Providing such surrogates for one's body image is no doubt one of the functions of spectator sports as well as other forms of bodily display and parade, such as fashion, beauty, and bodybuilding competitions, as well as animal and automobile shows and races. The powerful emotional investments that nonathletes in school and beyond have in sports teams is one such instance, as is the more vulgar form of patriotism that celebrates bombs bursting in air (and elsewhere) and destroying the enemy's real as well as surrogate bodies.

Also of great significance is the surrogacy function of virtual bodies, such as those we see on the movie or video screen or encounter in the pages of a book. Video games in which bodies and vehicles of various sorts attack each other, defend themselves, hurtle through treacherous terrains, and try to avoid getting blown up or vaporized allow players to engage with, and perhaps work through, various desires and fears concerning their own bodily integrity and agency. The same is true of certain movie genres, such as slasher and martial arts films, which provide teenage boys, in particular, with experiences of greater bodily integrity and agency than they in fact possess, just as sporting events and dance performances do for their spectators. These different modes appear to reinforce each other and are often almost indistinguishable from each other in important ways. Fighting and killing the enemy, for instance, can now be carried out by someone hundreds of miles away watching blinking dots on a video screen.

In addition to these various means of enacting bodily image and agency, bodily identity is also pursued and maintained through efforts to provide one's body with the physical, spatial, and visual settings in which its identity is optimized. Many people seek to live or vacation in natural environments having features—such as lakes, woods, rivers, mountains, deserts, or snow—that provide optimal visual and spatial support for their body-imagistic identity and its mode(s) of agency. The same is true of the built environment in which we live and work. In selecting, designing, or decorating our homes (and, when possible, our workspaces), we operate, sometimes only intuitively and unselfconsciously, other times quite selfconsciously and systematically, to provide ourselves with the sorts of visual and spatial scale, density, forms, textures, and colors that best support our bodily identity—that is, that make us feel most ourselves. Conversely, the identity-supporting function of spaces and places can also be inferred from those instances in which a place threatens identity, as when it produces claustrophobia, acrophobia, or agoraphobia: since anxiety is precisely the emotion we experience when our sense of self is endangered, the phobic anxiety in these cases is a direct indicator of the threatening effect that certain types of physical places have for certain types of identity. In light of these considerations, the physical places and spaces of learning take on additional significance. We must recognize the possibility that some students may avoid going to the library and even to class because of the unsupportive or even threatening effect that these places have on their imagistic identity contents. And likewise, students may be drawn to other spaces—such as off-campus housing, bars, or restaurants—where it is difficult for them to study but where their imagistic identity is more secure.

We consume virtual spaces and places for the same identity support that we find in actual ones. One reason we enjoy viewing certain types of places in paintings, photographs, films, and videos, or simply imaging them (with or without the aid of verbal descriptions) is that such images help us maintain our bodily sense of self, by allowing us to imaginatively project our bodies into such places in the same way as we do in real places when we scope them out as possible habitats or fields of action. The identity-supporting effects of such virtual places can be inferred from the sense of well-being that viewing or imaging them produces.

Engaging in such forms of identity support for long periods of time, as many students do, can clearly interfere with learning. Such activities, as well as the other forms of engaging bodily environment and prostheses, are often more attractive to students than learning because they can provide stronger and more immediate support for their identity in the form of both enactment and recognition than do alterations of the conceptual-linguistic register. For this reason, students are often more motivated to excel at music or sports or even video games than academics: such endeavors offer the potential of much more immediate and powerful support for their identities, through both enactment and recognition.

Social Problems

Maintaining one's body images also contributes to social problems. Katz finds that both gangs and individual street criminals invest heavily in enacting and eliciting recognition for identity-bearing body images. Some establish their autonomy and distinction through unusual ways of walking: "the ghetto bop and the barrio stroll identify the walker as a native of a place that is outside and antagonistically related to the morally respectable center of society" (Katz 88). Tattoos and distinctive postures serve much the same purpose. The body image of the "badass" identity is also evident in accoutrements such as leather, metal, and sunglasses, which enact autonomy and impenetrability, not only by the other's physical force but also by the other's gaze (Katz 89ff.). Both individual tough guys and street gangs also enact their identities of deviance and hypermasculinity via body images and insignia. Hence the importance of postures, parading, and uniforms, which are designed to invoke recognition in the form of dread (see Katz 128, 138).

Violent behavior is a quick, surefire way to establish one's imagistic identity, and this fact is an important reason why it is often so appealing for people who have few other means of enacting their identities. Engaging in physical violence both protects and (re)establishes one's bodily integrity and agency, especially when they are insecure or threatened. Physical violence immediately reverses one's bodily status from impotent, passive, damaged victim to active agent of the other's bodily disintegration. The damage done to the other's literal, prosthetic, or surrogate body not only proves one's power and agency but also demonstrates, by contrast, the relative integrity, invincibility, and impenetrability of one's own body. In this case the damaged body of the other serves as a receptacle into which one can externalize all of one's own bodily anxieties and insecurities.

A similar imagistic-identity-supporting function is part of the appeal of warfare, terrorism, and other forms of collective violence. Maiming and destroying other bodies can provide a (false) sense of one's own body's agency, power, and integrity. Another appeal of warfare, both to military personnel and to the general public, derives from the powerful prosthetics not only of weapons such as guns, tanks, ships, planes, smart bombs, and precision guided missiles but also of sensory extensions such as radar, sonar, satellite surveillance, laser scopes, and night-vision goggles. And insofar as war involves protecting the surrogate body of one's homeland and invading and destroying the homeland of the other, it provides additional support for one's imagistic identity in the form of its surrogates.

Teen pregnancy, too, provides imagistic identity support in several ways. First, during pregnancy the girl's body changes in ways that some girls (and women) experience as identity-enhancing. With pregnancy comes a different wardrobe, which can itself offer support for one's imagistic identity. In addition, pregnancy is in many ways the ultimate instance of bodily agency: one's body literally creates another body, another person. This enhancement of the girl's bodily agency is extended, after the baby is born, to the life-sustaining care she gives her baby, through nursing, holding, bathing, comforting, and protecting it. In this relationship, the baby further enhances the mother's imagistic identity by serving as both a prosthetic and a surrogate body for the mother, an extension or an avatar of herself in the world.

The fundamental conclusion to be drawn by educators is obvious: providing more benign, less destructive means of enacting one's imagistic identity—whether through curricular activities such as dance, art, shop, or fashion design or through extracurricular activities such as sports, camping trips, or certain types of internships or jobs—can contribute significantly not only to enhancing student learning and general well-being but also to reducing social problems.

Chapter 4
Identity Integration
and Defenses

Identity Integration, Intelligence, and Learning

Although identity contents are fundamental determinants of learning, resistance to learning, and social problems, the relations among the various contents are also important determinants of these phenomena and of the development of intelligence as well. Specifically, both identity security and intelligence depend on the organization and integration of identity contents within and across registers. Integration is necessary for a strong identity because such identity requires multiple and diverse contents, and if these are not organized and integrated, they can conflict and interfere with each other. Having a multiplicity and diversity of contents strengthens identity by rendering it less vulnerable to threats encountered by any one identity component (see Hoyle 62ff.) and by providing more opportunities for identity to be enacted and recognized. Such an identity is less in need of destructive, antisocial behaviors to maintain itself. And such an identity can also facilitate learning: the more multiple and diverse one's identity contents are, the more implicated and hence interested one is in the various academic subjects and activities. But diversity of contents can also undermine identity insofar as some contents are incompatible with, and thus threatening to, other contents. When two contents are not coordinated with each other—and even more, when they are in conflict with each other—the identity-bearing function of each is impaired, because they entail two mutually exclusive sets of behaviors to achieve enactment and recognition. The most obvious instances are those in which a content of one's affective-physiological register is in opposition to a content of one's imagistic or linguistic register, such as the oppositions between affects of tenderness and an identity-bearing signifier such as "tough." In such an instance being tough demands one kind of behavior while having tender affects inclines one toward the opposite kind of behavior, so that enacting or receiving recognition for one content would undermine the other. It is thus important that the three registers be coordinated, so that when a content of one register is enacted, the other registers correspond rather than conflict with that content. When conflicts exist, defenses are mobilized to eliminate or weaken one or both of the conflicting contents, thus often sabotaging identity.

When integration is lacking, the result is thus an impairment of identity, which manifests itself as psychopathology. The psychopathology can take various forms, depending on the nature and degree of integration deficiency within and across the registers. Neurosis, according to Bucci, involves disconnection of specific affects from the imagistic and linguistic systems of organization and meaning (202). According to Stanley Greenspan, neurosis and other forms of psychopathology involve inadequate representational capacity. Obsessionals, Greenspan has found, have a comprehensive system of meaning and identity in place, but it lacks sensitivity to affective nuances and perceptual details and hence fails to include key dimensions of these registers. More severe pathologies—such as autism, Attention Deficit Disorder, and various forms of depression, psychosis, and narcissistic personality disorders—result from other forms of inadequate development and/or integration of the registers.

Lack of integration within and between the three registers also impairs intelligence and learning. As the work of Greenspan and that of Bucci demonstrate, the various functions that we refer to as intelligence depend, like identity, on the development of comprehensive codes in each psychological register—those of affects, images, and words—and the development of relatively adequate and complete translations between the codes of the different registers. Greenspan defines intelligence as a function of two capacities: the capacity to generate ideas by abstracting from and naming affects and images, and the ability to integrate different categories of experience by building bridges between their respective (primarily linguistic) concepts (*Growth* 16, 125). The generative function of intelligence, of which inductive thinking and learning is one manifestation, is crucial for all levels and areas of performance in education and in life in general. General intelligence, professional expertise, and socially effective and responsible behavior are all based on the capacity to abstract from one's affective and perceptual experiences and create linguistic concepts, ideals, and principles that govern, guide, and motivate both one's major strategic decisions in life and profession and one's daily operations as well. "The ability to form abstractions," Greenspan says, "is actually the ability to fuse various emotional experiences into a single integrated concept" (*Growth* 25). Bucci argues that creative work in both the sciences and the arts involves working back and forth among the three registers, and she cites Jacques Hadamard's account of creativity in mathematics to show how advances in even the most purely symbolic of fields rely on subsymbolic and imagistic processes in interaction with the symbolic-verbal register (Bucci 223–227).

Eugene Gendlin makes a similar argument concerning the importance of accessing "felt meaning"—meaning that has not yet been verbalized or even imaged—for producing what he calls "fresh thinking":

> In genuinely fresh thinking one pursues a new edge that is only vaguely sensed. At the edge of a scientific discovery, at the furthest end of a logical progression, there is something troubling, new and exciting, not yet articulate or organized. To think freshly involves *sensing*, after every step of thought: Does that get at it? Does that open something up? Does that enter into the unclear lead that I am pursuing? Or does it cover up my sense of that lead? . . . Fresh thinking is like psychotherapy in this respect. In both cases all categories are open in principle. If it could be thought of entirely in the old categories, it would not be an unclear edge. (*Focusing* 245)

Gendlin identifies the three registers of experience as the logical and symbolic, the perceptual and operational, and the directly felt (*Experiencing* 1). "Very little of what we are, mean, or feel is ever in the form of explicit verbal symbols or visual images," he observes. "Even the most intellectual ideas and arguments as well as situations and behaviors involve a felt apperceptive mass" (*Experiencing* 27). Gendlin points out that not only creativity but virtually all mental activity and all action depend on translation and communication among these three registers. Every speech act, for instance, is guided by a felt sense of one's intention, a fact that becomes palpable when we cannot find the words to express our felt intention, or when we feel that what we have just said does not adequately convey our intention (*Experiencing* 69–70). Not only "fresh thinking" but virtually all thinking depends on this felt sense:

> We cannot even know what a concept "means" or use it meaningfully without the "feel" of its meaning. No amount of symbols, definitions, and the like can be used in the place of the *felt* meaning. If we do not have the felt meaning of the concept, we haven't got the concept at all—only a verbal noise. Nor can we *think* without *felt* meaning. . . . Only a very few considerations can be held in mind in a verbalized form, yet thinking involves the simultaneous role of many considerations. We "think" them all in a felt way. "Let me see, now, there is this, and this, and that," we may say to ourselves, meaning a whole complexity by the word "this" and by the word "that." We know what we mean by "this" and "that" because we directly feel the meaning. This felt experiencing, now verbalizations, makes up all but a small part of what we think. Concepts are not meanings at all, except in relation to experiencing. (*Experiencing* 5–6)

Comprehending someone else's ideas also requires translating between the three registers. When we read or listen to others, we understand them only insofar as their words elicit in us the corresponding felt meanings (*Experiencing* 101).

Integration of and translation among the three registers is thus essential not only for generative thinking and inductive learning but also for linguistic comprehension itself. To the extent that the affective and imagistic registers of one's experience are not integrally connected to one's linguistic register, all of these functions will be impeded.

Communication and translation among the affective, imagistic, and linguistic registers are also necessary for emotional intelligence, which, since the appearance of Daniel Goleman's best-selling book by that title a decade ago, has been increasingly recognized as a crucial factor in education, personal well-being, and social relations. As Goleman explains, emotional intelligence involves the capacity to control and direct one's own emotions and their consequent behaviors and to recognize the emotions and intentions of others and respond fairly and effectively to them. Such intelligence is based on the abilities to recognize affects, to distinguish among them, to name them, and to see their connections to thoughts and actions (see Goleman 268–270). And these abilities, it is clear, all presuppose adequate communication and translation between the three registers, particularly between linguistic and affective-physiological experience.

Rich, vibrant, creative, emotional thinking involving all three registers in a synergistic process is thus ideal. But it is unfortunately very rare, even in educational settings. According to Gendlin, most people do not even know that such thinking is possible:

> We have been taught to think at a great distance from experience. Even when we want to think about a specific experience, we often leave our direct sense of it behind, in order to think about it. As soon as we have one thought about it, we think from that thought to another and another, without ever returning to the experience to see if our thoughts do justice to it. (*Focusing* 240–241)

A large number of people, according to Greenspan, have significant deficiencies in representing their affective experience in words. Obsessional types, instead of experiencing a feeling such as anger, may simply experience a certain bodily state or feel the urge to act aggressively. They are often quite adept at manipulating symbols in math or even in intellectual (or intellectualized) discussions concerning human motives and relations but are incapable of applying these concepts and mental operations to their own affective experience (Greenspan, *Psychotherapy* 49–50). Such individuals are insensitive to emotional subtleties, nuances, and details. They "see a big picture, but it is faded and lacking in affective detail" (Greenspan, *Psychotherapy* 269), because their affects are not adequately connected to their imagistic and linguistic registers. Such a person—like a stereotypical absent-minded physics professor—may be an accomplished abstract thinker and adept at operating with spatial concepts, but inept at reading his own affects or communicating them in body language or facial expressions as well as words (*Psychotherapy* 285–86). Students (and teachers) of this sort may be masters of the complexities of history, philosophy, literary history or theory, or any of the physical or social sciences but experience no affective or imagistic intensity regarding this knowledge and hence fail to grasp its human significance.

While these obsessional individuals have difficulty grasping and generating adequate concepts of their own affects, narcissistic individuals are unable to generate adequate representations of other people's needs and feelings: "The narcissistic individual's self-absorption is seen as arising from a lack of capacity to truly appreciate the affect, wishes, and intentions of another person. Other people are not seen as full human beings with wishes, intentions, and affects in their own right. . . . This inability to appreciate the affect of the other can be viewed as a deficit in the ability to categorize experience" (Greenspan, *Psychotherapy* 337). While such individuals may command wide-ranging knowledge in the humanities, arts, and social sciences, they remain largely impervious to the affective experience that has generated this knowledge and to which this knowledge refers, and they thus fail to achieve wisdom or even significant understanding. Examples include students (and teachers) who learn multiple and detailed facts about the suffering and deaths of people around the world from famine, disease, war, and terrorism and yet experience no significant affect and remain unmoved to do anything about these horrors.

Lack of integration of the linguistic register with the affective and imagistic registers has several causes. In some cases an individual may simply not possess words for certain affects and images—either because the language does not provide them or because the words may not be widely used in the individual's culture or subculture. In addition, even when one possesses all the words and other representational resources of language, one can never capture all the singularity, nuance, and detail of prototypic images, which themselves inevitably reduce the infinite variations of affects by "chunking" them into a finite number of discrete categories.

But while cultural limitations and structural incommensurabilities between registers are significant factors in the internal conflicts of identity, the most significant cause of such conflicts is to be found in the direct opposition of the socializing forces of the linguistic register to the vitality affects of the organic body. That is to say, the civilizing, socializing process forces us to sacrifice certain bodily gratifications in order to become human—for example, we must submit our bowels and bladder, as well as our mouths, our genitals, and our locomotion, to the regimes of the social order—and also in order to assume all of the various other social identities, most notably our gender and sexual identities, which requires limiting our desire and enjoyment to certain parts of our own body and to certain parts and types of other bodies. The outcome of this colonizing of the organic body by language is a fundamental division between those parts of ourselves that we accept and identify with—an identity-bearing signifier, such as "lady"—and those parts that the signifier forces us to reject—the vitality affects, such as sexual desire and enjoyment as well as aggression. The result is a profound ambivalence toward the rejected elements of self: on the one hand, we want to recover and reintegrate the lost vitality of the rejected parts (hence our fascination with things taboo), but on the other hand we want to completely banish and annihilate those parts, since embracing them would in one way or another destroy our established identity.

Lack of Integration and Social Problems

The failure to integrate important elements of the self into one's identity also contributes substantially to many social problems, since the unintegrated elements can pose a threat to identity from within the self. Regarding substance abuse, Henry Krystal declares: "The basic defect, the basic dilemma in the life of the drug-dependent individual, such as the alcoholic, . . . is that he is unable to claim, own up to and exercise various parts of himself" (Krystal, "Self- and Object-Representation" 302). A major integrative deficiency in drug abuse is alexithymia, the inability to name one's affective-physiological states and thus integrate them into one's identity (Krystal, "Self Representation" 109–110). Many addicts are also unable even to experience their affective-physiological state in the imagistic register, in the form of fantasies (Krystal, "Self Representation" 110). Being out of touch with one's feelings deprives one of the most fundamental evidence of one's ongoing being, the core of one's sense of self (see chapter one and Levin 138). It can also result in an unbearable somatic tension: "Feelings that cannot be verbalized are overwhelming, and one of the most common ways of dealing with the inability to withstand the tension of unverbalized affect is to drink or drug it away" (Levin 56).

Much violence, too, derives from the threat that unintegrated (and hence rejected) tender feelings, passive impulses, and dependency wishes constitute for masculine identity, as in the case from Gilligan described earlier, in which a man whose masculine identity was threatened by his passive wish to live with his mother and to be taken care of by her committed murder to demonstrate to himself and others that he was active and dominant, not passive and submissive (see Gilligan, *Violence* 82).

Many instances of interpersonal and group prejudice, hatred, and even violence are also driven in part by unintegrated affects and impulses that are antithetical to identity and thus threatening to it. Prejudice helps maintain one's identity by using externalization, projection, projective identification, and reaction formation to defend against the threats posed by those qualities and impulses of one's own that one has rejected in order to maintain one's identity as "man," "woman," "civilized," "human," "kind," "fair," and so on. Thus in racism one projects onto the racial other one's own "uncivilized," bestial, and "perverse" impulses that have not been integrated into identity in order that one might solidify a linguistic identity as "human" rather than "beast," "refined" rather than "crude," "good" rather than "evil," and so on. By avoiding the despised subaltern (e.g., through segregation), excluding it (e.g., through immigration restrictions), or destroying it (e.g., in genocide or war), one maintains the illusion that one has eliminated those unintegrated, identity-threatening elements of self that have been projected onto the subaltern, oblivious to the fact that in the very act of demonizing, scrutinizing, and persecuting the subaltern, one is enacting precisely these unintegrated, identity-threatening contents of self that one is trying desperately to escape.

Sexism is also the result of unintegrated elements of self. It is a way some men attempt to escape their own unintegrated attributes, desires, impulses, and enjoyments that have been coded feminine and thus threaten their identity as men. Such unintegrated elements include the desire to be passive or subordinate and to be taken care of rather than to be always active and dominant, as well as the enjoyment of being tender or receptive rather than tough and imposing.

Homophobia results, similarly, from the threat posed by people's unintegrated homoerotic impulses and fantasies. This fact is demonstrated by research showing that the most homophobic men are those who become most aroused when watching homoerotic films of gay men: the most severe hatred and violence toward homosexual men is enacted precisely by those men and boys whose own unintegrated homoerotic impulses and fantasies are the strongest.

Nor is the social damage done by unintegrated elements of self limited to the behaviors of addicts, criminals, and bigots. In fact, the most severe social harm comes from the lack of identity integration in the masses of "innocent," "law-abiding" people. Their—our—own lack of integration leads us to seek to maintain our identities through our own acts of externalizing our unintegrated contents, the only difference being that in our case the receptacles of the externalizations are the perpetrators of racism, sexism, and homophobia rather than their victims. We support our identity by demonizing a subaltern—for example, racists, sexists, and homophobes—in basically the same way as they demonize their subalterns. We refer to them as "low-life," "pigs," "animals," "predators," "assholes," "white trash," and so on and thus establish them as receptacles into which we can externalize our own unintegrated bestial, inhumane, and perverse impulses.

The same urge to escape our own unintegrated impulses is also driving our punitive desires, decisions, and public policies toward criminals. Gilligan notes that our intense urge to punish criminals, as opposed to restraining and possibly rehabilitating them, is identical to the motive of violent criminals themselves (*Violence* 184). Strean and Freeman make the same point about capital punishment. Since the death penalty has been shown to be unfairly applied, ineffective as a deterrent, and more expensive than life imprisonment, why do we not only continue to use it but also celebrate it (as demonstrated by, among other things, the spectators who rejoice at executions)? Because of our own unacknowledged murderous wishes: "The vengefulness we feel toward a murderer, which drives us to champion execution, is identical to the wish for revenge the murderer feels for what he believes to be the horrendous injustices in his life. . . . We feel as murderous toward them as they do toward those they have killed. We wish either to kill or torture them" (Strean and Freeman 244).

Punishing criminals helps us "good, upstanding, law-abiding citizens" deny our own transgressive and even murderous impulses by focusing on the more manifest and extreme instances of these impulses in others. "The intense desire by some members of society to punish criminals masks the fact that these 'respectable' members of society themselves have criminal inclinations. . . . '[T]he louder a man calls for punishment of the lawbreaker,' [Alexander and Staub write], 'the less he has to fight his own repressed impulses' " (Anderson 90). "We need criminals to be criminals," Bloom and Reichert explain. "They are playing a social role that we cannot presently do without. . . . They are acting out our submerged conflicts and if we dare to decide that they do still belong to the human race, we are in danger of having to deal with our conflicts ourselves" (240).

Such externalization of our own unintegrated impulses provides us with the illusion that we fully and consistently embody our identity-bearing signifiers such as "good," "civilized," "humane," "egalitarian," and "unprejudiced." But while it may help protect our identities from the repressed contents of our selves, such demonization of bigots and criminals does little to prevent or reduce their destructive behaviors. In fact, it does the opposite: enacting our own unintegrated, externalized impulses through hateful attitudes and punitive public policies toward addicts, criminals, and bigots merely exacerbates the identity vulnerability that drives them to their destructive behaviors in the first place.

Defenses, Learning, and Social Problems

As we have just seen, unintegrated impulses and affects threaten identity and thus elicit defenses, which help to maintain identity by isolating or dissociating it in various ways from experiences and impulses that threaten it. Defenses perform an essential function without which identity could not exist. All of us maintain a constant vigilance regarding our identity components, "safeguarding our coherent existence by screening and synthesizing, in any series of moments, all the impressions, emotions, memories, and impulses which try to enter our thought and demand our action, and which would tear us apart if unsorted and unmanaged by a slowly grown and reliably watchful screening system" (Erikson, *Identity* 218). Some forms of defense, however, while protecting identity in certain ways, ironically render it more vulnerable by preventing it from becoming more integrated, complex, and capacious. Some defenses, such as denial, wall an individual off from threatening external realities, while others, such as repression, isolation of affect, and intellectualization, separate identity from other affective, imagistic, or linguistic contents of the self that are threatening to various identity components.

Defenses can be serious impediments to learning. And as Deborah Britzman notes, "in education, the smallest detail or the tiniest word can provoke the ego's defenses" (87). In order to maintain their identity, students may, as we have seen, reject new knowledge and values (denial); they may take in new knowledge and values but immediately forget them (repression); or they may embrace new knowledge and ideals but compartmentalize them (disavowal, dissociation) in order to keep them from undermining certain of their identity components. In such cases a separation is established between two systems—such as scientific knowledge and religious beliefs, or sociological knowledge and prejudiced attitudes—a separation that maintains both sides of the contradiction without allowing either side to undermine the other. The identity components students are refusing to relinquish may be certain ideals (such as those of white supremacy, patriarchy, or nationalism) or the indulgence in certain affects, such as the high of contempt or dominance, or the rush of hatred and aggression.

Such defenses interfere with the acquisition of knowledge and understanding and even with the development of intelligence, by preventing precisely those inter-register connections that are essential for understanding and intelligence. And these effects can contribute in a profound way to serious social problems. Consider, for example, the ways different defenses interfere with students' (and teachers' and politicians') knowledge of war. An adequate knowledge and understanding of war involves the sort of multifaceted, emotionally informed awareness of the most distant events in their most concrete affective and imagistic detail that Upton Sinclair describes in *The Jungle*:

> Your senses are dulled, your souls are numbed; but realize once in your lives this world in which you dwell—tear off the rags of its customs and

conventions—behold it as it is in all its hideous nakedness! *Realize it, realize it!* Realize that out upon the plains of Manchuria to-night two hostile armies are facing each other—that now, while we are seated here, a million human beings may be hurled at each other's throats, striving with the fury of maniacs to tear each other to pieces!. . . . We call it War and pass it by—but do not put me off with platitudes and conventions—come with me, come with me—*realize it!* See the bodies of men pierced by bullets, blown into pieces by bursting shells! Hear the crunching of the bayonet, plunged into human flesh; hear the groans and shrieks of agony, see the faces of men crazed by pain, turned into fiends by fury and hate! Put your hand upon that piece of flesh—it is hot and quivering—just now it was a part of a man! This blood is still steaming—it was driven by a human heart! Almighty God! And this goes on—it is systematic, organized, premeditated! And we know it, and read of it, and take it for granted; our papers tell of it, and the presses are not stopped—our churches know of it, and do not close their doors—the people behold it, and do not rise up in horror and revolution! (288–289)

This sort of emotional knowledge is foreclosed for most people, especially students in classrooms, by a synergistic relationship between lack of generative/inductive/emotional intelligence and defenses against making the types of inter-register connection that constitute such intelligence. A number of defenses operate in people's thinking about war to keep them from realizing and owning their own hateful feelings and murderous impulses, which everyone has (see Strean and Freeman). Splitting divides people and reality in general into binary categories of good and bad, right and wrong, true and false, and so on, while externalization and projection attribute all bad impulses and qualities to the other and all good ones to oneself. In protecting one's identity from damaging realizations about the self, these defenses prevent the accurate knowledge of both self and other that is a prerequisite for an accurate and adequate understanding of war (and thus also for fair and just action concerning war). Such defenses are obvious in the views on the current war in Iraq that have been expressed not only by many students but also by many politicians.

Another prominent defense in education is intellectualization. Here the emphasis is on the dry facts, with affect, and the graphic images that express and elicit affects, excluded. Thus students who study history may learn of the millions of people who died in various wars, but they rarely if ever *realize* these deaths in the way Sinclair advocated, much less imagine themselves inside the skin of even one of the millions who writhed in desperation and agony after being riddled with bullets, or who experienced the horror of watching loved ones or comrades blown apart or shrieking with unbearable pain, or who endured the terror of facing his or her own imminent death. Such intellectualization, which protects students' identities from their affective-physiological vulnerabilities, also enables them to maintain their sense of themselves as intelligent, responsible, moral beings while doing nothing about the terrible human suffering and injustice of a war that is eminently avoidable.

Repression, which blocks memory and awareness of identity-threatening affects and impulses (and other personal qualities as well), operates synergistically with cultural denial to block memory and awareness of historical events and actions that manifest such impulses and affects on the part of one's own identity group. Repression is operating in all those cases in which the general public remains ignorant of instances of human suffering or injustice about which information is freely available in the public sphere. The United States, for example, denies most of its genocidal and imperialist history and emphasizes mainly the laudable aspects of its national identity so that Americans can remain blind to their own individual and collective genocidal and imperialistic impulses and actions. And inversely, Americans' individual repression of such impulses in themselves motivates this cultural denial—this willful forgetting—of historical events and actions that reveal Americans to possess these qualities in abundance. Results of this strategy of protecting one's identity by blocking out evidence that threatens it can be seen, for example, in the fact that the general populace in the United States, which in recent decades has grown extremely skeptical and even cynical regarding the federal government, has expressed very little concern regarding the motives of U.S. military interventions in Grenada, Panama, Haiti, Afghanistan, and until recently, Iraq. At present, with the war in Iraq, there are virtually no images or even verbal descriptions of the thousands of human beings, including children, who as a result of U.S. military actions are every day suffering agonizing deaths, terrible mutilations, unendurable pain, and soul-destroying losses of loved ones. Instead, U.S. news media disseminate information expressed in abstractions, euphemisms, and circumlocutions that completely obliterate this terrible human suffering. During the Persian Gulf War, the news media regaled the public with aerial films of "smart bombs" tracking into the air vents of bunkers far below and concluding with an innocuous-appearing puff of smoke, with no image or mention of the bloody fragments of the human bodies blown apart by the "smart" bomb, or of the human beings who suffered slow, terrible deaths as they lay crushed in the rubble or as they were burned to death by the fire. Thus even when students acquire knowledge of Columbus's barbarous torture, mutilation, and slaughter of indigenous peoples or of early American genocide of American Indians, they rarely recall this knowledge and use it to inform their understanding of contemporary American actions and actors who are themselves not totally free of such impulses.

Such truncation of understanding also makes use of various forms of dissociation—in particular, the separation of affect from conceptual knowledge.

Excellent examples of dissociation can be found in news reports of war. One frequently replayed video clip of an oil-soaked seagull in its death throes captivated American audiences and elicited an outpouring of pity and grief during the Persian Gulf War. This image facilitated displacement and affectualization. It dissociated affects of concern, pity, and even horror from the human victims who elicit these affects, because connecting these affects to their true, human objects would have threatened the identities of all the U.S. citizens who were exulting in the purely positive images of national identity that were being circulated and performed. The affectualization promoted by the image performed the same function: by evoking powerful affects in the audience without connecting those affects to any realities beyond the image itself, the image of the dying bird helped the audience to eschew all thinking—thinking that might have led them to identity-threatening realizations about some of the consequences of U.S. military action—by simply overwhelming them, or at least filling them, with poignant feelings.

Dissociation of one sort or another is ubiquitous in education. Learning and thinking involve establishing links—links both within and between the registers of affects, images, and words. But insofar as new knowledge threatens identity, learning and thinking are always accompanied by resistance, and one ubiquitous form of this resistance is what the object relations theorist Wilfred Bion referred to as "attacks on linking," "the destruction," as Mary Jacobus phrases it, "of the links that make thought possible" (qtd. in Britzman 100). This form of dissociation or resistance to integration, attacks on linking, prevents students from achieving either valid knowledge infused with emotional conviction or emotional conviction informed by valid knowledge, as well as from grasping the root causes or the distant consequences of actions and events, including those constituting our most significant social problems and our efforts to solve these problems. Thus people attack and eliminate the links between poverty and crime, between their own selfish lifestyle and others' poverty, between their vote and poverty, and so on, in order to sustain an identity free from guilt and from the negative elements it is able to externalize onto criminals and the poor.

Another, subtler form of attack on linking is a defense that the psychoanalyst Mardi Horowitz calls dyselaboration. Horowitz describes this defense, which interferes with learning, thinking, and understanding and can often be found in students' written and oral communications, as follows:

> Dyselaboration consists of verbal efforts to avoid disclosure or, if a disclosure has already occurred, to retract, obscure, or purposely dilute and distort its meaning. This can include hedging phrases, movement into a less vital and more peripheral aspect of meaning to draw attention away from central issues, and efforts to disavow or misattribute ideas and feelings that have already been stated. (Horowitz, Milbrath, and Stinson 1041)

A full and adequate understanding manifests itself in the clear communication of complete factual information, of the important implications of the information for other topics and issues, and of the full significance of that information and one's attitudes and emotions about the information and its significance and ramifications (Horowitz, Milbrath, Reidbord, and Stinson 281). In dyselaboration, one or more of these features is suppressed. Horowitz describes four levels of dyselaboration (Horowitz, Milbrath, Reidbord, and Stinson 282), each of which involves defensive mechanisms that can be seen operating in students' verbal comments in class discussions as well as in their writing, and that thus are also operating in their thinking even when this thinking remains unexpressed. The first level of dyselaboration is characterized by filling and hedging. Filler expressions, such as "uh," "I mean," and "you know," interrupt the flow of speech and hence of thought and understanding. Hedges, including minimizing terms such as "somewhat" and "maybe," vitiate the central point of one's statement. Such filling and hedging in students' comments and writing can signal defense against threats that the topic at issue poses to their identities.[1]

The second level of dyselaboration involves fleeing from topics that are threatening to identity by focusing instead on less significant ones. Such a flight from threatening topics, most noticeable in the use of a red herring, can also take the form of "jittering," which involves the rapid shifting among different perspectives toward and aspects of a topic. Students whose classroom comments or papers are unfocused, unorganized, or incoherent may be employing this defense against a threatening topic.

Dyselaboration at the third level distorts the significance of the information one is articulating and can take the form of disavowal, misattribution, or misunderstanding. In disavowal one expresses mutually contradictory views about the same issue. A prominent instance that gained much public attention was presidential nominee John Kerry's statements about his position on going to war against Iraq. Misattribution involves the invalid ascription of actions, intentions, or causal responsibility either to oneself or to someone else, as, for example, when one unjustifiably blames another or absolves oneself of responsibility for a negative result. Such misattributions occur frequently in the analysis of literary characters and historical events in classroom discussions and in student writing, and they are rampant in the apportioning of blame for criminal acts and other social problems, where they play a major role in preventing the pursuit of effective solutions to such problems. Misunderstanding involves a motivated failure to apprehend the meaning of a statement of one's interlocutor. Though students' misunderstanding is by no means always defensive, when it concerns information that is of a level of difficulty that a student has successfully negotiated in other situations, the chances are good that the current misunderstanding is defensive.

The fourth level of dyselaboration involves shifting the discussion to another topic in order to avoid the identity threats present in the current topic of discussion. Various sorts of non sequiturs enact this defense. Sometimes, for example, a teacher will ask a question about one topic and a student will raise his or her hand as if to offer a response but then will address a completely different issue. In other instances, one student will follow the comments of another with comments on a different topic. Such shifting is also not uncommon in students' selection of paper topics and in diverting the focus of their paper or their exam answers onto safer topics or aspects of topics.

Each of these forms of dyselaboration impedes learning by inhibiting understanding and communication. Moreover, by preventing students from linking multiple facts or bodies of knowledge with each other, or integrating their intellectual knowledge with their emotional knowledge and their behavior, dyselaboration defenses also prevent the development of the deep understanding, meaning, and wisdom that are necessary not only for achieving personal well-being but also for solving our most serious social problems. And overcoming one's more massive and primitive defenses and achieving greater integration is also a prerequisite for achieving the fullest and deepest forms of understanding, intelligence, and personal well-being.

CHAPTER 5
IDENTITY STRUCTURE

Structures of Identity and Intelligence

In addition to lack of integration between registers, identity is also rendered vulnerable by identity structures of inadequate complexity and inclusiveness. The structure of identity is crucial because even when conflict between registers is minimal, as a result of adequate imagistic and verbal representation of affects, there can be debilitating incompatibilities among identity contents. For example, linguistic identity contents such as nurturing mother, sexy and lustful lover, and professional woman may conflict with each other, as may affects of tenderness and rage (particularly when they are directed toward the same object). To prevent, or at least limit, such conflict, one's multiple identity contents must be variously coordinated, embedded, and hierarchized. Such coordination and subordination determine under what conditions and in relation to what other identity contents a given content will be enacted. The enactment of rage, for example, will be limited to certain situations and excluded from those circumstances in which tenderness is called for. The strongest identities are those whose structures are complex enough to incorporate all significant components of the self in a manner that minimizes conflict among them, providing a time and place, a context, and a mode in which each component can be enacted in a way that produces minimal threats to other components. The psychological benefits of such development are demonstrated by studies showing that individuals with more complex identity structures have fewer depressive symptoms and less stress than individuals with less complex structures (Hoyle et al. 66).

Such structure is also crucial for the second dimension of intelligence identified by Greenspan, the ability to create links among concepts, an ability that is essential for deductive learning and problem-solving activities central to most academic disciplines. To the extent that one's schemas of self, other, and world are simplistic and constricted rather than complex and extensive, one will be unable to attain more than a superficial understanding of any subject matter, be it in the physical sciences, the social sciences, the humanities, or the arts, and one will be fundamentally incapable of grasping personal, social, or physical realities in a multidisciplinary fashion. Such individuals have trouble seeing the big picture—that is, integrating diverse experiences and meanings within the linguistic register and/or the imagistic register into a coherent whole. These persons, often characterized as having hysterical rather than obsessional personality structures, may be very sensitive to the concrete details of phenomena and to the most nuanced emotional significances. But while they may see a tree clearly in all its details and register its existence with intense affect, they remain oblivious to the forest. "Forming higher level abstract categories may not be easily done by a person who sees only 'trees,'" Greenspan observes. Such individuals, that is, have trouble constructing and holding in mind a comprehensive linguistic system of meaning and identity that is sufficiently powerful to adequately integrate affects, images, and linguistic concepts into a more or less unified and coherent whole. As a result, "such a person will exhibit lots of tendencies to operate naively or concretely in the more fragmented patterns character-istic of school-aged children, rather than evidence the behaviors of a mature adult personality" (Greenspan, *Psychotherapy* 340). Students (and teachers) with such limitations may be moved deeply by stories of suffering people and may take personal action such as helping distraught friends or even strangers, or contributing money to relief organizations, but fail to under-stand how their nation's institutions, or the policies of the president they voted for and enthusiastically support, are a significant cause of this suffering, because they have difficulty seeing causal connections between multiple events and actions, particularly when these are spatially and temporally dispersed.

The capacity to construct a big picture in which multiple states of affairs, events, actions, or states of being are all present, together with their multi-ple and complex causal interconnections across both time and space, is a prerequisite for various ego functions such as the reality principle, impulse control, planning, and perseverance, as well as the capacity to understand complex phenomena and systems (see Greenspan, *Growth* 85–86 and *Psychotherapy* 317). And such capacities are themselves crucial not only for pursuing productive courses of action in one's personal life but also for recognizing, supporting, and formulating effective strategies in business and public policy. Shortsightedness in business and public policy—as in chasing short-term profits at the expense of long-term development and gains, or the pursuit of policies that offer short-term gratifications (getting tough on drugs and crime, or building more prisons) rather than long-term solutions (economic development, education, rehabilitation)—is often a consequence of inadequate capacities (either chronic or acute) on the part of both leaders and the general populace to form such connections. Such capacities are crucial for social responsibility: narrow, monolithic identities rely much more on projection and aggression to sustain themselves than do more multifaceted, complex, and capacious identities, and simple, monolithic representations of the other make the other a much easier target for projection, demonization, and hence aggression than do representations that incorporate numerous different dimensions and aspects of the other.

The most fundamental connections that identity structure makes are those between the positive and negative states that one experiences at different times. To be able to recognize at any moment that who I am includes not only my present affective state but also many other states, including the opposite of the present one, is crucial not only to avoid being overwhelmed by my mood of the moment but also for planning, concentrating, and persevering. And likewise, the capacity to link another person whom one experiences as bad (the bad object) with other, more positive qualities that one also knows or can surmise this person to possess (the good object) is crucial both for maintaining a sense of trust in and engagement with other people and for avoiding counterproductive hatred and demonization.

Personally effective and socially responsible behaviors require further linkings of self and other, connections that in effect extend the boundaries of both self and other, so that the two intersect and overlap in multiple ways at varying levels without, however, dissolving or merging into each other. Greenspan describes this development in terms of an increasingly large context within which one's identity is located. First the child differentiates a dyadic sense of me and you, where the child recognizes an other that is separate from but nonetheless linked with herself, such that her actions affect the other and the other's actions affect her. Another dimension is added to this structure when it is linked with the third party in the oedipal triangle, where, Greenspan observes, "the bridges built between different categories of experience are more complex than those linking dyadic experiences," and the behaviors of each person in the triad are seen to have implications for the other two persons (*Psychotherapy* 327). Next, the child constructs links between its identity and the group. This stage involves the abilities to group people into various categories, to experience "gradations of feelings," and "to integrate different feelings and see that those feelings can exist simultaneously" (*Psychotherapy* 329). Most importantly, perhaps, the linking of opposing feelings in both self and other helps contain enmity and aggression. While "many younger children will enter into all or nothing patterns . . . [because] they cannot tolerate both warm and aggressive feelings toward the same person at the same time," older children "learn that they can compete on the soccer field and still not be enemies" (*Psychotherapy* 329).

In addition to connections between different affects and aspects of self and others, individuals also construct connections to experiences and events that are ever more distant both temporally and spatially. As children move into adolescence and then adulthood, they incorporate into their sense of themselves not only a wider range of experiences from their past but also a more distant future, which is a necessary foundation for behavior such as studying hard in high school in order to be admitted to a good college. Spatial extension of identity occurs in phenomena such as young adults' linking of their sense of identity to their children, and in the ability of middle-aged people "to see themselves on a new time and space continuum in the middle of their own life cycle . . . , and feel not only a part of and leader in their own family but in their community and the world at large" (Greenspan, *Psychotherapy* 333).

Thus the ego functions of reality testing, impulse control, mood stabilization, concentration, and planning all depend on the establishment of links between different aspects of self and object, links that produce "patterns" of self (including multiple and conflicting drives and affects), object, time, space, and causality (Greenspan, *Psychotherapy* 317). Integrating different elements of oneself, that is, is a prerequisite for certain ego functions that are themselves the basis of the complex and multifaceted representations of identity (of both self and other) that are necessary for both a fulfilling personal life and a responsible, productive social existence. When such connections are not developed, basic ego functions such as reality testing and impulse control suffer, representations of self and other are inadequate (simplistic), and identity formation is hindered (*Psychotherapy* 318). And as a result, intelligence and learning capacity, as well as personal and social performance, are compromised.

Ideally, as one's identity develops, one's center of gravity moves gradually from the affective, through the imagistic, to the linguistic register, with a corresponding increase in complexity and flexibility of structure that can integrate a greater diversity of affective, imagistic, and conceptual components into a coherent whole (see Greenspan; Siegel). Thus, for example, an individual who can engage in sustained purposive behavior, delay gratification of impulses, maintain relatively stable notions of both self and others through diverse situations, and operate according to the principle that there is a time and place for everything will be able to enact and sustain a wider variety of identity components from all registers, and successfully negotiate a wider range of situations and environments, than a person who cannot operate in this way. Harvard developmental psychologist Robert Kegan, drawing on the work of Piaget, Erikson, and other identity theorists, has identified in this trajectory five increasingly complex structures of identity[1] that are progressively more secure and resilient and that are the bases for increasingly powerful forms of intelligence and understanding. These structures can be summarized as follows (see Kegan, *In* 314–315 and *Evolving* 118–119):

1. *Impulsive*: I am my momentary impulses. I experience any thwarting of them as a threat to my very being, and I will fight that thwarting force.
2. *Imperial*: I am my current ongoing need, intention, or project and am able to sacrifice my impulses, which I now *have* rather than *am*, for the purpose of enacting my need, intention, or project. I will fight anyone or anything that opposes my current need, intention, or project.
3. *Interpersonal*: I am my relationship with another person and am willing to sacrifice everything else, including my impulses and ongoing needs, to sustain this relationship and the other person who is essential to it. I will fight anything that threatens the relationship.
4. *Systemic or Institutional*: I am the system in which each of my multiple interpersonal relationships, my projects, and my impulses has a place, but none of which by itself constitutes who I am. I will sacrifice everything not for a particular relationship, project, or impulse, but rather for the system or institution that I am or that I have identified with, and I will fight anything that opposes it.
5. *Trans-systemic or Interindividual*: I am, like Walt Whitman, a self that contains multitudes. When I operate in the interindividual mode, I care about all other individuals, no matter what their group or interpersonal identity may be. In this structure, I can no longer attack other groups or systems or the individuals who constitute them, because I experience every individual as sharing and constituting the being that I am, just as in the interpersonal structure I experience a specific individual as sharing and constituting my being.

Each successive structure incorporates the previous structures within wider boundaries of identity, such that the earlier, simpler, more limited identities remain embedded within the later forms. Thus impulses, projects, relationships, and systems continue as indispensable components of interindividual identities. Because this is the case, it is also the case that in many instances and domains of life, these less complex stages regain their ascendancy.[2]

Impulsive Structure

Very young children, in what Kegan calls the impulsive stage, have an incipient identity based in their impulses and perceptions, which change from one moment to the next. Such identities thus have no real continuity between the impulse or perception of one moment and that of the next, no coordination between competing impulses and perceptions in the same moment, and no adequate means of regulating the intensity and expression of their impulses or of coordinating their impulses and perceptions with the responses of other people, whom they depend on for recognition.

People with prominent impulsive identity structures often struggle in education endeavors. Learning requires deferral of gratification and continuous, focused attention, and impulsive identities are incapable of such actions. Students suffering from Attention Deficit Disorder frequently function at this level, with their inability to pay attention in class or to remember to do their homework. When operating from an impulsive identity structure, students are unable to sustain a line of inquiry, discussion, or argument, nor can they truly listen to or respond to the teacher or other students; instead, they may blurt out impressions, reactions, and free associations that often have little connection with each other or with the comments of others in the class. Learning is largely limited to the acquisition of facts or bits of information. While they may take interest in and learn about discrete facts, personages, and events that embody or elicit affects, images, or concepts integral to their identity, insofar as students are operating with an impulsive structure, they are unable to link these elements of information to form an understanding of chains of causation, or to take interest in people, facts, or events having no immediate relevance to them.

Impulsive identity structures are often implicated in social problems as well. Lack of capacity to restrain aggressive and/or libidinal impulses can be seen to underlie many criminal acts, ranging from shoplifting to assault and murder, and it also plays a central role in many instances of drug abuse and teen pregnancy.

Imperial Structure

The problem of continuity encountered by the impulsive structure is ameliorated by the imperial form of identity, in which a synchronic and diachronic consolidation of impulses produces needs and wishes that are ongoing rather than transitory. A person with an imperial identity structure has the capacity to maintain her sense of self in the face of stymied impulses and also to take other people's wishes into account when pursuing her own wishes, thus reducing the frequency with which she provokes negative responses from others or is caught off-guard by the behavior of others. But the imperialist still views others primarily as forces to be negotiated on the path to his own goals rather than as people whose wishes have a legitimacy equal to that of his own wishes, and as a result he frequently engages in actions that are unacceptable to others and that thus deprive him not only of their recognition but also of further opportunities to pursue his own wishes.

At the imperial level, students have a more temporally extended sense of self and are thus able to experience the importance of events at greater distance from the present and take interest in phenomena having no immediate impact on their present state of self. This greater extension of self makes them interested in a much wider range of phenomena and events. Anything that they perceive as significant for their ongoing identity and its projects becomes an object of interest and understanding. Imperial identities can thus produce impressive accomplishments in endeavors where singleminded pursuit of specific goals is called for. Such identities lack the capacities, however, to recognize the larger contexts of their enterprises and to discern the harm done to themselves as well as others by their singlemindedness. They are unable to dialogue effectively with others or even to see the other as an intentional being like themselves. Insofar as their identity does not include other people, much that is of great significance—including, to a large degree, other people with their different circumstances, capacities, and needs—is excluded from their sphere of interest and hence from their realm of learning as well. Examples of imperial identities in education include not only the bookish children who are immersed in their own fantasy worlds but also myopic scientists who are oblivious to the human suffering that may result from their work, and humanities professors who industriously but unreflectingly pursue scholarly and pedagogical activities that have minimal if any benefits for their students or society at large.

The imperial mode of identity also contributes significantly to various social problems. It underlies crimes that require plotting and planning, including premeditated murder, robbery, and burglary, as well as white-collar crimes such as fraud, embezzlement, and tax evasion. And it also plays a prominent role in practices that may be legal but that nonetheless cause considerable harm to other human beings, including exploitation of labor and other ruthless business practices and, most notably, the imperialistic policies, institutions, and actions of entire nations and civilizations.

Interpersonal Structure

Though the imperial structure takes account of other people, recognition and consideration of the other's subjectivity do not figure centrally in an imperial identity, nor are one's own multifarious dispositions and wishes integrated with each other. The third stage, the interpersonal, bridges these disjunctions, making identity itself a function of its interpersonal relationships, and self-consciousness of one's own needs and subjectivity in relation to those of other people becomes central to identity. In this structure, the other's demands are internalized, and meeting them is explicitly recognized as essential to having a secure identity. This form of identity centers on strong one-to-one relationships of mutuality and reciprocity and manifests itself, for example, in the "all you need is love" mentality. But while this structure solves the problem of being deprived of crucial recognitions and opportunities, it produces several serious new problems. First, it is unable to decide between mutually opposing demands by different others (e.g., parents and peers, parents and partner, partner and children, partner and friends) or between social demands and one's own wishes. And second, people with interpersonally structured identities are vulnerable to severe depression and aggression when their symbiotic bond with their significant other is broken or threatened, because loss of the relationship is experienced as loss of self. The depression and aggression that can be provoked by such a loss, whether real or imagined, can be readily observed in the responses of jealous lovers, such as Shakespeare's Othello, Browning's Porphyria's Lover, or the duke of Browning's "My Last Duchess."

Students with a well-developed interpersonal structure of identity are motivated to understand a still wider range of subject matter, including anything that is significant to people they care about, such as their teachers and classmates. Students with a strong interpersonal structure are easily infected by the enthusiasm of their teachers and peers, and this enthusiasm can be a powerful impetus for learning, resulting in significant achievements for students insofar as they identify with a powerful authority figure who teaches and inspires them. Unfortunately, such a relationship can also turn the inspired students into virtual puppets or clones of their masters and lead them both to overlook the needs and contributions of other potential sources of knowledge and growth and to forsake the enactment and development of key identity components and capacities of their own. Thus while it extends identity and motivates a broadening of interest, the interpersonal structure can also suppress independent thinking and curiosity.

Ironically, it can leave one just as impervious to the realities of other people—those who fall outside the interpersonal relationship—as the impulsive and imperial structures do. Furthermore, the interpersonal structure can amplify and reinforce antisocial impulses and agendas, as can be seen from the various instances of partners in crime and *folies à deux*, both literal and figurative. Adolescents are particularly vulnerable to being led by various sorts of partners into drug use, unsafe sex, shoplifting, and other harmful or dangerous practices.

Institutional or Systemic Structure

Freeing oneself from such submission to others requires an identity structure of still greater inclusiveness and complexity, one that adjudicates among the competing claims of multiple others and between the demands of these others and the individual's own impulses and projects. In this, the systemic or institutional structure, identity is no longer a function of its relationships but is rather a personal ideology or system of ideals, values, desires, and enjoyments that assesses and prioritizes these various ideals, desires, and values along with the demands of the various others from whom one desires recognition. Identity is now able to involve not only self-consciousness but also enhanced self-regulation and self-formation, which are guided by the ideological system that governs this structure of identity. This systemic or institutional form of identity can be seen most clearly in one's immersion in, or identification with, a discipline, profession, organization, or other group identity.

In education, the institutional structure constitutes the basis for a virtually limitless range of interest and hence learning, insofar as it makes the boundaries of self coterminous with those of the academic group or discipline. Thus anything that affects the group or discipline, directly or indirectly, is automatically of interest and a potential object of learning. In addition, at this level understanding becomes more complex and hence more adequate to its objects, because individuals who experience themselves not just as an impulse, or an ongoing project, or a relationship with another person but as an organic system of multiple interconnected impulses, projects, and relationships are able to apprehend other phenomena in terms of similar systems, as multifaceted and with multiple relationships with other phenomena. Thus while an impulsive person grasps phenomena only in terms of the *immediate* gratification or frustration they provide, an imperial individual views them as objects of *potential* gratification or frustration, and an interpersonally structured person apprehends them in terms of actual or potential relevance to self or significant other, a person operating with a systemic self understands everything from a fundamentally ecological perspective, in which everything is composed of multiple and complexly interconnected phenomena (e.g., molecules, atoms, subatomic particles, etc.) and is also ultimately connected to and significant for everything else. A tree is thus not merely a source of fruit (as it may be for an impulsive individual), or a source of wood for building a house (as it may be for an imperial identity), or a form of protection offered by Mother Nature (as it may be in an interpersonal structure), but also an unbelievably intricate organism, composed of processes of photosynthesis in its leaves, capillary action in its roots, and so on, which, moreover, has an incredibly complex (contemporary and historical) relationship with the rays of the sun, the minerals of the earth, the water from the earth and sky, the animals that inhabit it and disseminate its seeds, and so on. The institutional structure thus provides the basis for grasping phenomena as systems composed of subsystems and operating within suprasystems.

Such a perspective is a prerequisite for truly understanding the subject matter of any discipline. In fact, as Nick Tingle observes, university education requires that students be able to assume this systemic structure at least provisionally if they are to master their subjects of study, because disciplinary knowledge and academic discourse in general issue from this structure (Tingle 17ff.). And this requirement, Tingle argues, exerts an interpellative force that in and of itself facilitates the move of some students into the systemic structure:

> The great bulk of students will not devote themselves to the pursuit of truth as their sustaining ideal. But we can expect that the university's embodiment of this ideal in its formulation of disciplines, methodologies, and general epistemology will [affect] students' sense of selves and might, as I argue, assist in the transformation of narcissism [or their sense of self] from relatively archaic to relatively more mature forms at the level of intellection. (Tingle 34)

Unfortunately, most people, including most of our students (and quite possibly most teachers as well), think, feel, relate, and act most of the time from impulsive, imperial, or interpersonal identity structures, with institutions and systems serving as a cover or instrument for the satisfaction of their impulses, the achievement of their goals, or the consolidation of personal bonds. And this constricted identity structure takes a significant toll not only in education but also in the world at large. This can be seen clearly in the way many public figures, including our current president, and much of the general populace operate with regard to the major systems they identify with: rationality and science, Christianity, democracy, and "free enterprise" capitalism. In each case, people's identification with the system often stops as soon as the system conflicts with their impulses, imperialist aspirations, or personal alliances. Thus when rationality and science conclude that global warming is dangerous, the president rejects science and rationality in favor of his (individual and collective) imperialist interests and personal alliances with corporate and business interests. And when science says that stem cell research could save many lives and spare many people from great suffering, the president abandons science (and suffering and dying people) in deference to his identification with a religious belief system that places greater value on a few hundred embryos than on thousands and even millions of fully formed, living people. Yet when his religion tells him he should love his enemies, he abandons this religious identity in favor of his impulse to hate terrorists and his imperialist mission to overthrow Saddam Hussein. His identification with democracy operates mainly as a cover for these same impulses and imperialist agendas, as well as for other impulsive and imperialist acts on the domestic front, such as the Patriot Act. The fact that over half the voting electorate supported this man, and that there has been no impeachment of him and relatively little outrage and scandal in the United States over such behavior, is an indication of the level of identity structure most Americans are operating with and a measure of the importance of promoting the development of institutional/systemic identity structures.

Even this degree of complexity, however, may not produce an adequate understanding of a given phenomenon. While it may be necessary for wisdom, the systemic structure is not sufficient. Its deficiency is twofold. First, the institutional/systemic identity, while grasping itself as a complex system, may nonetheless exclude certain important parts of the self from its sense of itself, or identity. And second, while experiencing itself as an integral part of a social system, it may fail to apprehend other social systems—alternative, competing systems, or systems within which this system is embedded and of which this identity is therefore also a (presently unacknowledged) part. In education, a systemic identity often manifests itself in identification with a particular discipline or system of knowledge. Insofar as the system is benign and productive, the results of such identification may be positive. But if the system is less than benign, or if identification with it prevents one from making important discoveries or engaging in more beneficial practices, then the systemic/institutional identity is itself a problem.

While systemic identities may have sufficed for most people during most of the twentieth century, this structure, as Kegan points out, is no longer adequate for people living in an increasingly global and multicultural world. For in this structure, individuals and groups that challenge, ignore, or abandon our system, or that embody or enact systems that are other than our own, constitute a threat to our (individual and group) identities and thus elicit aggression and even violence. The harm done by institutional/ systemic identities ranges from the monumental atrocities perpetrated by totalitarian regimes such as those of Hitler, Stalin, and Pol Pot to the silent soul murder perpetrated on, and by, the "organization man." It is thus necessary to develop an identity structure that transcends identifications with particular systems and that encounters and attempts to do justice to individuals, groups, and other phenomena that exist outside whatever systems one has internalized.

Interindividual Structure

In Kegan's fifth and final form of identity, the interindividual structure, this need is met by identity's assuming a form of interdependency and intimacy in love and work. Kegan does not elaborate on where such an identity would itself be grounded or embedded, but it would seem that it would necessarily be based on some sense of common humanity that transcends the differences of both individuals and systems. Rather than being one system or another, interindividual identity is universal empathy for, or identification with, all humans (and perhaps nonhuman creatures as well). This structure allows one to transcend one's own disciplinary and ideological systems and judge all systems, including one's own, on the basis of the benefit and harm they entail for other human beings. Erikson saw the various liberation movements of the 1960s as grounded in this sort of awareness, which he described as "a new *religious element* embracing nothing less than the promise of a mankind freer of the attitudes of a pseudospecies: that utopia of universality proclaimed as the most worthy goal by all world religions and yet always re-entombed in new empires of dogma which turn into or ally themselves with new pseudospecies" (*Identity* 318; emphasis in original).

Such an identity can be grounded in any or all of the three registers and is most powerful when it is anchored in all three. In the linguistic-conceptual register, it can reside in the very concept of common humanity, or the notion of the human species. In the imagistic-perceptual register, it is located in the involuntary identification we have with other human bodies, particularly those that are vulnerable or suffering, as well as those manifested in mirroring activities such as the infant's mirroring of its caregivers' facial expressions. And in the affective-physiological register, it manifests itself in the empathy we feel for other humans, including the affective resonance that occurs between infants and their caregivers. For such an identity, all forms of violence and indifference are more difficult than they are for other identity structures, because harming another is tantamount to harming oneself.

In education, the interindividual identity is no longer in thrall to fleeting impulses, imperial projects, interpersonal enthusiasm, or disciplinary identification. For an interindividual identity, learning is motivated not by the need to support one's identity by pleasing others (teachers or peers) or by expanding the particular discipline or body of knowledge one has identified with. Rather, learning is motivated by the need to benefit other people—ultimately all other people—because the interindividual identity is constituted by its care and concern for all of humanity. And understanding cannot be constructed within the boundaries of a single discipline, or a single isolated phenomenon, or a single moment of time, but must rather extend outward indefinitely, both spatially and temporally, from whatever its (always necessarily contingent and provisional) focal point might be.

Conclusion

We see, then, that the integration and organization of identity contents play crucial roles in learning and understanding, with the former being crucial for generative and emotional intelligence and inductive thinking and the latter playing a key role in deductive reasoning and comprehensive, systematic analysis and synthesis. But it is important to realize that while the most highly integrated, inclusive, complexly structured, and nondefensive identities are (all other things being equal) more secure than their opposites, identity security, and hence learning and understanding, may ultimately depend less on structure and integration than on identity contents and whether or not they receive sufficient support, in the form of recognition and opportunities for enactment. Even the most highly structured and integrated identities will be resistant to learning and development unless significant identity contents involve or entail learning and are provided with ample opportunities for recognition and enactment.

The impediments to learning, understanding, and the development of intelligence entailed by the various identity needs and identity deficiencies we have discussed suggest that education at all levels should have as its most fundamental mission the real basics: the construction, maintenance, and elaboration of students' identities, with identity being understood as a function of a certain continuity and coherence within and between an individual's affective, imagistic, and linguistic enactments and recognitions. By focusing on supporting and developing students' identities, educators can not only reduce the fundamental impediments to learning but also contribute significantly to the reduction of key social problems, which are the consequences of weak, vulnerable, and threatened identities.

PART TWO
IDENTITY-UNDERMINING PEDAGOGIES

CHAPTER 6
TEACHERS' IDENTITIES AS OBSTACLES TO RADICAL PEDAGOGY

Good teaching cannot be reduced to technique; good teaching comes from the identity and integrity of the teacher.

—Parker Palmer 10

I feel that one of the things blocking a lot of professors from interrogating their own pedagogical practices is that fear that "this is my identity and I can't question that identity."

—bell hooks, *Teaching* 134–135

Whereas, for my entire teaching life, I had always thought that what I was doing was helping my students to understand the material we were studying, . . . what I was actually concerned with and focused on most of the time were three things: (a) to show the students how smart I was, (b) to show them how knowledgeable I was, and (c) to show them how well-prepared I was for class.

—Jane Tompkins, "Pedagogy" 170

I was especially bothered by the four eighteen-year-old male students who sat next to each other, leaning back in their desks against the wall . . . Whenever I tried to create drama or intensity, they joked or smirked . . . I retaliated (note the aggressive language) by indirectly threatening them. I interrupted the class one day to give an angry and sarcastic speech on how anyone who was not taking the class seriously would fail and end up taking it again . . . I looked right at them when I made the threat . . . They were threatened by me, I told myself, so insecure that they had to stick together and act tough . . . I had allowed myself to get caught up in a macho competition with these students and I was losing . . . Clearly this had as much or more to do with my insecurities and unconscious responses as it did with theirs.

—Lad Tobin 33–35

We teachers are motivated by identity needs the same as everyone else, and our pedagogical aims, strategies, tactics, and reflexes all in one way or another serve to maintain or enhance our identities. Our identity contents, structures, and maintenance strategies are thus crucial factors determining the extent to which education helps students maintain and develop their identities. If our identity needs lead us to engage in pedagogical practices that promote optimal support and development of students' identities, then we teachers, our students, and the public at large all benefit, for reasons that have been explained in the previous chapters. If, on the other hand, our identities and modes of their maintenance lead us to engage in practices that fail to provide optimal support and development of our students' identities, then everyone loses. Ideally, the identity needs of both teachers and students would coincide with the fundamental aims of education, so that in pursuing our own identity needs, we teachers would automatically provide maximum benefits for both our students and society in general. Unfortunately, such coincidence does not always occur, and it is therefore incumbent on us to make every effort to discern the respective identity contents, structures, and maintenance practices that underwrite each facet of our teaching, and in particular to make every effort to determine when and how our identity needs and strategies may be driving us to engage in pedagogical practices that are unproductive or even harmful to our students and/ or society in general.

There are two fundamental aims of education. One aim is to benefit students by helping them learn and develop in ways that lead to empowerment and fulfillment. This aim involves

1. providing students with—and getting them to desire to acquire—the information, knowledge, and skills necessary to flourish in the given social conditions;
2. helping students develop, and thus desire to embody, the ideals and values—and perhaps also the desires, fantasies, enjoyments, drives, and defenses—necessary to survive and prosper in their society; and
3. helping students develop the more complex psychological capacities necessary for fulfillment in society—an aim that depends upon students' desire to grow and to enhance their capacities.

The second aim is to help students develop in such a way that they will benefit society as a whole. This aim entails

1. providing students with—and getting them to desire to acquire—the information, knowledge, and skills necessary for them to be productive members of society and, in some cases, to solve particular social problems or meet other collective needs;
2. socializing students into—that is, fostering their desire to take on—the roles needed by society and its mode(s) of production, including the roles of critic, reformer, and even revolutionary; and
3. contributing to the "civilizing" process—that is, helping students become more civil, circumspect, critical, self-critical, moral, compassionate,

and responsible—through the inculcation of particular values, ideals, desires, and fantasies and through the development of more complex structures of cognition, affect, relationship, and identity.

Many teachers operate—and educational conditions, institutions, administrators, and policymakers often encourage or even force them to operate—as though there were no conflict between these aims and either their identity needs or their students' identity needs. Ultimately, as will be discussed more fully in chapter 11, all these aims do converge: the fullest enactment of our (teachers') identities occurs to the extent that we enable our students to develop their identities in ways that enable their greatest possible personal fulfillment, which is itself found (as great literary works such as *Faust* demonstrate) in prosocial activities that benefit others. Unfortunately, most of the time neither we nor our students fully recognize this convergence, because we lack an adequate understanding of our own identity needs, and it is thus rare for all three factors—our (teachers') identity needs, students' identity needs, and the aims of education—to fully coincide. Often, in fact, there are in practice substantial discrepancies and even oppositions between two or even all three of these factors.

Opposition between Teachers' and Students' Identity Needs

The conflict between identity needs and the aims of education can take several forms. The form most obvious to teachers is that in which our efforts of identity maintenance enact the aims of education but our students' modes of identity maintenance conflict with these aims—when, that is, students are uninterested in or downright hostile to pursuing the aims of education furthered by the activities we try to engage them in. Like Lad Tobin in the epigraph above, we often experience such recalcitrance and hostility, consciously or unconsciously, as a threat to our identities, however subtle or insignificant the threat may be:

> I have on occasion, felt very hurt by my students' seeming inability to value what I value or to understand what I ask of them. . . . [T]eachers are wounded every day, and hearing this wounding is not at all hard if one listens. One hears, "I had a crappy class today." One also hears, sometimes explicitly, "because the are a pack of idiots." Or "because they lack civility." Or "because they have not been raised properly." (Tingle 78–81)

We often react to our wounded identity with anger or even rage, even if we are not aware of these feelings:

> I have felt such rage and still do. I have had occasion in hallway conversations with my colleagues to refer to students in terms most unflattering to

them. . . . Most instructors do not recognize the rage in their rage to teach. The rage, still there and unconsciously buried, does not rise to the instructor's consciousness, because the very way he or she conceives of the pedagogical relationship shields the instructor against any conscious awareness of possible wounding by students. (Tingle 78, 80)

Such rage, needless to say, is an impediment to effective teaching and learning. And even when we do not respond with rage or aggression to students' recalcitrance or lack of interest, we often attempt in various other ways to get them to embrace our agenda by either submitting to our demands or identifying with us. Either submission or identification on the part of students constitutes a powerful support for our identities, in the form of tacit recognition by the students of certain key identity components of ours. Unfortunately, such tactics are usually less than optimal for promoting either learning or our students' identity development.

Another form of impediment to learning occurs when students' modes of identity enactment are in concert with the aims of education but conflict with our (teachers') acts of identity maintenance. Such practices of identity maintenance on our part are most easily detected when they lead us to narcissistic and/or aggressive behaviors that are clearly unproductive or even counterproductive for learning, such as when we berate or belittle students (as in Tobin's example above), parade our knowledge or personal histories in an effort to impress students (as in the Tompkins epigraph), or try to turn students into clones of ourselves by getting them to major in our discipline or take up our line of research. Such narcissism and aggression are attempts to elicit recognition from students. As we have seen, all aggression, including violence, is motivated by the need to protect or enhance a vulnerable identity, and in many cases, aggression aims to elicit recognition—from either the person(s) or institution that is the object of aggression or from observers whom the aggressor is trying to impress. Teachers who feel threatened or deprived of recognition that they believe is their due sometimes respond with unwarranted aggression toward their students, in the form of harsh or belittling comments, punitive grading practices, or assignments that are excessively long or difficult. While such action will not usually make us loved or admired by the students who are its victims, it will elicit recognition from them, in the form of fear or resentment: whereas before our aggressive behavior these students may have ignored us, now they at least have to take us into account, a significant albeit negative form of recognition. Our aggression toward students may also elicit a more positive form of recognition—perhaps even in the form of admiration—from other students, administrators, parents, and the general public. Students often enjoy seeing their rivals reprimanded and punished, especially if they have themselves been victimized by these rivals, and they may feel their stock rise when another student is put down. Administrators often appreciate—and show their appreciation for—teachers who force students to conform, and parents are also grateful to teachers who punish students who may be a threat to their children. And the general public admires teachers and principals who control their students with an iron fist, as witnessed by the publicity and acclaim accorded such individuals.

Collusion between Teachers' and Students' Identity Needs

Opposition between teachers' and students' efforts to maintain their respective identities is thus a significant impediment to realizing the aims of education and enhancing students' identities. Often, however, the main impediment to education is not the opposition but rather the collusion between the two sets of identity needs, resulting in teachers and students engaging in activities that both parties find supportive of their identities but that do not contribute significantly to realizing the aims of education: learning and identity development. Such pedagogical failures usually go unnoticed, because the primary parties are both satisfied: when students' identities are affirmed, they are happy, produce good teaching evaluations (important forms of recognition for teachers), and remain in school (valuable instances of recognition for administrators)—results that, in turn, produce further recognition for teachers in the form of awards, honors, and salary increases.

A prime example of such collusion is the conviction we often have that a class in which students are engaged and enthusiastic must inevitably be a productive class for the students (and perhaps also for society at large). Experiencing our students' engagement and enthusiasm as a spontaneous and thus irrefragable acknowledgment that we are good teachers, we overlook the fact that while their enthusiasm may indicate that they are experiencing significant identity support, it does not indicate that this support is benign and productive, helping their identities to develop in the direction of greater personal capacities and fulfillment and prosocial action, rather than malignant and/or regressive, directing them toward personally limiting and socially harmful courses of aspiration and action. After all, people are engaged and enthusiastic at professional wrestling matches, white supremacist rallies, and public executions, but few teachers would claim that such events are personally or socially beneficial.

In some instances, the complicity between teachers' and students' practices of identity maintenance seems relatively benign, but stagnating, as in the acquisition of trivial knowledge or relatively insignificant skills, or the performance of classroom knowledge-games accomplished at the expense of acquiring more valuable knowledge, skills, and development. An example of the acquisition of trivial knowledge is recalled by David Richter, whose eighteenth-century literature professor once distributed a ten-page list of dates in English literature from 1660–1800, a significant portion of which students were expected to commit to memory (Richter 121). An example of the acquisition of a skill of dubious value is the development of the ability to scan poetry and label the various metrical forms and devices employed. And an example of the performance of classroom knowledge-games of questionable benefit is the activity in which students and teacher compete to formulate the most ingenious reading of a line of poetry. In such instances, performance of the knowledge or skill by both teacher and students elicits mutual identity-supporting recognition, as well as providing other forms of identity support, such as a sense of participation in a meaning-giving system and an experience of mastery, but it does little if anything to develop more valuable identity contents or structures.

A more harmful instance of such collusion is found in the common pedagogical practice of criticizing the various antisocial types of people and characters. That such practices are an easy, cost-effective way for us as well as many of our students to affirm our own and each other's identities can easily be verified by recalling the sense of well-being we feel when we ferret out and denounce some element of colonialism, racism, sexism, homophobia, or other injustice in the issues and texts (and sometimes also in the students) we teach, or when we explain to our students the traumatic consequences or the psychological or social dynamics of these forms of violence. We often come away from such moments feeling self-righteous and self-satisfied, confident that we have done more than our fair share to make the world a better place. In fact, we may have done the opposite. For by focusing exclusively on harmful behaviors and bad character and failing to recognize the traumas that are responsible for bad character, we have deprived these traumatized perpetrators (directly, for those who may be sitting in our classroom, and indirectly, for those outside the classroom who will be victimized by the more critical manner in which many of our students will engage them) of a benign recognition that might have helped render their recourse to their harmful behaviors unnecessary.

Collusion in the Transference

Perhaps the most powerful factor contributing to the complicity between teachers and students in identity-undermining pedagogical practices is the phenomenon of transference. Transference inclines students to seek recognition from authority by adopting certain alien identity contents they believe the authority approves of and abandoning, suppressing, or rejecting elements that are integral to their selves but that they believe the authority disapproves of. Pedagogical transference is particularly insidious because it provides powerful recognition to both the teacher and the student: its dynamics tempt teachers to use students as sources of affirmation for themselves by encouraging students to set aside their own identities and either identify with their teachers or become other sorts of objects that support their teachers identities rather than enacting and developing their own. In recent years, teachers have become increasingly sensitive to such coercive, identity-damaging effects of their transference authority.[1] Many teachers have attempted to solve the problem by devising strategies for eliminating the force of their authority, because authority is not an acceptable identity component for them. In an effort to enact a more benign, nonauthoritarian identity, some teachers attempt to negate their authority by becoming, as much as possible, just another member of the class, allowing their students considerable power in determining class goals, activities, and even grades, and engaging in the same activities as the students do (doing the writing assignments, submitting their writing for student critique, sharing personal experiences, and so on). As Lad Tobin notes, "Many writing teachers deny their tremendous authority in the classroom because it does not fit the image they would like to project. . . . [Such teachers] describe themselves as 'facilitators' (as if they have no agenda of their own, or rather, as if their agenda is not important) or as 'just another member of the writing workshop' " (20). The ideal feminist teacher, as Constance Penley points out, often "carries out a very deliberate self-undermining of her own authority by refusing to be an 'authority' at all" ("Feminism" 138). Other teachers try to be forthright about their authority and explicit about their values and political views, on the assumption that if they and their students recognize and acknowledge the teacher's power and bias they both will be able to escape the coercive force of the teacher's authority. And still other teachers attempt to vitiate the coercive effects of their authority by engaging their students in a discussion of its contingent, constructed nature, thus hoping to transform their authority from a substantial reality into an illusion that they and their students can then discard. Jane Tompkins confesses, "In order to win my students' love, I would try to divest myself of authority by constant self-questioning, by deference to students' opinions; through disarming self-revelation, flattery, jokes, criticizing school authorities; by accepting late papers, late attendance, and nonperformance of various kinds" (*Life* 3).

None of these strategies, however, succeeds in negating the subtly seductive and coercive effects of the teacher's authority. The reason teachers cannot shed the mantle of authority lies in the nature of transference.

Teachers function as powerful and inescapable transference objects for their students because, as Lacan observed, transference arises whenever there is a "subject supposed to know."[2] From such subjects, Lacan explained, we seek both validation of our identities (e.g., as "smart" or "brilliant") and knowledge of how to recover the enjoyment and vitality that we had to sacrifice when we assumed these social, symbolic-order identities during the process of socialization. In transference, we suppose that the authoritative or powerful person who is the object of our transference can grant us fullness of being by validating our identity and/or by providing knowledge of how to regain the enjoyment that we forfeited in assuming that identity.[3]

Transference is present in all pedagogical situations, but it is often particularly powerful in humanities classes. Unlike many other disciplines, the study of humanities often attracts students who bring to our classrooms a demand for knowledge of much the same type as analysands bring to psychoanalytic treatment. Many of our students suffer, as bell hooks observes, "from a crisis of meaning, unsure about what has value in life, unsure even about whether it is important to stay alive" (hooks, *Teaching* 76). They come with implicit (and sometimes explicit) questions: What should I do with my life? What's the point of it all? Why am I here? How can I give my life meaning? What does it mean to be a man or a woman, or to be gay or straight? How can I as an individual, or we as a group, reduce our suffering and destructiveness and achieve greater fulfillment and justice? Most of our students desire answers to questions of this sort even if they have not expressly posed the questions to themselves, and when they find a subject (person, group, or discipline) that is presumed to know the answer, transference arises. And since the humanities offer students a multiplicity of such "subjects presumed to know"—with teachers, authors, characters, and critics being the most notable—transference is ubiquitous in humanities classes.

In such a situation, strategies designed to reduce or eliminate the coercive and seductive force of authority actually have the opposite effect, because they provide subterranean routes for the enactment and recognition of teachers' authority. The first strategy, the democratic, egalitarian gesture in which the teacher attempts to function as just another member of the class, encourages students to suppose that this subject, the egalitarian teacher, really does know—knows or understands something about students' abilities that other, more traditional teachers do not. As a result, students' admiration for and enthrallment by such teachers is often increased rather than decreased by the teachers' gestures of giving up their authority. The second strategy, the candid acknowledgment and expression of the teacher's own political or epistemological positions, with its assumption that students can counter the teacher's authority with their own if they can recognize the teacher's bias, mistakenly assumes that disagreeing with an authority neutralizes its force. In actuality, such admission of bias on the teacher's part often simply transmutes the force of overt authority into a more subtle transferential form even more powerful than the overt form: students are so taken with the teacher's honesty (or insight, or self-awareness) that their faith in the teacher's authority is made even stronger. The third strategy, that of exposing the contingent, constructed nature of authority, also results in increasing the force of the teacher's authority through reinforcing the transference, because such discussions, like the acknowledgment of one's authority and the egalitarian gesture, succeed above all in confirming the students' supposition that the teacher is a subject who really knows—in this case, knows epistemological truths that not only the students but also most other teachers do not know.

Each of these gestures of divesting oneself of the seductive and coercive effects of authority actually increases the force of one's authority because whether one announces, renounces, or denounces one's own authority, the *énonciation* (act of enunciating) by which one rejects one's authority in the *énoncé* (statement) functions to reenact and reinforce the authority of the subject of the *énonciation*. The authority that is being eschewed or critiqued can never coincide with the authority that is producing the divestiture or critique, and this active, enunciating, critiquing subject not only remains an object of transference, but actually has its power enhanced by the act of self-critique.

Someone who is an object of transference, then, cannot escape operating from a position of imputed authority, for the very attempt to escape this position surreptitiously reinscribes one within it. For this reason, Lacan held that the analyst should not seek to interpret the transference for the analysand, as traditional analysis often advocates, but should instead *operate ethically* with the transference, since even interpreting the transference, explaining to the analysand the illusions that support it, ultimately involves an uninterpreted *operation* of the transference that simply reinforces the supposition that this subject (in enacting the *énonciation* of self-critique) really knows.

Most current literary pedagogies operate with transference in ways that inevitably result in precisely such seduction or coercion, however subtle, in spite of the best intentions of teachers. The reason is the teacher's own identity needs, because the crucial factor determining the effect of the transference is what the object of transference, the subject supposed to know, desires. In transference, the teacher's desire determines the student's desire in one of two ways[4]: either the student identifies with the teacher's desire, thus coming to desire, perceive, value, and enjoy what the teacher does; or the student identifies with the *object* of the teacher's desire, thus trying to become the sort of object that will satisfy the teacher's identity needs. In the first case, we have the cloning effect, with students becoming, in one way or another, a replica of their teacher—coming, for example, to desire and enjoy the same authors, characters, texts, critical approaches, or preferred interpretations as their teacher. In the second case, we have students who try to become like their teacher's favorite writer or character, or write texts like those for which their teacher has expressed admiration, or assume roles (in class or outside of class) that they imagine will win their teacher's approval. Any pedagogy, then, in which a teacher desires to promote particular identities, ideals, values, enjoyments, or positions will subtly entice and/or coerce students into replicating this aspect of the teacher's identity rather than developing their own identities, all in an attempt to gain the recognition from authority that the students need in order to maintain their identities.

The crucial question, then, is whether—and if so, how—teachers can pursue enactment and recognition for their own identities in ways that can escape the deleterious effects of the transference and instead promote optimal development of their students' identities. I believe that they can, and that the way to do so is found in what Lacan defined as the psychoanalyst's desire and the resulting mode of operation, which he called the discourse of the analyst. Before pursuing this point, however, I will sketch out in the next two chapters four of the most prominent pedagogical strategies currently in operation and explain how each undermines and inhibits the development of students' identities precisely by providing them with certain nonproductive types of recognition through the operation of transference. The first three strategies—authoritarian pedagogy, establishment pedagogy, and resistance pedagogy—are instances of the three other major discourses identified by Lacan: those of the master, the university, and the hysteric. The fourth strategy, that of critical pedagogy, offers a first approximation of Lacan's discourse of the analyst, but it is unable to fully enact it, because it fails to adequately address the full complexity of the students' and (especially) the teachers' identities and their needs.

CHAPTER 7

AUTHORITARIAN AND ESTABLISHMENT PEDAGOGIES

Authoritarian Pedagogy: The Discourse of the Master

The potentially harmful effect of transference on students' identities is most evident in traditional forms of pedagogy in which the teacher overtly celebrates a certain identity, ideal, or value. Such a pedagogy corresponds precisely to what Lacan called the discourse of the Master, and Lacan's articulation of this discourse structure can help us clarify the forms taken by the teacher's and the students' respective efforts to maintain their identities. In the discourse of the Master, the teacher foregrounds and valorizes a certain identity, or identity components, such as ideals and values—which Lacan calls master signifiers and designates as S_1. What the teacher desires above all is the recognition and validation of this identity, which the teacher may present explicitly, in the form of concepts, or implicitly, as embodied in certain writers, characters, or the teacher himself. This desire aims at finding or producing a system of secondary signifiers (text, discourse, or body of knowledge), designated as S_2, through which the power of the master signifiers is established and extended:

$$\text{Agent (Teacher)} \qquad \text{Other (Student, Literature)}$$
$$\frac{S_1}{\$} \longrightarrow \frac{S_2}{a}$$

The most blatant form of this master pedagogy is what Gerald Graff has referred to as the "cult of the great teacher" (114), in which the teacher offers himself as the primary object for students' admiration and identification. The teacher's central motive here is what Roger Simon describes as "a desire to provide [one]self with a 'love object' who is a reflection of [one]self" (96). In such a pedagogy the teacher attempts to enhance his own identity by having students acknowledge him as embodying a master signifier (S_1) such as "brilliant," "wonderful," "wise," or "understanding." The ultimate satisfaction of this desire is for our students to decide to become teachers like us, and the strength of both our desire and our satisfaction is demonstrated unmistakably in our triumphant announcement of such clonings when they occur.[1]

In a less overtly narcissistic form of this master pedagogy, the teacher aims to garner recognition not of herself but rather of the authors, works, or values (S_1) that she identifies with so strongly that they actually form part of her identity. The form of recognition being sought here is for our students either to aspire to become great authors, scientists, or public leaders or to engage in that devotional form of scholarship that we are all familiar with, in which one dedicates oneself to the utterances of a subject presumed to know (the great author or researcher), producing an interpretation, S_2, built upon the master's signifiers, S_1. This is the traditional, and in many ways still dominant, desire of literature teachers in particular. It manifests itself most often in the pedagogical aim of bringing our students "to love what we have loved," as Helen Vendler, quoting Wordsworth, put it some years ago in her presidential address to the Modern Language Association (Vendler 28). We literature teachers often see our primary goal as being to bring our students to replicate our recognition of the value of particular works and authors, or of "Literature" in general. Many teachers still assume that such love or appreciation is the be-all and end-all of literary study.[2] And while this pedagogy is most often associated with traditional, even Arnoldian, views of literature, the same desire can be seen to animate many teachers who challenge the traditional canon but maintain a traditional pedagogy, simply embracing a different canon or tradition, as, for example, women's literature, African American literature, Native American literature, or postcolonial literature.

In a third form of master pedagogy, the teacher aims not to demonstrate his own personal greatness or the greatness of particular works, authors, or schools, but rather to establish the hegemony of certain identity-bearing master signifiers per se. This effort expresses itself in a pedagogy that approaches literary works in such a way that they appear to celebrate or demonstrate the significance of the teacher's master signifiers, such as "genius," "creativity," "courage," "authenticity," "indeterminacy," "subversion," "empowerment," "hybridity," and so on. Such teaching exemplifies Graff's observation that "no matter how humble and self-effacing teachers may try to be, they inevitably teach *themselves* in the process of teaching Plato, Dante, or any other text or subject" (74).

Each of these three forms of authoritarian pedagogy subjects students to the same coercive, seductive transferential force, which can undermine their identities: the teacher presents an S_1—either herself, or certain great writers, great books, great ideas, or privileged identities, or certain ideals or values— as privileged identity components for students to appreciate, enjoy, celebrate, emulate, and ultimately incorporate into their own identity. The student responds either by identifying with the S_1 or by producing a network of secondary signifiers (S_2), in the form of class discussion, answers to exam questions, papers, theses, and dissertations that provide implicit recognition of these identity-bearing signifiers of the teacher's by giving them pride of place, using them as the key signifiers around which the students' own discourse is constructed.

Authoritarian pedagogy engages students' desire for recognition by promising that if they can successfully embody the authority's ideals, values, desires, or enjoyments, they will merit recognition and validation by that authority or its avatars (e.g., the teacher). Despite the negative connotations of its label, authoritarian pedagogy is not necessarily all bad. Depending on its content, it can be quite beneficial, and in any case it is in certain instances unavoidable. It can be beneficial, for example, if, taking Jesus, Buddha, or Gandhi as one's authority, one embraces identity-defining ideals such as love or nonviolence, rather than the ideal of dominance and the feeling of hatred embraced by those who took Hitler as their authority. And authoritarian pedagogy is inevitable insofar as all infants must submit to the protective demands of their caregivers ("Don't bite the electrical cord!" "Don't touch the fire!") in order to survive, as well as to the socializing process in order to become civilized. Authoritarian pedagogy, in fact, has its roots in our infantile experience with our caregivers, in which our well-being was totally dependent on their actions. From this situation in which our very survival depended on the actions of others, we learned that acceding to others' demands results in the provision of identity validation and support by these others. This same desire—to protect and support one's identity by pleasing the other—is at the heart of authoritarian pedagogy. The authority in such cases, as we have seen, can be the teachers themselves functioning as masters, gurus, or mentors, or it can be great scientists, entrepreneurs, writers, thinkers, historical figures, or literary characters whom the teachers idealize. Students who have already embraced the identity components embodied in these authorities identify with the authoritarian teacher more or less automatically. And students who do not already have these elements as components of their identities are coerced and/or cajoled to make them such by the powerful recognition (in the form of grades and other indications of teacher approval) that accrues to their presence and the lack of recognition that attends their absence. For such students, authoritarian pedagogy promises to satisfy the desire for recognition by supplying new identity components that will elicit greater recognition, and perhaps agency—at least in the immediate situation of the classroom and perhaps the academic community—than these students currently possess. Students who resist the (implicit, tacit) summons of the teacher to assume the authority's identity components may be subject to exclusion from the teacher's recognition and interest and perhaps ultimately from the education system as well.

But although it is impossible to completely avoid the authoritarian dynamic, and although the particular identity components one is coerced to embrace may be quite positive, acceding to the authoritarian teacher's desire and embracing his or her identity-defining master signifiers always comes at a price. For in order to embody the authority's identity components, students must enact them—through their reading, their writing, or their thinking, and/or in their political and interpersonal actions. And this means that they often have to suppress or allow to atrophy those parts of their selves that are different from those of the authority's identity. These abandoned and rejected components, of course, continue to insist that the students (unconsciously) enact them, thus producing alienation, a split between the rejected (and still insistent) elements of their self and the identity components promoted by the authority.

A further suppression of students' identities derives from the fact that authoritarian pedagogy trains students to take a fundamentalist approach to problem solving and inquiry and to seek identity support by conforming to or identifying with authorities and masters. In directing students to desire enlightenment from the teacher or from an authoritative thinker or text—be it the Bible or the Koran, or Marx, Freud, Lacan, or Foucault—authoritarian pedagogy inculcates the assumption that the best way to understand a phenomenon or solve a problem is to devote oneself to reading and interpreting the writings of a master. This promotion of fundamentalism is evident in Vendler's authoritarian pedagogy, where the mode of reading that Vendler desires for both herself and her students is one of submission to the text and suppression of their own identities:

In every true reading of literature in adult life we revert to that early attitude of entire *receptivity and plasticity and innocence before the text*. . . . The state of reading . . . is *a state in which the text works on us, not we on it*. . . . *It is this state of intense engagement and self-forgetfulness that we hope our students will come to know*. From that state, at least ideally, there issue equally the freshman essay, the senior thesis, the scholarly paper on prosody, the interdisciplinary paper on social thought and literature, the pedagogical paper on compositional structure, the variorum edition, and the theoretical argument. No matter how elementary or how specialized the written inquiry, it originated in problems raised by *human submission to, and interrogation of, a text*. . . . It is from that original vision—of the single, unduplicatable, compelling literary object—that we must always take our final strength in university life and public life alike. (Vendler 32, 37; emphasis added)

In this case, authoritarian pedagogy aims to perpetuate itself by establishing in students a desire for authority, teaching them that when they face practical problems in their jobs or difficulties in their lives, they should turn to authoritative texts rather than to their own experience, understanding, and cognitive and emotional capacities. Such training in fundamentalism, here made plain, is produced by all teaching practices that emphasize reverential, devotional interpretation at the expense of critical analysis and encounter with and exploration of the things themselves. And this indoctrination into fundamentalism holds for authoritarian pedagogy whether it is reactionary or progressive (or even radical) in its aims.

Even more significantly, it trains students to seek not only identity support but also the very content of their identities from authorities, masters, and gurus. Whatever benefits students obtain from such a pedagogy, to the extent that they are engaged by it, they sacrifice those parts of themselves (desires, enjoyments, beliefs, values, ideals, designated by the small a in Lacan's schema) that conflict with the master signifiers they have incorporated into their identities. Thus, while the aim of this pedagogy may be laudable, its mode of operation is ethically questionable, because it functions to surreptitiously impose the master's identity on the student.

Professionalism, or Establishment Pedagogy: The Discourse of the University

Although authoritarian pedagogy is by no means uncommon today, it is no longer the idealized and dominant practice that it was in previous decades and centuries. Today, in both theory and practice, the ideal teacher is often viewed as a servant of knowledge rather than its master. Thus many teachers view their function as that of initiating students into the discourse of their particular discipline or into academic discourse in general, a process that they see as empowering students. In such cases, teachers desire that their students establish their identities not upon certain ideals or values but within an established system of knowledge, know-how, and/or practices:

$$\text{Teacher} \qquad \text{Student, Literature}$$
$$\frac{S_2}{S_1} \longrightarrow \frac{a}{\$}$$

In this mode of pedagogy, as Lacan's formula indicates, the teacher foregrounds not particular identities, ideals, or values, but rather an identity-bearing system of knowledge, of disciplinary rules, or of professional practices, designated by S_2. Teachers deposit their identity-bearing knowledge, S_2, in students, a, for recognition in the form of adoption and preservation. The teacher is here seeking to maintain his identity through enforcing the system that constitutes a crucial dimension of his sense of self. To ensure the security of this system, and to enhance its recognition-conferring effects, the teacher needs to colonize otherness; he needs empty vessels into which his knowledge may be poured, blank slates onto which the system can be inscribed, amorphous material that his discourse can inform and form.

These blank slates or empty vessels can be either literary texts, reality, or the students themselves. We see literary texts taking on this role in pedagogies in which literature functions as grist for the teacher's critical mill, with the texts often being selected according to how well they can be seen to embody, or offer an occasion for enacting, the teacher's particular identity-bearing system of knowledge or critical methodology. When teachers look to students rather than texts to perform this function, they manifest what Roger Simon calls a "desire for an intellectual partner" ("Face" 96) or a "desire for solidarity" ("Face" 97). Such teaching summons students, in the first instance, not to produce any discourse at all but to offer themselves as empty vessels or blank slates (the a in Lacan's formula) that can simply accept and preserve the new knowledge and mirror it back to the teacher. This pedagogy appeals to students' need for identity support by offering them a system that, when internalized, constitutes an internal source of recognition and provides a sense of agency, and when inhabited, provides, like membership in a club, an identity-bearing sense of orientation, connection, and significance.

But while mastering a field of knowledge and becoming fluent in a particular discourse can produce agency and significance, it also produces harmful effects. One harmful effect of establishment pedagogy is that the knowledge and skills through which it provides agency and significance in the classroom actually produce little agency and significance in life beyond the classroom. Teachers and students, and laypersons as well, can very easily get caught up in learning and performing a particular knowledge or discourse not because of its value for addressing human needs or solving problems but simply because of its social currency in a particular academic discipline: possessing it allows one to join the club or be a member of the gang. The knowledge itself may be completely trivial, the discourse utterly useless except as social currency within a narrow academic sphere, and yet teachers and students, and even laypersons, will devote significant portions of their lives to acquiring, performing, and disseminating them. This dynamic is quite common in the field of literary studies, where the Scholastic competitions between rival interpretations and theories are often enough to capture students' desire for agency, recognition, and other identity-supporting dynamics.

The combined passion and insignificance of such controversies over interpretations of particular literary works should remind the contestants of the bitter dispute between Swift's Big Endians and Little Endians over which end of the egg should be cracked. Usually, however, such conflicts have the opposite effect, energizing both teachers and students to construct their identities out of the trivial knowledge and skills that allow them to compete in these Scholastic games. Gerald Graff, for example, reveals that he first became interested in literature and history through exposure to the internal debates of these disciplines (66). It is evident from Graff's account of his conversion to literary study that the debates were attractive to him because they provided him with identity-supporting experiences of stature, agency, aggression, and belonging. Explaining that he found the study of literature uninteresting until his class was informed that critics disagreed with each other concerning the merits of the ending of *Huckleberry Finn*, Graff recalls:

> Reading the critics was like picking up where the class discussion had left off, and I gained confidence from recognizing that my classmates and I had had thoughts that, however stumbling our expression of them, were not too far from the thoughts of famous published critics. I went back to the novel again and to my surprise found myself rereading it with an excitement I had never felt before with a serious book. Having the controversy over the ending in mind, I now had some issues to watch out for as I read, issues that reshaped the way I read the earlier chapters as well as the later ones and focused my attention. And having issues to watch out for made it possible not only to concentrate, as I had not been able to do earlier, but to put myself into the text—to read it with a sense of personal engagement that I had not felt before. Reading the novel with the voices of the critics running through my mind, I found myself thinking things that I might say about what I was reading. . . . It was as if having a stock of things to look for and to say about a literary work had somehow made it possible to read one. (67–68)

Graff goes on to observe that "reading books with comprehension, making arguments, writing papers, and making comments in a class discussion . . . involve entering into a cultural or disciplinary conversation, a process not unlike initiation into a social club" (77), and he advocates that literature classes should therefore "teach the conflicts."

The identity maintenance strategies and the corresponding ethical consequences of professionalist pedagogy are quite evident from Graff's account of teaching the conflicts. Graff argues against master pedagogies and their promotion of particular cultural ideals, political goals, or teachers, which he calls "the course fetish and the myth of the great teacher" (14). His desire is for a powerful S_2, a coherent curriculum in which students are brought to participate in the professional debates and disciplinary controversies of the day. What positions students take in these debates is less important to him than the fact that they participate. "I suspect," Graff states, "that my best courses have been those which helped my students articulately to disagree with me" (44). In contrast to the master teacher, Graff does not need to get students to venerate him, or to love particular books or authors, or to embrace particular political positions (S_1); he needs rather to initiate students into the discourse of the university, to "socializ[e] them into the academic intellectual community" (76), or S_2. Here students' identification with a subject supposed to know produces a sense of membership in a club and hence an increase in identity security. This is one of the main attractions offered by professionalist pedagogy. Students who allow themselves to be colonized by their teacher's knowledge become subjects ($\$ $ in Lacan's schema) in the new field: they now can speak the language of the discipline and reap the corresponding enhanced identity security through agency and community with others in the field.

This strategy of identity maintenance can easily lead to what has been described as "a kind of perverse consummation of professionalism, the last refinement on the isolation and self-referentiality of academic studies: it makes what professionals do the subject of what professionals do" (Menand 109). And even when joining an academic club or gang through mastering its discourse is empowering beyond the walls of academe, it can nonetheless ultimately be disempowering, even psychologically eviscerating, insofar as membership, like identification with an authority, entails renunciation of certain key components of one's self. Students wind up emptying themselves of their own identity-bearing beliefs, knowledge, values, ideals, and key concepts and being colonized by the new system. "Good students" in such a pedagogy are often those who are the most quickly and fully colonized, getting rid of their "naive," "biased," or "uncritical" ways of reading, thinking, feeling, and perceiving and assuming the responses called for by the new system. Thus students such as women, minorities, and others who have significant identity components that are devalued by, or incompatible with, the teacher's system, or with the more general educational or cultural system of which the teacher's system is a part, may resist learning because to learn would be to sacrifice crucial identity components. And if they do learn, one consequence is the sacrifice of certain identity components, as when female students who studied American literature in its patriarchal form "learned" that women and their accomplishments were less important (and hence less worth writing about) than men and their achievements (see Fetterly).

Thus while establishment pedagogy may give students a voice, it also produces a self-division ($) in them, because part of the being (*a*) that they submit to the discipline (S₂) cannot be assimilated by the discipline and is thus excluded by it. As Scholes observes, "What we have to offer our students is an entry into discursive formations that will give them a certain power: [but it is] a power that can be exercised only at the price of being subjected to the rules and limits established by that discourse. . . . And we have no magic that will spare them the price, that will preserve their initial apprehension of themselves from fading as they acquire their new subjectivities" (109). This is why, as Lacan says, students are inevitably alienated, separated from crucial parts of their identity.

Such alienation, as Nick Tingle points out, is a frequent consequence of a form of establishment pedagogy practiced in thousands of college writing classes across the United States: the craft approach. One of the primary proponents of this approach, Donald Bartholomae, states, "The struggle of the student writer is not the struggle to bring out that which is within; it the struggle to carry out those ritual activities that grant one entrance into a closed society" (qtd. in Tingle 95). This means, as Tingle comments, that "the student's struggle to move into the alien discourse of the university requires that he lose himself. As a result, the chronicles of those who have made that move are tales of loss, violence, and compromise" (96). One of the reasons many students experience a loss of identity in learning to write like an academic is because such writing elicits no recognition from those who are the primary sources of recognition for these students:

> [I]n writing academically, . . . one may begin to express oneself in a way that is not intelligible or comprehensible to those audiences most deeply embedded in oneself. . . . One is trying to learn to write and to think in a way (to gain entry to that closed society) that cuts one off exactly from those audiences from which one most desires recognition. No wonder students become enervated. No wonder they write things they don't understand and don't care about. The psychological roots of BS run very deep. No wonder some might experience themselves as becoming someone they are not. (Tingle 111)

Professionalist, establishment teachers, like authoritarian, master teachers, usually manage to remain ignorant of such alienation, often focusing on student enthusiasm as evidence of the supposed personal benefits of this pedagogy. But this enthusiasm is no proof of any sort of student benefits, for it is the result of the same subtly seductive and coercive transferential forces that are operating in the more overtly authoritarian and oppressive master pedagogies. Professionalist pedagogy, too, is operating in an ethically questionable manner that can be harmful to students' identities, and no amount of student satisfaction or enthusiasm can erase this fact. To put it bluntly, in both the authoritarian master pedagogy and the professionalist establishment pedagogy, the spectacle we offer our students of authoritative, knowledgeable, and enthusiastic subjects passionate about literature—that is, as subjects who appear to know how to become whole and recapture lost *jouissance* through literary study—functions in the same way as an advertisement of an attractive and satisfied individual enjoying a cigarette: both the teacher's performance and such advertisements elicit identification with the subject supposed to know, which promotes replication in the students or the advertisements' audience of this subject's identity. While our conscious pedagogical intentions might be more noble and the direct results less destructive than those of cigarette advertisements, the transferential effect and identity damage of such pedagogical practice are the same as those of the advertisers when we parade our passions or those of other subjects, real or fictional, before our students: both practices seduce our charges, through transference, to renounce important parts of their identities and embrace identities other than their own. The recognition received can seem quite fulfilling, but in reading as in smoking, there can be negative long-term consequences—such as those that Judith Fetterley termed the "immasculation" of female students (xx)—that become apparent only much later.

CHAPTER 8

PEDAGOGIES OF RESISTANCE AND EMPOWERMENT

Resistance or Protest Pedagogy: The Discourse of the Hysteric

Reaction against precisely the sorts of problems with authority and establishment discourses and systems of knowledge discussed in the previous chapter has produced a third, increasingly prominent pedagogical mode, that of resistance and protest. In such a pedagogy, teachers seek recognition for their own identity vulnerability or deprivation, or that of a subaltern group with which they have identified, and oppose the authorities and the establishment systems that are presumably responsible for this deficiency. This pedagogy is most prominent in relation to various subaltern identity components, including those of gender, class, ethnicity, and sexual orientation, as frequently found in feminist, Marxist, postcolonialist, and queer pedagogies.

Any such pedagogy that centers on utterances (those of teachers, students, or texts) of alienation, anxiety, suffering, or injustice is an instance of what Lacan calls the discourse of the Hysteric, in which the speaker's self-division or alienation, $, is the central element of the utterance:

$$
\begin{array}{cc}
\text{Teacher} & \text{Student, Literature} \\
\dfrac{\$}{a} & \longrightarrow \dfrac{S_1}{S_2}
\end{array}
$$

Here the teacher's aim is 1) to gain recognition of his or her own identity damage (or that of a group the teacher has identified with), indicated by $, 2) to expose the identity-bearing master signifiers (S_1) responsible for the identity damage, or self-alienation, and 3) to acquire new master signifiers that would recognize and allow enactment of those parts of the self that the current identity-bearing signifiers reject.

The most common and fully developed instances of this strategy of identity maintenance can often be found in feminist pedagogy, where the first aim—to gain recognition for one's identity-damaging self-division—is expressed in the very existence of women's literature courses, as well as in the personal, confessional element found in much feminist teaching and writing. In some cases, teachers aim explicitly and self-consciously to get their students to identify with the teacher's alienation, suffering, or oppression ($). One feminist teacher, for example, declares: "As a teacher, I begin with the assumption that I should train students to be discontented with a culture that tolerates and perpetuates oppression" (Waxman 149).

The second aim, to expose the identity-damaging effects of the identity-bearing signifiers allocated to women, is manifested quite clearly in what has been called the images of women approach, or feminist critique (see Showalter). The purpose of this pedagogy is to show that the dominant images and signifiers (such as "lady," "girl," "babe") harbored either in texts or by students themselves are woefully inadequate to women, distorting, caricaturing, or ignoring crucial elements of women's being, their experience, and their worlds.

The third aim of the discourse of the Hysteric, the desire for a new identity-bearing signifier that would include elements of the self that the old signifiers require women to reject—such as aggressive and sexual impulses ("lady"), maturity and autonomy ("girl"), and subjectivity rather than objectification ("babe")—is most evident in the cultivation of knowledge of and identification with women writers, the practice that Elaine Showalter named gynocritics (Showalter 248). Such writers offer, through their own lives, their characters, their ideals and values, and other elements of their writing, new signifiers of "woman" with which readers can replace their old master signifiers, and these new identity-bearing signifiers can then become the nodal points of a new S_2—a new system of knowledge, social organization, and/or identity-bearing narrative.

Such a pedagogy can be wonderfully empowering for students in whom subaltern elements are a significant part of their identity. And it can be empowering for others who are not themselves subalterns but who identify with the subaltern plight and thus strengthen their own identity through acquiring a) the group membership and solidarity the identification provides, b) the sense of agency produced through being an advocate for justice, and c) the particular identity-bearing signifiers (e.g., "good," "just," "courageous," "caring") that such advocacy enacts. Both subaltern students and those who identify with them have experienced by the thousands the identity support and development that such a pedagogy can provide. Moreover, the establishment or reinforcement of such identity components also contributes to social change, insofar as their identity vulnerability motivates students to take action to change the authorities and systems that are responsible for the damage to their identities.

Such reinforcement of one identity component, however, can also have disempowering effects, such as when it leads students to invest their identities almost exclusively in the subaltern categories and thus ignore other capacities and attributes the development of which might be of great value both personally and socially. In addition, such a pedagogy can support socially destructive forms of identity politics that pit different groups against each other in a competition for recognition as the greatest victim (including the tacit recognition embodied in concessions granted by the establishment). Taken to its extreme, this logic can lead to disastrous results, including genocide, as David Richter has pointed out (130). And in cases where students identify with the teacher's desire to expose the deficiencies of the master or the master signifiers, the result will be at least partially negative for them, for their identification will almost inevitably result in the repression of some of their own feelings, impulses, or qualities, as we saw in the cases of authoritarian and establishment pedagogies.

Even more problematic is the teacher's desire for a new master signifier. For whether students identify with the object of this desire, or with the desiring subject (the teacher), in either case they will seek (to find or to be) a master signifier provided by a subject who is supposed to know. This, as Lacan pointed out to student protesters in 1968, is an inherent danger courted by the discourse of protest: it can very easily become a demand for a new master—a new identity or identity element provided by a subject supposed to know. In feminist pedagogy, although the new master may be a mistress, in the form either of newly canonized women writers or of feminist critics, the process is the same: the subtle coercion or seduction of students to identify with someone else's S_1. While the new master signifiers offered by feminists may in our view be much less distorting and constricting than the old, our students, both male and female, often feel threatened by the accounts of men and women they encounter in writing by feminists. They experience such accounts, that is, as a new identity element that these writers—and the teacher, too—are trying to impose on them and that, if successfully imposed, would produce a significant loss of important elements of their identities.

A fundamental problem of protest pedagogy thus becomes clear: as Lacan warned, it often eventuates in the acceptance of a new master signifier from someone else, a subject supposed to know. Feminist critique leads to gynocriticism, and as soon as gynocriticism establishes a new canon, a new tradition to be taught—which we know has occurred when Norton publishes an anthology devoted to the tradition—we are back on the grounds of authoritarian and establishment pedagogy with their attendant threats and damages to identity. The same process occurs with literatures of other oppressed groups, such as African American literature, as Michele Wallace has observed (660–661).

The most significant identity damage produced by protest pedagogy, however, may come from teachers' need to expose and reject master signifiers that they regard as oppressive. The harm produced by this practice is most notable in cases where students themselves appear to embody the master signifiers that the teachers find oppressive. In such cases, teachers often respond with "oppositional pedagogy," which entails "identifying and confronting the subject positions of [the] students" (Strickland 119)—a practice that constitutes a direct assault on the students' identities. In criticizing or denouncing individuals or groups that perpetrate various forms of violence—racists, sexists, homophobes, fascists, murderers, rapists, terrorists, child molesters—protest pedagogy, operating with the best of intentions, unwittingly fans the flames of violence by further threatening the already damaged identities of its most notable perpetrators. We literature teachers are complicit in the perpetration of the various forms of physical, institutional, structural, and cultural violence by virtue of our almost total failure to provide—and help our students understand why and how to provide—recognition for the perpetrators of each type of violence.

This complicity is quite ironic, considering all the recognition that has been accorded to "the Other" in literary theory, criticism, and pedagogy—especially protest pedagogy—in recent decades. Beginning with feminist criticism in the 1960s, concern for the Other has grown exponentially in literary studies, becoming a focal point in most literary historical periods and critical methodologies and addressing the status of virtually all demographic groups other than that of the hegemonic white, Euro-American, middle-class, heterosexual, conventionally abled man. Our aim has been to promote greater social justice for these Others, who have been traumatized—often severely—by being denied recognition of every sort. Thus literary study has during the past four decades taken major steps toward providing significant recognition for certain groups that were traditionally marginalized and disrespected by its institutionalized practices as well as by American society and culture as a whole. One of the most visible and progressive of these steps has been the opening up of the canon to (or the rejection of the canon in favor of) authors of marginalized identities such as women, gay, lesbian, and queer writers, as well as writers with African American, Hispanic, Asian American, and other racial, ethnic, and national identities. The inclusion of such writers in the canon constituted in and of itself a significant act of recognition and respect where earlier there was either lack of recognition or active disrespect of such writers. In pursuit of justice for these Others, we routinely instruct our students about the traumas that these Others have sustained, and we express—and encourage our students to feel—sympathy, respect, and admiration for groups that have been variously deprived of recognition—excluded, marginalized, disempowered, ignored, denigrated—by the (predominantly white, male, heterosexual, economically secure American) mainstream. We take particular pains to discern and respect these Others' differences from ourselves, explaining how failure to do so has led to the imperialistic imposition of parochial categories, values, and beliefs in the name of a universal humanity. It is precisely the Other's otherness, we say, that must be recognized and respected; if we recognize only those aspects of the Other that are the same as our own, then we are engaging in an act of narcissistic, Other-denying cultural imperialism, social exclusion, and psychological oppression.

Despite this lip service to difference, however, the Others that we literature teachers focus on and sympathize with tend to be much like ourselves—or rather like those parts of ourselves that we acknowledge—in their core moral and behavioral characteristics: while their race, ethnicity, nationality, class, religion, gender, and/or sexuality may be quite different from our own, we imagine them, as we imagine ourselves, as being fundamentally humane, benign, nonviolent. Rarely do we express or attempt to engender sympathy for those individuals and groups—murderers, rapists, child molesters, terrorists, or the perpetrators of genocide and ethnic cleansing—who appear to be the most different from us humane, nonviolent literature teachers, the most fully Other in terms of what we consider to be the basic human qualities. Nor do we grant respectful recognition to those identities that are most responsible for institutional, structural, and cultural violence (primarily angry white males). In fact, in literature classrooms these identities are more often the objects of criticism and even condemnation than they are the recipients of recognition in the form of sympathy and understanding. And when racism, sexism, homophobia, classism, imperialism, and militarism are criticized in class discussion or in texts under discussion, students whose identities include one or more of these elements sustain yet another traumatization, however mild it may be. In addition, the students whose identities do not incorporate these (negative) qualities are being trained and habituated to ignore these qualities within their own selves and to externalize them and attack them in the other, thus perpetuating the Other's traumatization and making him more rather than less likely to engage in cultural, structural, institutional, and even physical violence.

This shaming process is perhaps most pronounced in the response many of us literature teachers have given to claims by straight, white, Euro-American men that they are the true victims, oppressed by the efforts (such as affirmative action) to help various marginalized groups: we have met such claims with consternation, indignation, and even anger and ridicule, as well as categorical rejection. Of course, such responses are in one sense justified, since it is clearly the case that most members of this group have escaped the more obvious, dramatic, mass traumas experienced by marginalized groups. The problem is that our dismissal of their claim of victimization ignores the traumatic effects that can be produced by experiences that appear mild and undramatic. Moreover, by denying recognition to this dominant group's identity and feelings of vulnerability—at the same time that we criticize men in general for not recognizing and acknowledging their vulnerability—we make members of this group more rather than less prone to continue perpetrating cultural, structural, and institutional violence. Our refusal to recognize and sympathize with their experiences of vulnerability constitutes another increment of trauma that makes their identities more vulnerable and thus more prone to violence. The refusal of recognition simply reinforces their macho denial of feelings of vulnerability, a denial that provides a further impetus to violent behavior. Thus the ridiculing and dismissing of the angry white male, while morally justified from one perspective, is from another perspective yet another instance of putting the Other down (a milder form, but nonetheless an instance, of traumatizing violence) that constitutes another turn in the vortex of trauma that produces violence. Hating and demonizing the devil, whether in the form of the violent criminal or of the angry white male, simply makes the devil more diabolical. Recognizing and providing sympathy for the devil, on the other hand—whether he be a murderer, a rapist, a terrorist, or an angry white man—provides him with a more benign form of what he needs and is trying desperately to obtain by means of his violent behavior.

Depriving (physically, institutionally, structurally, or culturally) violent others of recognition is thus not only profoundly unjust but also powerfully self-defeating. By participating (even if only passively, through our lack of opposition) in our society's demonization and punishment of such individuals rather than trying to understand them and provide them (directly or indirectly) with the recognition that would help them enact the benign elements of their identities and in doing so eschew violence, we literature teachers harm ourselves and our students. We harm them and ourselves morally by engaging in precisely the process of othering that we condemn when it is directed toward supposedly benign others; we harm our students and ourselves psychologically by activating primitive defense mechanisms such as projection and projective identification, which diminish both our self-awareness and our sensitivity to Others; and we harm our students and ourselves personally and socially by precluding the understanding and motivation necessary to reduce rather than escalate violence.

In this way, teachers' identity needs are profoundly implicated in the failure to pursue effective solutions to social problems. One reason that the traumas sustained by the perpetrators of physical, institutional, structural, and cultural violence are not sympathized with and thus prevented or healed is because those of us who are in the best position both to recognize these traumas and thus help prevent or heal them—that is, cultural workers such as artists, teachers, scholars, journalists, poets, novelists, screenwriters, lyricists, and recording artists—are ourselves driven by our own identity needs to demonize these Others rather than provide them with the trauma-preventing or healing recognition and sympathy that would reduce their need to perpetrate institutional violence (such as the humiliation and punishment of criminals), structural violence (such as the perpetuation of poverty and economic inequity), and cultural violence (such as the promotion of ideals of masculinity, individualism, independence, self-reliance, and toughness). When we seek the reasons for our failure to provide recognition for these types of people, we find our own identity needs playing a prominent role.

Critical Pedagogy and the
Discourse of the Analyst

The fourth prominent pedagogical mode is critical pedagogy, which might be described as resistance pedagogy combined with the Socratic method. Like resistance pedagogy, it aims at liberation from the oppressive forces and structures that constitute racism, classism, colonialism, sexism, and heterosexism. But in addition to liberating students (and others), it also aims to help students develop their full potentials, to become empowered. A careful reading of critical pedagogical theory reveals that a central motivation animating this pedagogy is the teachers' desire for a strong identity for their students, whose identity needs the teachers have identified with.

This motivating force is essentially the same as the psychoanalyst's, which Lacan called the desire for absolute difference. What Lacan's phrase means is, first of all, that the analyst desires not to clone herself or to replicate her own identity components in her analysands: rather, she desires that they develop and enhance their own identities, which will be fundamentally ("absolutely") different from hers in multiple ways, rather than just moderately different variations on the basic themes of her identity. And in order to enable her analysands to develop such an identity, the analyst desires a second absolute difference: those capacities and qualities in the analysand that remain undeveloped, repressed, or disowned because they are "absolutely different" from the analysand's dominant, socially sanctioned identity components, and which the analysand must recognize, own, and accommodate in order to find relief from suffering and to progress and develop in life. Thus what an analyst would desire in relation to an analysand struggling with his sexuality would be not that the analysand "become" heterosexual, homosexual, bisexual, transsexual, or any particular sexual identity at all but rather that he come to own all of his impulses, desires, ideals, and other elements of self—many of them fundamentally different from both the analyst's and the analysand's own identity components—and arrive at an accommodation of these "absolutely different" elements that he is satisfied with. By thus fostering identity development in her patients, the analyst's identity enacts itself and receives recognition from the real, in the form of her patients' identity development.

Similarly, critical pedagogy, unlike the other three modes of teaching we have discussed, aims not for students to embrace particular identity components but for them to become aware of their present identity components, of repressed qualities that could become new aspects of identity, and of the consequences of both types of elements for themselves and for others. Such a pedagogy is like the discourse of the psychoanalyst in that it offers not prefabricated identity components but rather a process for discovering one's own potential identity components and developing them into an identity of one's own.

This aim of helping students to enhance their identities is revealed by a careful reading of the writings of a number of the leading proponents and developers of critical pedagogy. Henry Giroux and Roger Simon, for example, state,

> Our project is the construction of an educational practice that expands human capacities in order *to enable people to intervene in the formation of their own subjectivities* and to be able to exercise power in the interest of transforming the ideological and material conditions of domination into social practices that promote social empowerment and demonstrate possibilities. (189; emphasis added)

Another prominent advocate of critical pedagogy, Peter McLaren, articulates a similar desire to enhance students' identities, emphasizing that "students especially need to be provided with opportunities to devise different assemblages of self" (214). McLaren points out that such a project is not only an important end in itself but also a necessary component of any effort to achieve liberation and social justice: "The remaking of the social and the reinvention of the self must be understood as dialectically synchronous— that is, they cannot be conceived as unrelated or only marginally connected. They are mutually informing and constitutive processes" (210). Likewise, Abdul JanMohamed describes the aim of critical pedagogy in terms of "the incipient constitution of a new identity" and the clarification of students' "nascent identities" (245).

There is a crucial difference between such desire for (one's students') identity and the identity-supporting desires animating the other three pedagogical modes. The other pedagogical modes aim to get students to identify with some aspect of the teacher's identity, such as the teacher's ideals, values, or enjoyments (authoritarian pedagogy), the teacher's knowledge or belief system (establishment pedagogy), or the teacher's opposition to, lack of, or desire for a particular identity (resistance pedagogy). In critical pedagogy, in contrast, teachers identify with their *students'* identity needs. Whereas the first three pedagogies serve teachers' identities in ways that may fail to help or may even harm the students' identities, critical pedagogy involves practices that, strictly speaking, provide support for the teacher's identity only insofar as they benefit the students' identities.

Rather than offering students new identity components, as the other three pedagogies do in one way or another, critical pedagogy aims, like psychoanalysis, to help students understand (1) the nature and origins of their own identity components, (2) the consequences of these components for themselves and others, and (3) the nature, potential source, and likely consequences of alternative identity components that they might embrace or pursue. The aim is not to change students in any particular way but rather to provide them with the opportunities and resources to change and develop according to their own identity needs. As Lawrence Grossberg puts it, critical pedagogy

> aims not to predefine its outcome (even in terms of some imagined value of emancipation or democracy) but to empower its students to reconstruct their world in new ways and to rearticulate their future in unimagined and perhaps even unimaginable ways. It is a pedagogy which demands of students, not that they conform to some image of political liberation nor even that they resist, but simply that they gain some understanding of their own involvement in the world, and in the making of their own future. (18)

This same desire informs the political dimension of critical pedagogy, according to Grossberg:

> If political struggles are won and lost . . . in the space where people and groups are articulated, both ideologically and affectively, to social identities, cultural practices, and political projects, then it is here that pedagogy must operate. The task of a politically engaged pedagogy is, after all, never to convince a predefined subject . . . to adopt a new position. Rather, the task is to win an already positioned, already invested individual or group to a different set of places, a different organization of the space of possibilities . . . We cannot tell our students what ethics or politics . . . to embrace. Again, we must connect to the ethics and politics they already embrace and then struggle to

rearticulate them to a different position (without necessarily knowing in advance that we will be successful, or even what that different position will actually be). (19–20)

The central process through which this desire is pursued is the mapping of students' identities, a process that is also central to psychoanalysis. McLaren states,

Educators need to stare boldly and unflinchingly into the historical present and assume a narrative space where conditions may be created where students can tell their own stories, listen closely to the stories of others, and dream the dream of liberation. Identity formation must be understood in terms of how subjectivity is contextually enacted within the tendential forces of history (Grossberg 1992). The exploration of identity should consist of mapping one's subject position in the field of multiple relationships. (217)

This mapping can be pursued in several ways, including helping students identify and question their own individual and collective meanings, values, histories, cultural investments, desires, and affective responses (see Giroux 47ff.; Giroux and Simon 182ff, 195; and JanMohamed passim). As in psychoanalysis, such mapping can help students become aware of their own intrapsychic conflicts. As Giroux puts it, in the form of critical pedagogy he advocates, "students would study their own ethnicities, histories, and gain some sense of those complex and diverse cultural locations that have provided them with a sense of voice, place, and identity. In this way, students could be made more attentive to . . . the struggles that inform their own identities" (51). JanMohamed notes that overcoming hegemony requires engaging the internal division within oneself: "Denial of identity operates most effectively . . . through the construction of hegemonic rules and regulations that are 'internalized' as normal operating procedures. Thus, on the sociopolitical register antagonism exists on the 'inside': it cleaves the subject" (247). An important step in critical pedagogy is thus for "students to develop relationships of nonidentity with their own subject positions . . . , [which] amounts to the development of an antagonism with oneself" (246). By activating students' self-division, critical pedagogy can promote their development of new, alternative identities: "their new subject positions," JanMohamed explains, "begin to cathect around the project of excavating and reading their own social and physical bodies, which are in fact texts of the history of their oppression. Thus their new subjectivity emerges in the process of drawing borders around their old subject positions" (248).

In this way, the key processes of critical pedagogy resemble those of psychoanalysis: mapping one's identity leads to a recognition of oppositions and the experiencing of conflicts between different identity components, and working through these conflicts in relation to one's present realities and future possibilities promotes the alteration of one's identity, or the development of an alternative identity—a result that liberates people from a constricting identity and thus empowers them both personally and collectively.

I have quoted extensively from its leading advocates to make the point that critical pedagogy is ultimately driven by the same motivation—the same form of identity enactment—as the psychoanalyst is. But my selective quotation has made critical pedagogy seem to be a much more unified, coherent, and fully theorized practice than it actually is. And it has also made it seem more psychoanalytic and more effective than it really is. For though the core identity-enacting strategy of critical pedagogy is that of psychoanalysis, its practice, and hence also its results, often diverge significantly from those of psychoanalysis, in ways that are potentially harmful to the very identities that they are aiming to nurture.

In the first place, critical pedagogy often equates identity with subject position, which is largely a function of the socially determined signifiers of group identity. By thus largely ignoring students' imagistic-perceptual identity components, their affective-physiological identity components, and their particular, individual (as opposed to collective) linguistic identity components, critical pedagogy runs a significant risk of undermining their identity rather than supporting and developing it. Such alienation is already quite familiar and well documented and criticized when it involves, for example, a feminist pedagogy that tries to help women own their identities as women but ignores differences of race, class, nationality, and sexual orientation among women, with the result that some female students feel that they are being pressured to embrace identity components that are not really a part of their self. But even if one is sensitive to these multiple differences—distinguishing, for example, the subject position of black, lesbian, working-class, South African women from the subject position of black, lesbian, working-class American women—one still runs the risk of excluding key and even core identity components of the individuals occupying these subject positions as well as the risk of imposing other identity components on them that are not part of their self. A more adequately theorized notion of identity such as that provided in earlier chapters helps avoid such exclusion and imposition by recognizing, first of all, that identity is a function not of one's *subject* position but of one's *subjective* experiences in three different registers. That is, one's identity and the desires and needs that it entails, while multiply and powerfully influenced by one's social positioning, are not a direct reflection of that positioning but are rather a function of the way one's social positioning has been internalized by the particular subjectivity one brings to this position (a subjectivity that is itself a function of a succession of previous similar encounters between subjectivity and environment, all the way back to the first encounter of the zygote and its genetic givens with its intrauterine environment). The psychoanalytic model of identity articulated above further militates against reducing identity to subject position through its identification of three registers of identity, each incorporating multiple identity components. Armed with this model, teachers can avoid the identity-damaging reduction of students to their subject positions that critical pedagogy risks.

The absence of an adequate theory of the nature of identity and of how it is developed and altered also leaves critical pedagogy with little indication as to how it might best enable students to more fully own and develop their various elements of self. More specifically, critical pedagogy lacks a theory of how to determine which elements of self should be included in identity and developed (and how) and which components should be subordinated, excluded, or eliminated (and how). Without such guidance, teachers easily fall into reinforcing either whatever identity components a student happens to express or enact or those identity components that mirror the teachers' own, thus undermining student identity components that conflict with their own as well as elements of the students' self that may be good candidates for including in identity but that need to be supported by recognition before such integration can occur. An example is a politically correct classroom in which some students feel silenced.

As noted above, some practitioners of critical pedagogy appear to avoid this problem by recognizing the importance of helping students identify and explore their own internal conflicts. But critical pedagogy is largely silent about how to do this, saying little about the ways in which the transference and countertransference forces that pervade classrooms can be most effectively and ethically negotiated. As a result, there is no safeguard against teachers simply following the vectors of their own identity contents when addressing their students' internal conflicts. And when critical pedagogy does articulate a strategy for operating with internal conflict, such as the strategy described by JanMohamed, it reduces it to a reflection of, and a means to pursue, the external conflict between dominant and dominated groups. The problem, in the view of critical pedagogy, is not internal conflict per se; internal conflict appears to exist only because of external, social conflicts: the oppression of one group by another. The way to resolve the internal conflict as well as the external oppression, it is assumed, is thus to oppose the oppressive group and its culture, which cause internal conflicts by infiltrating the subjectivities of the dominated subjects. It is through such opposition that subjectivities are altered, according to JanMohamed (245–247). By reflecting on the (objective) "conditions of their existence," oppressed people "in effect become archeologists of the site of their own social formation; their new subject positions begin to cathect around the project of excavating and reading their own social and physical bodies, which are in fact texts of the history of their oppression. Thus their new subjectivity emerges in the process of drawing borders around their old subject positions" (JanMohamed 248). Such a strategy overlooks the fact that, precisely through the subjectivity-infiltrating hegemony of dominant culture, one's "own social and physical bodies" may include, as central components, elements of the dominant, oppressive culture. In such cases, opposing the dominant culture involves rejecting an integral part of oneself. And it also overlooks singular identity components that may have no determinative relationship, pro or con, with the dominant or the subordinate culture.

The central difficulty with critical pedagogy is thus its tendency to reduce individual identity to its social coordinates, thus effectively leaving out of account the core of identity as we have defined it—namely, one's sense of oneself, which can be neither reduced to nor deduced from one's social coordinates. It is understandable why critical pedagogy should try to collapse individual identity into its social factors, given not only the importance of such factors in the construction and maintenance of individual identity but also this pedagogy's commitment to social justice. The most important reason for this reductive move, however, and a major impediment to implementing a pedagogy of identity support and development in the humanities, is the hegemony of the historicist paradigm, to which we now turn.

CHAPTER 9
HISTORICISM AS IMPEDIMENT
TO RADICAL PEDAGOGY

In addition to the identity-undermining modes of pedagogy discussed in the previous two chapters, another major impediment to student identity development is historicism, which has long been the dominant educational paradigm in the humanities in general and in literary studies in particular. Despite the dominance of New Criticism in the 1950s and 1960s and the theory revolution of the 1970s and 1980s, literature curricula, syllabi, and faculty positions are still organized largely by historical categories. Moreover, many teachers and scholars who want their work to promote social justice view historicism as an essential weapon in their battle against injustice and oppression. When socially committed critics began in the 1980s to speak out against the hegemony of what they perceived to be the apolitical and hence conservative positions of structuralist and deconstructive modes of literary and cultural analysis, historicism was the primary banner under which they united. Since that time, such critics, taking advantage of historicist disciplinary and curricular structures that have continued to dominate the humanities, have largely succeeded in displacing their apolitical, formalist rivals, with the result that historicism continues to be hegemonic in literary and cultural studies. Fredric Jameson's slogan "Always historicize!" first uttered at the beginning of the 1980s, now goes without saying in many quarters and goes almost without question in all.

Though there has been some questioning of various historicist assumptions and procedures, there has been relatively little inquiry concerning the human consequences, psychological and social, of historicism as such. Forgotten is Hayden White's observation (now some forty years old) that "it is worth asking . . . why the past ought to be studied at all and what function can be served by a contemplation of things under the aspect of history, [i.e.,] why we ought to study things under the aspect of their pastness rather than under the aspect of their present-ness" (48). For the past two decades at least, the answer to this question has seemed obvious: we need historicism either to provide people (ourselves or others) with a sense of identity or to help them escape the narrow confines of their present identities and become more appreciative of otherness and difference (see Southgate). To what degree are such claims justified? And how do the processes through which historicism pursues these aims compare with the processes through which a radical pedagogy of identity development would pursue the same goals? A number of psychoanalytic critics have questioned whether historicism's hegemony is justified,[1] and if we are to make progress in formulating educational strategies for promoting social justice and equality, we need to develop this questioning further, in order that we may have a clear understanding of precisely how various modes and aspects of historical knowledge and inquiry might function as resources for, or as obstacles to, the attainment of this goal. We need sustained and systematic inquiries into questions such as: what are the benefits to students' identities, and what are the costs, of having students learn histories and view present social and cultural phenomena in relation to the past?

It seems clear that historicism can provide a number of crucial—indeed, indispensable—benefits for both individuals and groups. Three fundamental uses of history are particularly significant. First, what Nietzsche called monumental history can provide ideals and heroes to emulate, models that are crucial for the formation of both individual and collective identities (see Nietzsche and Southgate). Second, critical history, in demonstrating that the givens of the present are actually contingent social constructs rather than essential, eternal, and universal realities, can both reveal alternatives to the status quo and provide proof that human activity can change the world, thus inspiring reform and even revolution (see Nietzsche and Southgate). Critical history has proven to be a useful corrective to the oppression caused by ignorance of differences and of alternative possibilities— including, we should note, the ignorance that has both informed and been promulgated by psychoanalysis.[2]

Third, history can provide an antidote for what psychologists call the "fundamental attribution error," the tendency to ignore the multiple causal factors embodied in past and present circumstances and to attribute responsibility for a given event or state of affairs solely to a (collective or individual) human agent. Thus we blame the poor for their poverty, criminals for their criminal actions, terrorists for their terrorism, and so on without recognizing the causal roles played by the past conditions, including genetic endowment and circumstances of birth and upbringing, that have made these individuals and groups what they are (i.e., poor, criminals, terrorists, etc.). The blame resulting from such faulty attribution of causality leads, in turn, to ineffective and unjust efforts to deal with social problems by attacking those individuals and groups who are the immediate causes of the problems (e.g., the poor, criminals, and terrorists) and ignoring the root causes that produce poor people, criminals, terrorists, and so on in the first place.

But the ability of history to promote the development of prosocial ideals, agency, and responsible causal attribution has led some critics to ignore the question of whether history provides the only (or even the most efficient) basis for achieving these effects and to assume that historicism should always have the last word (and in some cases the only word). Nietzsche was of a different opinion; he contended that while the lessons of history are indispensable, they can be learned from a relatively small piece of history, and that, furthermore, "the historical sense makes its servants passive and retrospective" (49). Although Nietzsche's criticism was directed at late nineteenth-century German historicism, it rings disturbingly true of much historicism, old and New, in literary and cultural studies today:

> The monotonous canon runs thus: the young man [sic] must begin with a knowledge of culture, not even with a knowledge of life, still less with life and the living of it. This knowledge of culture is forced into the young mind in the form of historical knowledge; which means that his head is filled with an enormous mass of ideas, taken secondhand from past times and peoples, not from immediate contact with life. He desires to experience something for himself, and feels a close-knit, living system of experiences growing within himself. But his desire is drowned and dizzied in the sea of shams. (67)

This is a sobering counterpoint to the enthusiasm for historicism, and it raises questions that need to be pursued. Specifically, what effects does historicism have on the identities of those engaged with it (scholars, teachers, students), and what are the personal and social consequences of these effects?

Identity Constriction through Historicism

One of the primary effects of historicism throughout history has been to constitute and consolidate a sense of group identity, thus providing identity support for the individual members as well as for the group as a whole. As David Perkins observes, literary histories "define the identity of the group in a certain way, . . . [and] this definition has extreme importance since it affects the way a person views himself and is viewed by others" (181). That historicism is an excellent way to articulate and consolidate group identity is an assumption that has been promoted by cultural warriors on both the right and the left. Those on the right, such as William Bennett and Lynne Cheney, see the study of history as a way to produce a unity (if not uniformity) out of multiplicity and diversity, by overwriting various different identities (racial, ethnic, class, gender, sexual) with a common identity.

Those on the left, many of them representing one or more of the various identity groups that the right would like to homogenize, look to the study of alternative histories as a way to preserve and enhance precisely those identities that are threatened by the historicism of the right. As Walter Benn Michaels has observed, the "sense that we study history in order to learn who we are is as powerful among those, like [Annette] Kolodny, who explicitly oppose Bennett's version of that history as it is among those who support it" (117–118).

This identity-consolidating function of history would seem to be quite useful and even necessary at certain times for certain groups and individuals. We must ask, however, whether the mode of identity-consolidation promoted by historicism is cost-effective. That is, do the benefits of this mode of identity-consolidation (in terms of human flourishing and fulfillment) outweigh the costs (in terms of human suffering and injustice)?

In many cases, the answer would seem to be no. If we examine the psychological mechanisms involved in historicism's consolidation of identities, and the various psychological and social effects produced by these mechanisms, we discover a number of significant undesirable consequences. The major one is identity constriction, which entails repression of both internal and external difference. Historicism promotes identity constriction in several ways. It does so first of all by constructing a system of knowledge in which one can situate one's own identity securely and in which an identity group to which one belongs, or values and ideals that one has identified with, are the protagonists. Like other systems of knowledge, including science, philosophy, and psychoanalytic theory, history offers people the opportunity to see their identity-bearing signifiers circulate in discourse in a dominant position, thus providing them with recognition and validation by the generalized other, the authoritative system or institution. When those signifiers that bear our identity (e.g., "American," "Anglo-Saxon," "white," "man"—or "African," "black," "woman," etc.) are dominant in a discourse, we experience a validation of our identity (see Bracher, *Lacan* 23–28). This tacit recognition that we get from historical knowledge is one of the main reasons for the enjoyment and security we and our students may feel when reading, studying, lecturing on, or just recollecting history— not to mention the uneasiness and perhaps even anger we may feel when the validity or the value of this knowledge is questioned. This recognition is also one reason we labor within historical knowledge with such intensity and attempt with such zeal to initiate our students into it.

Historicism also promotes identity constriction by appearing to ground one's master signifiers, and hence one's identity, on the bedrock of the real itself. Despite protestations to the contrary by some "New" historicists, history inevitably masquerades as a system of signifiers that, unlike philosophy or literature, represents the real. "Literary history," as Michel de Certeau observes, "meticulously links the literary text to 'realistic' (economic, social, psychological, ideological, etc.) structures . . . [and] thus contrives the belief that the text articulates the real" (31–32). New Historicism exhibits the same belief through its attention to details, even when it professes great skepticism concerning the possibility of grasping the real. Hence the New Historicist belief that, as Alan Liu characterizes it, "criticism can, and must, engage with context in a manner so close, bit-mapped, or microbial (to use some of the method's paradigms) that the critic appears no farther from the cultural object than a cybernetic or biological virus from its host at the moment of code exchange" (78). By giving us the sense that our identity-bearing signifiers are grounded in the real, historicism, old and New, encourages us to deny the radical contingency and relativity of our own identity and thus to repress internal and external difference: if our own identity is either cause or effect of the real, then it is not in need of or capable of embracing or even tolerating internal or external otherness.

There are several ways in which this identity constriction that results from historicism's consolidation of identity is detrimental, not only to society at large but also to the very individuals and groups who are supposed to benefit from it. The damage to those outside the group whose history is in play is widely recognized. For example, as feminist, African American, and other critics have pointed out, Dead White European Male literary histories promote suppression and oppression of, and repression in, those (women, racial and ethnic minorities, and others) whose attributes are not recognized in these histories. But this repressive force is not just a characteristic of certain particular literary histories; it is intrinsic to historicism as such, with histories of marginalized groups exercising a similar, although usually much less damaging, repression of other groups.

Nor are members of other groups the only ones denied recognition by histories. Histories also entail a significant refusal of recognition for various individual members and subgroups of the supposedly recognized group. For example, as feminists have long realized, feminist representations of "feminine" identity can themselves be repressive insofar as they are written from the perspective of a heterosexual white middle-class American woman. By articulating certain attributes as essential to a particular identity, such histories produce a situation in which "desire is drowned and dizzied in the sea of shams," as Nietzsche put it: individuals for whom certain elements of self are excluded from or marginalized by these histories experience an erosion of these elements and their exclusion from their identity.

But as serious as denial of recognition can be to disenfranchised groups, if this were the primary damage done by historicism, historicism itself could solve the problem by simply supplying histories that offer recognition to heretofore excluded or marginalized groups and subgroups. Indeed, this supposed solution has been pursued, and as a result we now have substantial histories of several groups (e.g., women, Hispanics, Native Americans, and African Americans) that had been largely excluded from previous histories. The repressive, identity-constricting effects of historicism do not disappear, however, as a result of this proliferation of histories. This is because the damage done by historicism is not limited to the *denial* of recognition with which it victimizes some groups and individuals. Another form of damage, arguably more serious because it is more difficult to remedy, is produced precisely through historicism's *providing* of recognition.

By *providing* strong recognition of a particular identity group, historicism renders members of that identity group vulnerable by tempting them to put all their identity eggs into this single narrative basket. Such overinvestment in a single identity (racial, gender, sexual, national, etc.) produces two negative consequences. First, it renders one's identity quite vulnerable, because if this single investment does not pay dividends in the form of recognition and enactment opportunities in society at large, one risks identity depletion, in the form of feelings of frustration, hopelessness, fatalism, meaninglessness, depression, and other passive and defeatist states.

Such overinvestment in a single identity is also debilitating insofar as it leads people to develop only a very limited number of their various interests, abilities, and attributes and to neglect many others that could bring them greater fulfillment and also produce greater social benefits. Perhaps the most destructive instance of this effect among disenfranchised groups is the cultivation of a victim identity. Feminists have become quite wary of the danger of overidentifying with one's victimization, as have some African American critics. Shelby Steele,[3] for instance, maintains that this sort of narrowing of identity has been very damaging for African Americans:

> The civil rights movement and the more radical splinter groups of the late sixties were all dedicated to ending racial victimization, and the form of black identity that emerged to facilitate this goal made blackness and victimization virtually synonymous. Since it was our victimization more than any other variable that identified and unified us, it followed logically that the purest black was the poor black. . . . All other blacks were, in effect, required to identify with him in order to confirm their own blackness. . . . [Racial identification thus] became more self-conscious, more narrowly focused, more prescribed, less tolerant of opposition. It spawned an implicit party line that tended to disallow competing forms of identity. (100–101)

Historicism's consolidation of identity thus closes off access to the otherness, internal and external, that, as we have seen, must be acknowledged and accepted if one hopes to enhance either one's own identity or that of others. Identity politics, as Henry Louis Gates has pointed out, is thus incompatible with a politics of liberation: "Identity politics, in its purest form, must be concerned with the survival of an identity, . . . [while] the discourse of liberation often looks forward to the birth of a transformed subject, the creation of a new identity, which is, by definition, the surcease of the old" (8). By promoting such identity constriction, historicism exacerbates some of the very social and psychological problems that it is supposed to ameliorate. Thus as Michaels notes, "Contemporary historicism plays a real if limited role in the ongoing racialization of American life. . . . The identitarianism of much current historicist thinking—the conviction that in studying the past we are studying ourselves— . . . requires technologies of identity that do play a role in contemporary politics and that may indeed produce real victims" (118–120).

At this point, two objections may be raised. First, it may be pointed out that psychoanalytic theory—or any other type of knowledge, for that matter—can also function to promote repression and identity constriction. In fact, psychoanalysis has functioned in precisely this way since its origins, insofar as it has essentialized or valorized whiteness, maleness, and Europeanness. It is precisely historicism, it will be argued, that has rescued us from this identity constriction and repression perpetrated by psychoanalysis.

Second, it may be argued that although historicism can promote repression and identity constriction, it can also have precisely the opposite effect, if people simply engage the histories of identity groups other than their own or histories that demonstrate the contingency of their own identity groups (see Southgate 56–57). This is the assumption behind many of the current programs promoting multiculturalism and cultural diversity. Many educators believe that historicism produces recognition and acceptance of difference and thus promotes the benign social and political change that these critics aspire to. Perkins expresses this view when he declares that a major function of literary history is "to set the literature of the past at a distance, to make its otherness felt" (185). "To learn to read with the perspective of literary history," Perkins asserts, "is like growing up. We encounter a wider, more diverse world of books, expressing mentalities that challenge us by their difference" (184). Jerome McGann makes a similar claim: "Works of the past are relevant in the present, it seems to me, precisely because of this difference. We do not contribute to the improvement of social conditions or even to the advancement of learning . . . by seeking to erase this difference, but rather by seeking to clarify and promote it" (*Romantic* 2). Through historicism, McGann believes, "the abstractions and ideologies of the present are . . . laid open to critique from another human world" (*Romantic* 3).[4] Brook Thomas, in the same vein, asserts that "the problem with American culture is not . . . narcissism but amnesia" and argues that New Historicism offers a solution to this problem: "Immersed in the immediacy of one present after another, students lack a sense of otherness necessary to start a dialogue with a text that allows their position in turn to be judged and altered. Tapping the historical quality of literature, the New Historicism attempts to provide a perspective from which we can judge the very conditions of our judgments" ("Historical Necessity" 99).

As these remarks suggest, historicism is often thought to promote change in a way similar to that of psychoanalytic treatment. Like psychoanalysis, historicism is seen as confronting subjects with differences that have been repressed and thus engaging subjects in a self-critical process that leads to modes of identity that are less constrictive and oppressive for oneself and for others. As Jameson puts it, literary history finds its value "in restoring to the surface of the text the repressed and buried reality of th[e] fundamental history [of human oppression]" (20). McGann takes a similar view, describing the historicizing of literary works as, in effect, a cure for the constrictive effects of the literary tradition. Historicism, McGann says, demonstrates to us "that secret histories, forgotten facts, other imaginations operate in all that we do and make, and that our massive ignorance of these Othernesses is working to undermine what we do" ("Third World" 88).[5] Historicism would thus appear to be a kind of collective psychoanalysis: like psychoanalysis it aims to lift repression and promote acknowledgement and ownership of the otherness that causes us anxiety and to which we therefore respond with repression. Seen in this light, historicism and psychoanalysis seem equally capable of promoting either identity constriction and repression or openness to otherness and encounter with difference: it would all seem to depend on how one uses the two practices.

"Self"-Criticism in Historicism and in the Psychoanalytic Process

This apparent similarity between historicism and psychoanalysis, however, is an illusion, supported by several pivotal equivocations. First, the "psychoanalysis" that promotes repression and identity constriction is psychoanalytic *theory* when it operates, as it often does for academicians, as an end in itself—that is, as a truth discourse functioning as a fortress to inhabit and display, or as a weapon with which to colonize other subjects or discourses. The "psychoanalysis" that promotes the lifting of repression and the opening up of identity is the psychoanalytic *process*, in which psychoanalytic *theory* functions as a means by which the analyst helps individuals achieve recovery and integration of previously excluded elements of the self, rather than as a body of knowledge to be developed, validated, or celebrated as the bearer of one's identity. It is crucial that we maintain this distinction between psychoanalytic theory as a *means* and psychoanalytic theory as an *end.* The former *challenges* identity constriction, while the latter often *produces* it. Operating as an end in itself, psychoanalytic *theory* often functions psychologically and ideologically much like historicism; the psychoanalytic *process,* however, is quite different from historicism.

This difference between the psychoanalytic process and historicism, however, is obscured by three additional equivocations: those concerning "self-criticism," "repression," and "recovery." While historicism promises, like psychoanalysis, to engage people (individually and collectively) in a process of "*self*-criticism" through the "recovery" of "repressed" elements, all three components of this process—the "repressed" elements, their "recovery," and hence the "self"-criticism as well—differ markedly from their counterparts in psychoanalysis.

First, in historicism, the position from which an individual is criticized lies (in the first instance, at least) outside the individual. In psychoanalysis, in contrast individuals are challenged or criticized by another part of themselves, which has been repressed.

Second, the repressed elements recovered by psychoanalysis are fundamentally different from the "repressed" elements recovered by historicism. This is the case, first of all, because historical events that I never experienced (e.g., those that occurred before I was born) have not really been repressed by me. As Michaels puts it,

> Since almost none of the things done in the past were in fact done by us, why do any parts of it have either more or less to do with our identity? When we learn things that we never knew, why should we think of ourselves as remembering them? Who is the historical subject who, when he learns about some things that didn't happen to him, thinks he is studying his own past and, when he learns about other things that also didn't happen to him, thinks he is studying someone else's past? (118)

Too often, historicists (and psychoanalytic critics too) assume that a nation's repression of its inhumane deeds operates through the same mechanisms, produces the same psychological consequences, and yields to the same kinds of interventions as does an individual's repression. But the act my forbears committed and repressed before I was born—for example, their brutality toward their African brothers and sisters—however significant their effects may still be for my own psychodynamics, do not have the same intrapsychic function for me as do my own repressed acts of brutality toward my siblings.[6]

Finally, because of this important difference in the nature of the "repressed" elements dealt with by psychoanalysis and historicism, respectively, the "recovery" that historicism promotes of these forgotten events is also quite different from that of psychoanalysis. In historicism, "recovery" of "repressed" elements means filling in gaps in our knowledge and thus correcting misrepresentations of our own identity group and/or that of the other. What is needed to combat intolerance and injustice, it is assumed, is for people, especially members of dominant groups, to correct misrepresentations of themselves and of others. Intolerance and injustice, this belief would have it, derive from unrealistically virtuous representations of oneself and inadequate knowledge of the other; thus by confronting the dominant culture with excluded or marginalized information and voices from the past, one can undermine the intolerance and injustice. The basic function of both historicism and psychoanalysis, in this view, is to overcome inadequate representations of oneself and of the other, by filling in the gaps in our knowledge and correcting inaccuracies in that knowledge.

Unfortunately, as anyone who has experienced the psychoanalytic process knows, filling in the gaps in our knowledge and thus correcting misrepresentations of oneself or the other do not necessarily produce significant psychological change. Nor do such actions get rid of intolerance, as many historicists would like to believe, for inadequate representation, either of the other or of oneself, is not the root cause of intolerance. The root cause of intolerance is fear of one's own rejected wishes, impulses, and enjoyments—what Jacques-Alain Miller, following Lacan, refers to as one's extimacy. Racism, for example, "is founded on what one imagines about the Other's jouissance; it is hatred of the particular way, of the Other's own way of experiencing jouissance" (Miller 125–126). As Slavoj Zizek, elaborating on this point, explains, "What really bothers us about the 'other' is the peculiar way he organizes his enjoyment, precisely the surplus, the 'excess' that pertains to this way: the smell of 'their' food, 'their' noisy songs and dances, 'their' strange manners, 'their' attitude to work. To the racist, the 'other' is either a workaholic stealing our jobs or an idler living on our labor" (203). And our fantasy about the other's enjoyment, Zizek observes, is an expression of our own innermost unconscious enjoyment, or "extimacy":

> What are fantasies about the Other's special, excessive enjoyment—about the black's [supposed] superior sexual potency and appetite, about the Jew's or Japanese's [supposed] special relationship toward money and work—if not precisely *so many ways, for us, to organize our own enjoyment?* Do we not find enjoyment precisely in fantasizing about the Other's enjoyment, in this ambivalent attitude toward it? Do we not obtain satisfaction by means of the very supposition that the Other enjoys in a way inaccessible to us? Does not the Other's enjoyment exert such a powerful fascination because in it we represent to ourselves our own innermost relationship toward enjoyment? . . . The fascinating image of the Other gives a body to our own innermost split, to what is "in us more than ourselves" and thus prevents us from achieving full identity with ourselves. *The hatred of the Other is the hatred of our own excess of enjoyment.*[7] (*Tarrying* 206; Zizek's emphases)

If we recognize that our fear of the jouissance that we imagine the Other to possess derives from the resonance of that jouissance with our own most intimate but alien, repressed jouissance—our extimacy—the need to examine our own unconscious desire and jouissance becomes clear. Such an examination is precisely what the psychoanalytic process pursues through its recovery of the repressed, and it is precisely what historicism avoids and even prevents. That is, the psychoanalytic process—as distinct from psychoanalytic theory and in contrast to much psychoanalytic cultural criticism—aims to help individuals achieve insight into the contents and maintenance strategies of their own identities and recovery and integration of excluded elements. Psychoanalytic theory, and academic applications of that theory, quite often do not, as we have observed. And historicism per se has neither the aim nor the means to systematically promote such self-knowledge, recovery, and integration.

Moreover, when, in psychoanalytic treatment, one investigates the gaps and inconsistencies in one's personal history in order to recover what is repressed, the purpose is not simply to correct inadequate representations of oneself or of others but rather to own and integrate one's own repressed, unconscious impulses and qualities. It is through integration of these rejected elements into identity that psychological change comes about. The gaps, distortions, and contradictions in the different memories or stories that make up one's personal history are simply one of several types of indicators that are used to detect the presence of these elements that have been repressed because they were threatening to one's identity.[8] Recovering and integrating these repressed elements is what produces change. Simply filling in gaps or rectifying distortions in knowledge does not.

Psychoanalytic treatment, that is, is interested in gaps and distortions of knowledge only insofar as they point to excluded elements of self. In psychoanalysis, true "recovery" of repressed elements involves affirming, in effect: "I wanted or enjoyed that then, I did it, I desire it now, I enjoy it now, and in fact I have been doing it and enjoying it again and again in ways that I haven't been aware of, in assuming a certain subjective position or pursuing a certain object that is antithetical to my most precious values, ideals, and self-image." Only when there is the acknowledgment, "I am desiring this, enjoying this, doing this, here and now, even though I don't like this fact," will there be "*self*-criticism" of the transformative, psychoanalytic sort: consciousness of one part of one's being (a repressed element) challenging another part (one's current identity).

This is a very different psychological process, producing quite different psychological and social results, from the "self-criticism" produced by historicism's "recovery" of "repressed" knowledge. No engagement with collective history can bring about an equivalent assumption of one's own rejected elements unless one has personally lived through that collective history, and even then, it will be one's personal memories of that history that lead to such a recovery and integration, rather than the collective aspect per se of the history. Historicism can and does, of course, engage one's identity and its excluded elements, as can any historiography—or any story, historical or not. But the way historicism engages one is diametrically opposed to the way the psychoanalytic process—as distinct from psychoanalytic theory—does. Historicism engages one's identity and its excluded elements primarily in an externalized form. That is, when one's desire is engaged by some event or figure of history, one does not focus on this desire as one's own but rather sees it as the Other's desire—the desire of a particular figure or group, or even of History itself—and hence fails to recognize and take the same responsibility for one's own desire that one takes in psychoanalysis. Thus even though one's own desire may be involved in the history being analyzed, this desire is not recognized and recovered as one's own, because it is encountered in externalized form, as the desire of some Other, even if that Other is an identity group in which one claims membership. Coming, through the study of history, to recognize that white men, of whom I am one, have treated women and nonwhites in appalling ways is very different from coming, through psychoanalysis, to recognize and accept responsibility for the fact that I, a white man, have thoughts, feelings, or behaviors that are racist or sexist. The result of the psychoanalytic process is struggle and change; the result of the historicist process may well be further rejection and externalization of one's unconscious desire, the antithesis of the recovery and integration that occur in the psychoanalytic process.

Moreover, because historicism covers over rather than uncovers unconscious desire and jouissance, it not only leaves intact but actually fortifies the roots of intolerance, and thus prevents us from effectively addressing our most serious social problems. It does so because our need to maintain our constricted identities by continuing to repress our own harmful impulses and behaviors prevents us in two ways from seeing the root causes of social problems. First, it results in our need to project our own harmful qualities onto others, which in turn requires us to find others who appear to be suitable targets for such projections, which means others who appear to be "bad" or "evil"—that is, agents who harm innocent others. This need to blame others for their harmful behavior interferes with our recognizing the fact that these others are not responsible for the circumstances that made them what they are—that is, their genetic endowment and the circumstances of their birth and upbringing, from which everything about them derives—and hence cannot in the final analysis be morally culpable for their harmful behaviors (even though they must often be prevented from repeating their harmful behavior). As a result, we locate the cause of harmful behaviors solely in the perpetrators and seek to eliminate them, exclude them, or otherwise punish them, while leaving untouched the root causes of their behavior, including poverty, lack of jobs, and inequality, which will only produce more perpetrators like them.

Historicism's constriction of identity also contributes in a second way to this outcome: by repressing, rather than acknowledging and integrating, our aggressive impulses, it allows and almost forces this aggression to find surreptitious means of expression, which it does in the structural, institutional, and cultural violence our society perpetrates against criminals, the poor, the unemployed, the homeless, and other groups. To allow this sort of violence to be perpetrated by our society against such groups, we must first believe that they are deserving of the harmful conditions that our violent social and economic policies put them in. And to believe that this is what they deserve, we must block out of our awareness all the external causes, for which they cannot be responsible, that have made them into what they are and make them do what they do. Thus historicism, insofar as it reinforces a constricted identity, ironically prevents precisely the kind of grasp of cause and effect relationships that it should help, and is often touted as helping, people to acquire: a grasp of the full synchronic and diachronic range of causes and effects implicated in a given event or state of affairs.

What we and our students need to develop is not so much a knowledge of history as the ability to historicize, at every moment, the present people and events we encounter individually and collectively. True historicizing means seeing the present state of affairs as a) the product of multiple causal chains leading from previous states of affairs and b) a link in many causal chains leading to multiple possible future states of affairs. We need this capacity to historicize so that we can see and respond not merely to the harmful actions of criminals, terrorists, and so on but also to the (unmet or malformed) identity needs that have produced their harmful actions, such that our own responses will be productive—that is, helpful for meeting and/or further developing their identity needs—rather than destructive, that is, aggressive and thus reinforcing of the very causes—unmet or malformed identity needs—of their harmful behavior.

For most people, including most of our students, such historicizing is not possible with regard to the most serious social problems, because their own identity needs interfere with it. Specifically, their need for an Other onto which they can project their own unintegrated, rejected qualities prevents them from seeing certain others as being themselves victims of traumas, identity needs, prior circumstances, and so on over which they have had no control and thus for which they cannot be held responsible. This need for a receptacle for their projections, and the need to avoid guilt, cause people to break the links in the causal chains that establish their own guilt and responsibility and that ultimately exculpate the subaltern.

A prerequisite for true historicizing is thus a secure identity, that is, an identity that can contain negative qualities and accept responsibility for negative events without disintegrating into shame or escaping into repression. What is needed, to establish the capacity for true historicizing, as opposed to the mere ability to recite historical knowledge, is some sort of psychoanalyzing—that is, some process by which students can recognize, own, and integrate their own rejected impulses and qualities, so that they no longer have the need to reject these by projecting them onto others. Their identity, or sense of self, also needs to be strengthened and expanded before they are able to recognize the ways in which they themselves are responsible for these social problems and accept the guilt that comes with such recognition. Such expansion often requires modification of linguistic identity registers composed exclusively of absolutely positive signifiers such as "innocent," "good," "fair," "kind," and so on, to include negative signifiers such as "guilty," "selfish," "hateful," "proud," "mean," "lustful," and even "murderous" and "sadistic"—not as ideals, but as components to be acknowledged and controlled. If people have not integrated such signifiers into their identity, it is not because their selves are free of these qualities, for these qualities are part of every self to a lesser or greater extent. Rather, every identity that does not include these qualities is an identity founded on their repression and hence also on their projection onto a subaltern, a subspeciated individual or group of one sort or another. Conversely, people who have owned and integrated these qualities are able to recognize their own implication in the destructive behaviors of the "evil" other. And this recognition entails guilt. To be able to sustain this recognition and guilt, one must find a compensatory source of identity support, to make up for the identity erosion that the guilt entails. Where such erosion is not compensated for, one's entire identity is severely depleted, which produces not guilt but shame. And shame, the experience of identity decomposition, is precisely what causes the kind of destructive and self-destructive behavior that leads to social problems in the first place.

Transference and the Great Other in Historicism and in the Psychoanalytic Process

The crucial difference between the identity-constricting effects of historicism and the identity-expanding effects of psychoanalysis derives ultimately from a fundamental difference in the ways that the analyst and the historicist operate with transference. Historicism elicits a transference relation between individuals and certain historical figures (including writers) that it establishes as subjects presumed to know—that is, subjects presumed to know how to embody or to attain ultimate gratification and wholeness.[9] Both old and new historicism—and much traditional psychoanalytic literary and cultural criticism as well—promote psychological subjection to an external Other by engaging individuals in a transference relationship with subjects presumed to know: each historical period, figure, or work represents for its devotees (unconsciously, if not consciously) a time in which people possessed a fullness or wholeness of identity that is lacking in individuals today. One reason scholars study these subjects presumed to know—sometimes devoting their entire lives to a single figure or group of figures—is because at some level they assume that they can achieve wholeness of identity by identifying with these figures.

The transference in historicism often takes the form of a fantasy of an Other who is recognized as lacking omniscience and omnipotence but is nonetheless looked to for all the answers. The disavowal—that is, simultaneous denial and affirmation—of the Great Other's lack that characterizes New Historicism is expressed quite overtly by Stephen Greenblatt, one of the pioneers of New Historicism and probably its premier practitioner:

> In literary criticism Renaissance artists function like Renaissance monarchs: *at some level we know perfectly well* that the power of the prince is largely a collective invention, the symbolic embodiment of the desire, pleasure, and violence of thousands of subjects, the instrumental expression of complex networks of dependency and fear, the agent rather than the maker of the social will. *Yet we can scarcely write* of prince or poet *without accepting the fiction* that power directly emanates from him and that society draws upon this power. (Greenblatt 4; emphasis added)

The fantasy here, which Greenblatt is quite conscious of, is of an omnipotent father, Shakespeare. The statement, "at some level we know perfectly well . . . , and yet we can scarcely write of prince or poet without accepting the fiction" has the classical "I know very well, but nonetheless" structure of fetishistic disavowal (see Mannoni) and expresses quite clearly what Zizek describes as the "split between our conscious knowledge of [the Great Other's] impotence . . . and our unconscious belief in its omnipotence" (*Tarrying* 236). The purpose of this disavowal of the Great Other's impotence is to sustain the fantasy that one's own lacking wholeness can be attained through identification and union with the Great Other, the poet.[10]

In addition to supporting identity by producing identification with the subject presumed to know, the transference promoted by historicism also offers a second route to identity support, in the form of a fantasy of being the object desired by the Great Other. The prototype of this desire to be the object of the Great Other's desire is the infantile experience of being the object of our parents' desire (love, joy, and/or attention), which is the primal and ultimate experience of being recognized and affirmed. One of the grandest, most elaborated instances of this fantasy of being the object that completes or fulfills the Other can be found in Hegel, who sees all history—natural as well as cultural—as building toward its crowning achievement in the production of the Hegelian philosopher, who is the means through which Spirit achieves its ultimate fulfillment by becoming conscious of itself as Spirit.

Similar fantasies can be found in certain forms of Marxism, where the revolutionary is the instrument of the Great Other in the form of History. Such fantasies can also operate where no notion of history as progress exists. Where history is viewed as a decline, a cycle, or even as a random series of events, one can very easily entertain the fantasy of being significant precisely as the devalued object, the stone that the builders rejected. The existentialist and postmodernist views that human existence has no intrinsic significance vis-à-vis Nature or any other instance of the Great Other fit here. In such visions, human existence in general, or a particular race or group, is viewed as the detritus of history, which can unconsciously be transmuted into inestimable value, because it lies outside of what the Great Other in the form of History or Nature can assimilate.

This submissive, passive relation to the Great Other (as well as the identificatory one articulated by Greenblatt) can also be seen quite clearly in Marjorie Levinson's account of New Historicism, when she remarks; "We are the effects of particular pasts. . . . Might we not be part of a developing, leap-frogging logic? Are we . . . the consciousness of the Romantic movement produced as a moment in the accomplishment of that action?" ("New Historicism" 50–51). Charles Altieri fantasizes a similar position when he proposes "the ideal of showing how the social claims we propose for our work emerge from and partially fulfill the version of history we are trying to tell. This makes historical analysis the work of self-consciously taking on the burden of completing or resisting what we show we inherit" (54). The fantasy here, like the Hegelian fantasy, is that the New Historicist's existence constitutes the culmination or fulfillment of some aspect of the past—in this instance, through becoming the consciousness of (subjective genitive) the past: the past's consciousness.

At the same time, Levinson's question in the complete version of the passage just quoted—"Are we, or could we make ourselves the consciousness of the Romantic movement?"—betrays the active fantasy of identifying with the Great Other's agency—in this case, becoming the progenitor of the generative agency, History, that produced us. This fantasy is elaborated in Levinson's description of the past as "a structure that comes into being only through the dialectical practice of the present, which is read as the delayed effect of that structure . . . , a structure . . . which is really, suddenly, there in the past, but only by the retroactive practice of the present" (23). Such a sense of agency is powerfully supportive of the historicist's identity.

Levinson's rather esoteric formulation of this relation to the Great Other might tempt one to dismiss this position as characteristic of only a few overly intellectual academicians. But the fantasy of being both the object and the agency of the Great Other is not limited to a few intellectuals, as we can see from the popularity of the film *Back to the Future*, the title of which Levinson takes as the subtitle of her essay. Levinson herself notes a fundamental similarity between the plot of the film and the New Historicist notion of the historian changing the present by intervening in the past and thus altering the past's future, the present. Examining this aspect of the film can clarify the fantasy operating in New Historicism. Like New Historicism, the film owes much of its appeal to the fact that it helps its audience disavow their recognition of their own radical contingency, a contingency that derives from the even more disturbing fact that the Great Other (parent, society, race, God, History, etc.) is deficient and thus 1) incapable of providing validation for them and/or 2) devoid of desire for their existence, thus leaving them ontologically adrift. Both of these elements are present in the film, in Marty McFly's anxiety concerning his father, George. First, there is the fear that the father—Marty's Great Other here—is not omnipotent but impotent, castrated. This is the condition of George McFly at the beginning of the film, as well as of the young George McFly whom Marty encounters in the past. The central action of the film is devoted to producing a father who is not castrated. Second, there is the fear that the Great Other does not desire us, that we are nothing, nobody to him. In the film, this recognition is embodied in the fact that when Marty travels to the past and encounters his (future) father George, he is nothing to George, not even a gleam in his eye. George's impotence and his lack of desire for his son Marty serve to produce anxiety in Marty and through him, in the audience. The film then helps the audience overcome their anxiety by undoing the father's castration, through manipulating him to become both potent and desirous of Marty's mother. The audience's anxiety culminates when George seems to be drifting away from Marty's future mother rather than toward an encounter with her, and Marty sees himself begin to disappear in a picture he has brought with him into the past. At this point the audience experiences a powerful anxiety in the face of radical contingency, a contingency that is seen to be due to the Great Other's (the father's) impotence and lack of desire. Like Marty, the audience knows at some level that if things had been different—for example, if their parents had not gotten together—they themselves would not exist. Precisely what has to get established in order for Marty's existence to be guaranteed (and for the audience's anxiety to be contained) is for the father to overcome his castration so that he and Marty's mother will get together and then conceive Marty. The crucial action is the construction of the Great Other (the father) as a potent benefactor who not only desires the subject but also provides the subject with surplus jouissance (in the form, for example, of the phallic truck that Marty receives when he returns to the present). Members of the audience, in accompanying Marty back to the past and constructing a potent Great Other, achieve a sense of transcending their radical contingency, disavowing the Great Other's castration by experiencing, through the character of Marty, being their own progenitor: with Marty, the audience assures that the Great Other is not castrated and desires them as well.

Reading and writing New Historicist criticism offers a similar disavowal of the Great Other's castration, and an affirmation of the Great Other's desire for us and our students. In New Historicism, the fantasy is present together with an acknowledgment of the Great Other's deficiency. In this version of fetishistic disavowal, the Great Other, in the form of History or a particular past (e.g., Levinson's Romanticism), is acknowledged to be deficient, lacking. But fortunately, the New Historicist (in true Hegelian fashion) turns out to be just what the Great Other needs to fill its lack. Thus both the Great Other (e.g., Romanticism) and the New Historicist overcome their lack, and the New Historicist's fantasy of recovering lost wholeness through the Great Other is sustained.

Similar transference desires, both active and passive, operate in psychoanalytic criticism and in the psychoanalytic process. And many psychoanalytic critics reinforce this desire. The psychoanalytic process, however—in contrast to many psychoanalytic critics—operates quite differently with the transference. Rather than reinforcing such desires, analysts operate so as to enlist the analysand's transference in the cause of self-knowledge, self-criticism, and separation from the Other. Analysts produce this result through the same means by which psychoanalytic critics reinforce submission to the Great Other: through the analysand's identification with the analyst's/critic's desire. The crucial difference is in the nature of the analyst's desire. The desire of the analyst, as we saw in the previous chapter, is for "absolute difference" (276). That is, the analyst does not desire that the analysand embrace any particular desire, enjoyment, ideal, or identity that the analyst might value. Rather, the analyst desires that the analysand encounter and come to terms with the antithetical impulses, enjoyments, and identifications that are present in the analysand him- or herself.

The desire of the historicist (and the traditional psychoanalytic critic), in contrast, is to achieve identity security through identification with or submission to the Great Other, even if the resultant identity is more constricted and hence antisocial than the subject's present identity. More specifically, the historicist desires to procure from an Other the resources or substance to complete either the historian's own or someone else's identity. This desire is present in both old historicism and New Historicism. In old historicism, it takes the form of a fantasy, often conscious and overt, that one's favorite society, period, or figure of history is a subject that knows how to attain the wholeness that we lack. Virtually every historical period offers a version of this fantasy. For a medievalist, the fantasy may take the form of the notion that medieval subjects, living as they did in a world where the sacred and the profane were integrated in certain ways that no longer exist, possessed a unity and fulfillment that we are deprived of. For a Renaissance scholar, the fantasy may occur as the belief that such subjective unity, or escape from division and alienation, was attained by the multifaceted and well-rounded men—the "Renaissance men"—who gilded that age. Admirers of the eighteenth century find subjective fullness and self-possession in the period's supposed unity of sensibility (e.g., T.S. Eliot), or its supposed integration of public and intellectual life (e.g., Terry Eagleton). For Romanticists such as Harold Bloom, Romantic self-consciousness embodies a subjective fullness and self-possession that is unsurpassed before or since, and in the eyes of neoconservatives, Matthew Arnold and the Victorians possess a sense of cultural unity and integrity of values that we have lost.

New Historicism is motivated by the same desire to solidify identity by acquiring the secret of identity integrity from a subject that is presumed to possess it or to know how to procure it. Greenblatt recognizes this desire in his own work, as well as in the work of his old historicist forbears. "I began [as a more traditional historicist] with the *desire to speak with the dead,*" Greenblatt writes. "The textual analyses I was trained to do had as their goal the identification and celebration of a numinous literary authority [i.e., a subject presumed to know], . . . [and] the great attraction of *this authority* is that it *appears to bind and fix the energies we prize, to identify a stable and permanent source of literary power, to offer an escape from shared contingency*" (3; emphasis added). As Greenblatt's description of the function of the "numinous literary authority" clearly indicates, what is involved in this traditional historicist aim is a powerful desire to receive from the Great Poet the lost life or jouissance ("the energies we prize") that will make one whole and complete ("offer an escape from shared contingency").

Greenblatt acknowledges the continued presence of this desire in his present New Historicist enterprise. "In the book I have written," Greenblatt observes, "something of this initial conception survives" (2). What survives is the desire to recover lost jouissance or "escape from shared contingency." The only difference between the New Historicist desire and that of old historicism is that whereas the old historicist desire was explicit and often largely unqualified—and thus an easy object of criticism and even scorn today—the New Historicist desire operates under the shelter of disavowal. Like Freud's fetishist, who recognizes intellectually that the mother has no penis but who nonetheless continues on another level to believe that she does, New Historicists recognize quite clearly that the historicist quest for lost jouissance and wholeness is doomed to fail, yet at the same time they retain the fantasy that wholeness can be recovered from a subject (text, author, or period) that either possesses it or knows how to procure it. "This project," Greenblatt acknowledges, "endlessly repeated, repeatedly fails for one reason: there is no escape from contingency" (3). "All the same," he continues, "we do experience unmistakable pleasure and interest in the literary traces of the dead, and I return to the question how it is possible for *those traces* to *convey lost life*" (3; emphasis added). The function in New Historicism of historical figures such as Shakespeare is similar to that of Freud's omnipotent, uncastrated father of *Totem and Taboo*, as Greenblatt's observations indicate:

> The question then was how did so much life get into the textual traces? Shakespeare's plays, it seemed, had precipitated out of a sublime confrontation between a *total artist* and a *totalized society*. By a *total artist* I mean one who, through training, resourcefulness, and talent, is at the moment of creation *complete unto himself*; by a totalizing society I mean one that posits *an occult network linking all human, natural, and cosmic powers* and that claims on behalf of its ruling elite a privileged place in this network. (Greenblatt 2; emphasis added.)

Although Greenblatt realizes the untenability of the notions of "total artist" and "totalizing society," he admits that "something of this initial conception survives" (2) in his book. What survives, despite the acknowledgment of the Great Other's (Shakespeare's) castration, is precisely the core desire of receiving from the Great Poet the identity wholeness lost to all socialized beings ("lost life" or "energy"). The fantasy is that we too might have access to this wholeness if we can only become good enough readers and thus identify with that "most comprehensive soul" (as Samuel Johnson put it) of the Great Poet.

Historicism's disavowal of the Great Other's deficiency promotes a submission to the Great Other that underwrites even the most skeptical and critical forms of historicism, which, unlike Greenblatt's or Levinson's historicism, might seem to aim only at revealing the radical contingency of one's own subject position and of the Great Other itself. In "What Is an Author?" for instance, Foucault exposes the constructed and hence contingent nature of the notion of "author"—one of the most prominent instances of those avatars of the Great Other, subjects presumed to know— and thus offers us the possibility of escaping from the hegemony of this notion and the limitations it places on our freedom to own our rejected qualities and impulses and incorporate them into identity. What is liberating about Foucault's analysis, however, is not so much its historicism as its explanation of the interests presently served by, and the present consequences resulting from, the "author function."[11] Foucault's analysis is liberating, that is, not insofar as it is historicist but rather to the extent that it duplicates part of the psychoanalytic process—that is, insofar as it helps us to recognize the presence, and take responsibility for the consequences, of our use of the author function to support our identity.

Moreover, whatever liberation such critical historicist analyses might produce comes at the considerable cost of the surreptitious reassertion of the omnipotence of, and submission to, the Great Other in the form of History. This is due to the assumption by critical historicism that the only place we can find an alternative to present actuality is in the past (see Evans). Thus even if projects such as Foucault's, by duplicating part of the psychoanalytic process, do from time to time help to free the identities of some students from certain forms of domination by the codes and regimes of the Great Other—for example, in the form of its avatar the Author—the very fact that the identity enacted in such projects seeks authorization from the Great Other in the form of History enlists students in a profound clandestine resubmission to the Great Other, from which they are supposedly being released. Historicism, even Foucauldian historicism, inevitably reintroduces students into a transference relationship with some aspect of the past, thus promoting fantasies that constitute an obstacle rather than a conduit to an encounter with their own rejected elements of self—their extimacy—and hence with external otherness as well.

This belief in the Great Other, in directing students away from recognition of their own rejected elements of self—that extimacy that is the true ground of intolerance—constitutes the primary obstacle to the kind of self-knowledge, recovery, and integration that are necessary if intolerance and the violence and suffering it produces are to be reduced. Belief in the Great Other produces repression of one's extimacy, which produces intolerance and violence. For this reason, it may well be, as Zizek suggests, that "our very physical existence hinges on our ability to consummate the act of assuming fully the nonexistence of the [Great] Other" (237). Historicism, and most traditional psychoanalytic criticism, in denying or disavowing the nonexistence of the Great Other (even when, as in much of New Historicism and post-Lacanian psychoanalytic criticism, one simultaneously asserts this nonexistence), reinforces the psychological ground of intolerance and violence.

The ideological impact of historicism (and of much psychoanalytic criticism) here converges with that of poststructuralism, which, in pronouncing the death of the subject, assures us that we are willy nilly the object of the agency that is Language—which is poststructuralism's Great Other. Both the linguistic turn of structuralism and poststructuralism and the historicist turn of contemporary literary and cultural studies disavow the Great Other's impotence—disavow, that is, the fact that there is no absolute authority—by establishing an omnipotent Great Other in the form of a Language or a History that produces us and gives us our being and identity and thus holds the key to our lacking wholeness. From that perspective, the return of historicism to the foreground of literary and cultural studies was not so much a return of what had been repressed by the linguistic turn of structuralism and poststructuralism as it was a return—or a continuation in a new key—of the repression of desire and jouissance enacted by poststructuralism, and by older forms of historicism and formalism as well. In functioning in this manner, historicism constitutes a specific version of the social symptom that is the very substance of academic literary and cultural (including traditional psychoanalytic) criticism, which, in all of its formalist and historicist modes, has functioned to distance students of literature and culture from their own identity elements and exclusions that are engaged by cultural artifacts, not only allowing these elements and exclusions to be acted out without self-scrutiny, but actually precluding self-criticism through massive institutionalized procedures for rationalizing and externalizing one's responses to culture, rather than helping students acknowledge, recover, and integrate the excluded elements of self that are producing their responses.

Historicism thus cannot produce the same benefits as can a psychoanalytic pedagogy that is directed by the analyst's desire, the desire for "absolute difference." But it offers the illusion of doing so, and this illusion is a crucial source both of historicism's wide appeal and of its psychologically and socially detrimental effects. Historicism, that is, promises to produce—relatively painlessly, and on a grand, collective scale—what the psychoanalytic process produces painstakingly and often painfully, and on a more modest scale: namely, an encounter with and integration of one's excluded elements of self and hence an expansion and restructuring of identity. In fact, however, historicism, like traditional psychoanalytic criticism, functions as the inverse of the psychoanalytic process: the psychoanalytic process operates with *personal* history in such a manner as to *dissolve* a symptom (i.e., a mode of gratification that maintains substantial repression and thus produces more suffering than the gratification is worth), while historicism and traditional psychoanalytic criticism, in contrast, operate with *collective* history in such a way as to *construct* a symptom. In consolidating a relatively narrow sense of identity and in continually engaging our students' desire to acquire identity wholeness and security from the Great Other or its avatars, subjects presumed to know, historicism keeps our students from encountering and integrating their own rejected impulses and qualities, which is not only their best chance of developing their identities but also one of our best chances of reducing the intolerance and injustice that grow out of this repressed desire and jouissance.

Always Psychoanalyze!

In light of these observations, and contrary to the reigning assumption, it thus turns out that a nonhistorical approach to literature and cultural studies offers greater potential than a historical approach does for a psychologically and socially productive encounter with internal and external otherness. An encounter through literature and culture with their own internal otherness—their acceptance of which is necessary before they can accept and appreciate the otherness of other people—is more likely to occur if our students approach cultural artifacts unhistorically (naively and spontaneously), for in such an approach their rejected elements of self—their internal otherness, or extimacy, their own absolute difference from themselves—are engaged and thus made susceptible to examination of the sort that, as psychoanalytic treatment demonstrates, can lead to beneficial psychological change. Perkins notes that "in youth [when] we are all naive, unhistorical readers . . . , we do not place and explain a sonnet as the expression of courtly love conventions; it is a moving utterance of an emotion we identify with" (183). Such emotion is a manifestation of one's own internal otherness, or extimacy, one's hitherto unacknowledged and unintegrated elements of self. Approaching culture historically, in contrast, diminishes the degree to which one's excluded elements of self become engaged and manifest, as Perkins acknowledges: "When a text is placed in literary history, seen as belonging to the past, and especially to a past about which we are informed . . . , it locates itself at a distance from ourselves. . . . Literary history thus tends to prevent us, in some degree, from completely committing ourselves to any work" (183–184). Reading historically limits our students' encounter with internal otherness and hence their openness to and respect for external otherness.

These observations constitute a compelling argument for altering the paradigm of literary and cultural studies and eschewing even critical historicism in favor of a radical psychoanalytic pedagogy aimed at promoting the development of students' identities. Instead of always historicizing, we should always psychoanalyze, in the sense of desiring to promote our students' identity development. Insofar as we cultural critics and teachers can be directed in our teaching, our scholarship, and our criticism by the analyst's desire for absolute difference, rather than by the desire for sameness that animates historicism's consolidation of identity, or by the anxiety of extimacy that underwrites historicism's fantasies of acquiring a lacking wholeness, we will be more likely to help our students recover and integrate some of their excluded elements and thus reduce suffering and oppression—a goal that is the ostensible *raison d'être* of historicist scholarship and pedagogy.

PART THREE
DEVELOPING TEACHERS' IDENTITIES

CHAPTER 10
SELF ANALYSIS FOR TEACHERS

Our own identity needs, whether in collusion with students' identity needs or in conflict with them, are thus significant factors in pedagogical failures and, through such failures, in social problems. To remedy this situation, we need to do several things. First, we need to identify which of our teaching practices provide significant identity benefits for our students and which do not. Second, we need to understand as fully as possible all of the various forms of identity support that we seek through our current teaching practices, especially those practices that are not providing significant benefits for our students and the world at large. And finally, we need to understand how alternative, more beneficial teaching practices that do not currently provide us with identity support could provide such support if we reinterpreted such practices in terms of our identities and/or reconceptualized some aspect of our identities in light of such practices.

Unfortunately, pedagogical practices that meet our identity needs can be highly resistant to change or even to interrogation. As bell hooks notes, "one of the things blocking a lot of professors from interrogating their own pedagogical practices is that fear that '*this is my identity and I can't question that identity*'" (*Teaching* 134–135; emphasis in original). How can we overcome this resistance? Since merely interrogating our pedagogical practices threatens our identity, what can bring us even to identify and acknowledge, much less relinquish, the identity support we receive from the various nonproductive and harmful pedagogical practices we engage in? And supposing we are able to identify and acknowledge the identity support we get from demonizing rather than sympathizing with various types of "bad people," as well as from the various other unproductive and harmful teaching practices that we engage in, what can bring us to give up these practices and embrace new ones?

The Process of (Self-)Analysis

The most effective way, I believe, is through a process of (individual and group) self-analysis based on the psychoanalytic process outlined by Lacan.

This process comprises four moments: rectification with the real, the operation of transference, interpretation, and working through.

Rectification with the real involves coming to recognize that one's own actions, based on motives (identity needs) that one may know nothing of, have served to produce a situation that one consciously wants to prevent. That is, one is confronted with evidence that one has been unwittingly instrumental in bringing about the very reality that one complains of (see Lacan, *Ecrits: A Selection* 237). In our case, this involves recognizing the negative consequences of pedagogical practices that we had previously assumed were producing benefits for our students and society.

Once one begins to recognize that the problems one wants to solve are at least partially the result of one's own actions and of invisible motives that produce these actions, the task then becomes to identify exactly what this motive is. In psychoanalytic treatment, one of the best ways to apprehend such motives is to recognize them in the transference, the ways the analysand imagines or tries to manipulate the analyst into repeating the relationships and dramas that the analysand experiences as most supportive of his or her identity. In teaching, similar efforts are engaged in, not only by students but also by us, their teachers: we automatically and unconsciously engage in those pedagogical practices that we (unconsciously) presume will provide us with our habitual modes of identity maintenance.

While transference is the key to engaging and enacting unconscious motives, interpretation is crucial for bringing these motives to recognition and thus putting one in a position to avow and assume them as one's own. Interpretation can take many different forms. For us, it will involve translating our pedagogical aims, strategies, tactics, and reflexes into modes of identity maintenance—that is, into ways of enacting, eliciting recognition for, or defending certain components of our identities.

Finally, there is the process called working through, in which recursive movements through the first three steps lead to the development of a more capacious and integrated identity—perhaps with a more complex structure as well—and the establishment of new behavior patterns that more fully enact this revised identity.

Rectification with the Real

The discussion of teachers' counterproductive practices in the three preceding chapters has enacted the first step of analysis, providing a kind of collective rectification with the real by exposing the negative consequences of certain prominent pedagogical practices and pointing out some of the identity-supporting tactics that they enact for teachers. Recognizing, for example, how our demonizing practices impede student identity development and thwart social justice deprives these practices of their identity-supporting power by revealing them to be antithetical to key identity-bearing qualities, such as self-efficacy and fairness and justice. Such a realization renders such practices ego-dystonic, in the parlance of psychoanalysis; that is, instead of continuing to embrace and enact such practices, we now begin to experience discomfort with them and at least a slight aversion or hesitation in enacting them.

In addition to undermining the identity support provided by such harmful pedagogical practices, rectification with the real can also reveal alternative, positive sources of identity support to compensate for the support that is being lost. A number of new sources of identity support can come into play at this stage, including the perception that our self-scrutiny and behavioral changes themselves enact important identity-bearing qualities, such as honesty, humility, or courage, as well as another form of self-efficacy. But the most powerful new source of identity support for altered pedagogical practices will most likely come in the form of a recognition from the Real, by which I mean the deep, implicit acknowledgment of our significance that we receive when our actions produce important consequences for other people. Thus to the extent that we are able to formulate pedagogical practices that can be demonstrated to help promote identity development—and thus perhaps also help to eliminate the need for violence—knowing that we have contributed such benefits will constitute a form of recognition that more than compensates for the identity support we lose when we give up demonizing violent Others and externalizing our own disowned violent impulses onto them.

Thus the simple realization that some of our pedagogical practices are unproductive or counterproductive will motivate us to at least begin to alter them in more productive directions, since our most profound identity support (as is the case with everyone) comes in the form of recognition from the real: evidence that we have made a significant contribution to the lives of others. When confronted with the realization that one of our current practices fails to make such a contribution while an alternative practice would succeed, our investment in the current practice is automatically diminished, irrespective of whatever appeal it may still have due to various other ways in which it may support our identity. And we begin to invest in the alternative practice, whatever obstacles there may be to its enactment, because it promises to make such a contribution and thus to provide us with the most profound form of recognition, the recognition coming from the real itself. The mere identification of a) practices that are not helpful to students but that we pursue because of the identity support they offer and b) practices that would be helpful but that we do not engage in because they appear to offer us no identity support will thus itself begin to reduce our investment in the former practices and increase our investment in the latter.

Operation and Interpretation of the Transference

The next aspect of analysis, operation of the transference, is always already present in our teaching, as we inevitably organize our classes and interact with our students, subject matter, and other scholars in our preferred modes of identity enactment, recognition-seeking, and defense. We thus proceed to the third step of self-analysis, identifying the basic patterns of our pedagogical desires and behaviors and interpreting them in terms of their identity-maintaining functions. The previous four chapters have already provided fairly substantial collective self-analyses of the identity-maintaining functions of common pedagogical practices, and most teachers will be able to recognize at least some of their own individual identity-supporting strategies in these analyses. A more complete and effective self-analysis, however, must go beyond such collective self-analyses and pursue the individual teacher's own key personal identity investments in his or her own personal and even idiosyncratic teaching practices.

One way to proceed with this endeavor is for each of us to directly interrogate our identity as a teacher by engaging in a kind free association, which can be pursued in the form of focused free-writing in response to questions such as the following:

- What does being a teacher mean to me?
- What does it mean in terms of my social, economic, and material sense of self?
- How central to my sense of self are the lifestyle, the status, the social relations, the material circumstances, and the psychological tasks entailed by being a teacher?

To answer these questions, we can scan our memories and perform thought experiments, recalling or imagining how our sense of well-being was or would be altered by events bearing upon specific identity elements. We might recall, especially, the time in our life when we first became aware that we wanted to be a teacher, and ask:

- How did I decide to become a teacher?
- Why did I want to become a teacher?
- What identity needs of mine at that time were involved in my decision to become a teacher?
- Do those needs still have the same prominence for me?

- What other identity needs do I have now that are significant?
- What are the main identity needs that my teaching meets now?

Articulating our fundamental pedagogical aims and objectives can also be a bridge to significant insight concerning our identity needs and maintenance strategies:

- What kind of impact do I want my teaching to have for particular students or for a particular class?
- What memories of the impact of my teaching do I cherish?
- What do I want the effects of my teaching career to be?

Listing and interrogating our favorite pedagogical strategies, tactics, classroom practices, assignments, and reflexes can also provide significant insight into the identity components and modes of maintenance that drive our teaching. For each of these behaviors we can ask, how does this action enact, defend, or elicit recognition for my identity, and which identity elements are particularly important here? We should examine each pedagogical behavior or situation for the presence of one or more types of recognition, asking:

- Recognition from whom?
- Recognition in what form?
- Recognition for what identity contents?

We should try to identify instances and modes of recognition that we may be seeking and/or receiving unconsciously. We should consider the following potential sources of recognition:

- Students
- Peers
- Supervisors, administrators
- Students' parents
- Our former teachers
- Our parents
- Community, Society
- God (for teachers who are religious), Nature, the Real

We should be alert for different forms of (conscious and unconscious) recognition, including:

- Explicit (from students, peers, supervisors)
  - Praise, flattery
  - Deference
  - Admiration
  - Positive evaluations

- Implicit (from students)
  - Attendance
  - Attention
  - Interest
  - Responsiveness, cooperation
- Structural
  - Money
  - Position, rank, title
  - Space (work, recreational, living)
  - Time (quantity and quality allotted by the institution to one's activities)

We should also take cognizance of the various identity contents that we are attempting to enact or be recognized for. Our linguistic contents might include ideals such as "intelligent," "brilliant," "wise," "cool," "kind," or "helpful," as well as political, religious, ideological, and disciplinary systems of knowledge or belief and various sorts of narratives concerning our personal and professional lives. For many teachers, including Jane Tompkins, the key identity content is "smart" or "brilliant," and the unconscious aim directing teaching behavior is to elicit recognition as such from one's students. Looking back over her career, Tompkins realizes what drove her to teach the way she did:

> I often took students who liked me for granted, and longed for the admiration of those who were indifferent. Sometimes I even resented the ones who liked me if they weren't the smartest in the class, for if they weren't smart, then maybe I wasn't either. And smart was the most important thing to be. I cared for my students, but still and all, unconsciously I made them serve as my reflection. In return for the hard work I put into my classes, I wanted them to love me, to love the material I taught, and to talk about it in a sophisticated way so that I would look good by extension.
>
> Almost all my effort as a teacher went into finding things to say about the texts I'd assigned, since, as far as I knew, good teaching consisted of having brilliant ideas about the subject matter. This was the model I had been given, and it was what I tried to live up to. Year after year I strove to achieve that ideal of brilliance, and year after year I waited for a student to tell me that I had. (*Life* 89–90)

Imagistic contents involving physical appearance or bodily mastery or agency might also be significant, as might metaphorical derivatives such as the desire to be "looked up to" and prosthetic devices and surrogate bodies such as our office, house, or car. For Tompkins, maintaining identity in the body-imagistic register involved attracting the attention of others by speaking, whether at family dinners, faculty meetings, or in a classroom. Tompkins explains the feelings she experiences when she speaks in such situations:

> I felt and still feel more at home in such moments than in many others. For in that space of time, borne up by the audience's attention, my existence is guaranteed. I can't not *be*, intensely. . . . I began to become aware of my power to enslave another in the flow of language—always a person subordinate to me, usually a student—driven by need, the need to register my existence on the retina of another human soul. (*Life* 63)

In the affective register we may attempt to achieve recognition in the form of affective resonance with our students by sharing with them the excitement of discovery, the joy of insight, the warmth of shared understanding or commitment, the energy of a joke, or the enjoyment of the material being studied. Many literature teachers, including Tompkins and Helen Vendler (see chapter seven), have not only aimed to get their students to enjoy the same texts that they enjoy but have also conceptualized their job as literature teachers as being "to help students get the same pleasure out of literature that I had" (Tompkins, *Life* 87). We should also become aware of patterns in the dominant mood of our classroom, the emotions we display toward our subject matter, and those we express or merely feel toward our students. Tompkins recalls, for example, how in teaching a course in which students wrote their autobiographies and shared them with the class, she, like her students, was seeking affective recognition:

> The people who signed up for those courses wanted to tell their stories; they wanted someone to know their pain. I wanted the same thing, though I didn't know it then. My own unhappiness found relief as I read about theirs. It was the bond we shared. Through the autobiography courses I came to know my students at a deeper level and felt more connected to them, mitigating the loneliness and isolation of my first years at the huge urban university. (*Life* 93)

Interpreting Our Images and Experiences of Teaching

In addition to inquiring directly into the identity factors that drive and direct our teaching practices, we can also inquire indirectly. One method, used by Parker Palmer in faculty workshops, is to elicit images or metaphors of ourselves as teachers. Palmer elicits such metaphors by asking teachers to quickly fill in the blank of the following sentence: "When I am teaching at my best, I am like a—————." As Palmer explains, filling in the blank quickly and accepting whatever image occurs without censoring or editing it allows the unconscious to produce a metaphor embodying insights into one's identity that were not previously available to one's consciousness (Palmer 148). We can become aware of these identity contents and maintenance strategies by taking inventory of the specific features of this image/metaphor through a process of free-association. Palmer analyzes his own metaphor, a sheepdog, in terms of its functions: protecting the sheep, keeping them together, enabling them to graze, and moving them to new pastures. Further free-associations on his part, however, would no doubt reveal more fundamental identity qualities and needs involved in his teaching. A hint of such identity needs may be found in his initial description of his metaphor: "When I am teaching at my best, I am like a sheepdog—*not the large, shaggy, lovable kind*, but the all-business Border collies one sees working the flocks in sheep country" (148; emphasis added). Here, in the italicized phrase, we have an instance of the editing or censorship that Palmer warned against precisely because the elements we are inclined to exclude often embody the most significant unconscious material. Palmer's initial, uncensored image, which includes the qualities of large, shaggy, and lovable, may offer clues concerning his deepest identity investments in teaching, such as the desire to be loved, large, and shaggy (i.e., uncurtailed, spontaneous, completely natural) in the classroom, rather than "all-business" like the Border collie of his edited image. In addition, the image of tending the flocks has religious overtones, invoking Christian ideals of Jesus as the Good Shepherd that may be of considerable significance for Palmer, who is apparently a Christian.

We can also gain access to our key identity contents and maintenance strategies by examining specific experiences of satisfaction and dissatisfaction that we have had in teaching. Such an approach has the added benefit of focusing our attention directly on those factors that often prevent us from recognizing harmful or counterproductive effects of our practices or from developing pedagogical practices that are more beneficial for our students, society at large, and even ourselves. Examining our satisfying and dissatisfying experiences helps us to identify the kinds of identity support we are drawn to and the kinds of situation we find threatening and thus tend to avoid, which in turn enables us to give extra scrutiny to the consequences of pedagogical practices that provide us with these types of support and threat, for it is precisely regarding such practices that we run the greatest risk of deceiving ourselves concerning their worth. We can proceed with an exercise such as the following.

First, we can identify and jot down our most positive experience as a teacher. The experience might involve a particular classroom moment, a particular individual (student, parent, administrator), a class session, an entire course, a school event, and/or working conditions. We can simply jot down phrases, clauses, fragments of sentences as they come to mind.

Next, we can take a minute to identify and jot down our most negative experience as a teacher. Again, the experience might involve a particular classroom moment, a particular individual (student, parent, administrator), a class session, an entire course, a school event, working conditions.

We can then describe the experience that comes to mind in response to the following adjectives, taking thirty seconds or so for each word and jotting down as many objective and subjective details of the experience as we can in that amount of time, writing whatever comes to mind, even if it does not seem to fit the prompt. If no experience comes to mind for a particular cue, we can simply make a note of that fact.

1. Most pleasant
2. Most frustrating
3. Most exciting
4. Most humiliating
5. Most joyous
6. Most anxious
7. Proudest
8. Most unpleasant
9. Most fulfilling
10. Most depressing
11. Most satisfying
12. Most embarrassing
13. Most enraging
14. Most inspiring
15. Most uncomfortable
16. Most disappointing
17. Most shameful

Next, we can pick the most significant positive experience and the most significant negative experience from this list and flesh out the details of each, describing.

1. objective details of the event
   a. People involved
   b. Issues or subject matter involved
   c. Setting
   d. Activity

2. details of our state of mind immediately before, during, and immediately after the event, insofar as we can recall them:
    a. Our thoughts
    b. Our feelings
    c. Our fantasies
    d. Our impulses
    e. Our bodily posture, position, movements, sensations
    f. Our behavior

We can now focus on how the experience affects our sense of self, or identity. For the positive experience, we can ask the following questions:

- What specific recognition or validation did I experience? (Refer to the checklist above.)
- What other gratifications did I experience?
- What did I do to elicit this recognition or produce the validation or other gratification?
- What identity elements did I enact in the experience? (Refer to the checklist above.)

For the negative experience, we can ask the following questions:

- What specific recognition or validation did I desire but not receive?
- What damage or threat to my identity did I experience, and to what elements of my identity?
- What was my role in this event?
- Could the event have been avoided, or made less negative, if I had not been pursuing certain identity needs or other gratifications (such as being in control, or fearing to assert myself or take control)?

All of us who teach have such a desire for immediate recognition and affirmation from our students, and this desire can produce many pedagogical practices and reactions that undermine our efforts to facilitate student learning and development. A number of teachers have written about struggles in which their efforts to empower their students and/or help them develop were impeded by their need for immediate, express recognition from the students. bell hooks, who challenges her students and encourages them "to relate the information they are learning to the personal identities they are working to socially construct, to change, to affirm," recalls how her efforts were inhibited by "that longing for immediate recognition of my value as a teacher, and immediate affirmation. Often I did not feel liked or affirmed and this was difficult for me to accept" ("Toward" 82–83). Lad

Tobin recalls a situation in which a lack of recognition embodied in the behavior of a group of students threatened his identity as a good teacher and thus evoked an aggressive, defensive, counterproductive response from him:

> I was especially bothered by the four eighteen-year-old male students who sat next to each other, leaning back in their desks against the wall. . . . Whenever I tried to create drama or intensity, they joked or smirked. . . . I retaliated (note the aggressive language) by indirectly threatening them. I interrupted the class one day to give an angry and sarcastic speech on how anyone who was not taking the class seriously would fail and end up taking it again. . . . I looked right at them when I made the threat. . . . They were threatened by me, I told myself, so insecure that they had to stick together and act tough. . . . I had allowed myself to get caught up in a macho competition with these students and I was losing. . . . Clearly this had as much or more to do with my insecurities and unconscious responses as it did with theirs. (Tobin 33–35)

Tobin concludes that it is important to monitor both one's experiences of threat and one's feelings of pride in teaching:

> I respond more favorably to students—male or female—who make me feel secure than to those who threaten me. And that is what I need to monitor: as soon as I find myself giving up on a student or, on the other hand, feeling tremendous personal pride in a student's work, I need to question my own motives. I need to discover in what ways my biases and assumptions—both conscious and unconscious—are shaping my teaching. (38–39)

Working Through

After identifying our identity investments in our various teaching practices, we can begin the process of working through by examining whether the teaching practices that help to maintain our identities contribute significantly to our students' identity development. This repeated rectification with the real, together with an understanding of how our identity needs motivate and direct our various teaching behaviors, can enable us to identify more pedagogically effective practices to support our current identity contents, including:

1. demonstrating/enacting mastery not by putting students down or setting them up to fail but by devising ingenious ways to help them succeed;
2. demonstrating/enacting intelligence not through rehearsing our knowledge for our students but through understanding them, their

capacities, their needs, and how best to help them learn and develop;

3. devising practices that entail recognition from the real (e.g., through formal assessment of learning outcomes);
4. formulating practices that enact our student-enhancing identity attributes (e.g., empathy, generosity, compassion); and
5. constructing a consensus, a community, to provide recognition for teaching and being a teacher.

Working recursively through the process of self-analysis can also facilitate our development of new pedagogically enabling identity contents, such as

1. linguistic contents such as generativity (discussed in the next chapter),
2. linguistic contents such as knowledge of identity and its development,
3. a sense of agency and mastery in using our identity-developmental knowledge to facilitate our students' learning,
4. empathy, the ability to resonate with our students' affects and experience, and
5. a greater sense of being a resource that the system (school, education, society) cannot do without: being needed.

By working through these steps recursively, we come to integrate various parts of ourselves that were previously excluded. Such integration occurs between elements of one register and those of another (e.g., between affects and identity-bearing linguistic contents) and also between elements in the same register, such as conflicting values, ideals, or affects. One major benefit of such integration is that it reins in impulses that may be operating at cross purposes to our core identity contents and redirects them into modes, objects, and aims that coincide with these core contents—for example, redirecting our aggression away from unresponsive or hostile students and toward the forces that are making the students this way; sublimating our aggression, that is, transforming it from a destructive into a constructive, productive form of action; or redirecting our recognition-seeking away from behaviors that interfere with student development and toward behaviors that foster it.

In promoting such integration, working through also promotes development of the more complex identity structures, which enhance our capacity to be attuned to, to coordinate, and hence to more easily satisfy students' identity needs and the needs of the larger society together with our own identity needs as teachers. This capacity includes 1) the capacity for empathy, attunement to individual students and their needs (enhanced interpersonal structure); 2) the capacity to balance the needs of individuals and groups in our presence with the (often competing) needs of individuals and groups out of sight and even out of our sphere of acquaintances (enhanced institutional structure); and 3) the capacity to see beyond the rules and regulations of systems and institutions and attend to the needs of people who are often overlooked, marginalized, or ignored by the systems and institutions that we are involved with (enhanced interindividual structure).

CHAPTER 11

GENERATIVE IDENTITY AND THE NEED TO TEACH

Integration Leading to Altruistic Pedagogy

Why would the recovery and integration of rejected and marginalized parts of oneself necessarily lead one to become a better teacher, a teacher pursuing more consistently and effectively the aim of benefiting students and society by promoting students' identity development? After all, the rejected elements of the self include murderous and sadistic urges and desires together with primitive and perverse narcissistic and sexual impulses and fantasies. What is to guarantee that the recovery and integration of the rejected elements of self would not simply turn teachers into sociopaths or sexual predators, rather than more altruistic and benevolent servants to their students and society? Why will owning our narcissism, rage, and libidinal and murderous impulses prevent us from enacting these qualities, but owning our tender impulses will enable and even require us to enact these attributes in a prosocial manner?

There are two basic reasons. First, for most teachers, enacting the harmful impulses would not provide adequate identity support to compensate for the identity support (from prosocial identity components) that they would sacrifice if they enacted them. Most teachers have been socialized effectively enough so that their humane, prosocial identity components (in traditional psychoanalytic terms, their ego ideal, superego, and ego) will carry the day even against the most powerful of their perverse and antisocial impulses.

But more importantly, the analytic process recovers not only aggressive, narcissistic, and perverse impulses but also what psychoanalysis discovered as the instinctual, primal basis of morality itself, the involuntary impulse to protect and care for others that develops from the infant's primal bond with the mother. That is, if we pursue our desire to its deepest and most archaic instantiations, we uncover not only grandiose narcissistic desire, lust, and rage but also our need to receive recognition from the real, or what Erik Erikson called our need to be needed. We come to realize that our most profound gratification and fulfillment occurs when our need/desire for the (m)Other is reciprocated in her need/desire for us, a need that we experience not only when our need to be nursed meets our mother's need to nurse us, but also when our need/desire for loving recognition expresses itself in an intense or excited gaze, vocalization, or body motion that is responded to by a (m)Other's voice, gaze, or body language communicating her need to be needed by us.

This means that to the extent that teachers (or anyone else) can recover and own their deepest needs, urges, impulses, and desires, such ownership will entail not rampant asocial or antisocial narcissism, hedonism, or aggression but rather empathy, compassion, and altruism. This is a crucial point, which is made in different ways by both Lacan and Erikson.

Lacan: The Desire of the Other

In Lacan's view, the psychoanalytic process is guided by the question, which Lacan views as a fundamentally ethical question: have I acted in accordance with the desire that is in me (see Lacan, *Ethics*)? In the psychoanalytic process, Lacan says, the only thing of which one can be guilty is of having given up on one's desire. Now this dictum is often interpreted to mean that psychoanalysis legitimizes asocial or even antisocial self-indulgence and the acting out of impulses, and this construal has been given credence by—and offered as an excuse for—rude, arrogant, and self-indulgent behavior by some Lacanian analysts and theorists. But if one understands these comments of Lacan in the context of what Lacan says elsewhere about desire in general and the analyst's desire in particular, one arrives at a profoundly different conclusion.

The first point to understand about Lacanian desire is that our most fundamental desire is desire for recognition—a claim that, as we saw in chapter 1, is supported by numerous nonpsychoanalytic theorists of the self as well. This fundamental desire for recognition entails a second basic point that Lacan makes about desire: namely, that it is always desire of the other. This can mean a number of different things. Most significant for our purposes is the fact that the first and most basic desire that an infant has is to be desired by its mother, the mother's desire here functioning as the most powerful instance of recognition. Infants need evidence that they are desired, and they receive it through the mother's affective attunement with them, as well as through being gazed at and being held, touched, cared for, spoken to, and listened to. Some gratification of this desire is necessary for an infant's survival, both psychological and biological, and as a result of this necessity, a primal concern for the other's desire is built into our very constitution as subjects; it is in fact the basis on which we become subjects and come to have a sense of self or identity. Since the infant's very being is dependent on its responding to the other's desire, without a proto-ethical attunement to and concern for the other's desire, the infant would never become a subject. Thus one form, perhaps the most profound form, of desire as the desire of the other is empathy, or desiring *for* the other, in the other's place. Primal desire thus involves a primordial care for the other. As Lévinas puts it, ethics is prior to being. And the Lacanian ethical question, "Have I acted in conformity with the desire that is in me?" thus inevitably entails, at its deepest level, the question "Have I acted in conformity with the desire for the other's well-being that is built into me?"

Our desire for the other's welfare is reinforced by a third factor that Lacan emphasizes with regard to desire—namely, that human desire always involves desire in the second degree: every desire always entails a desire to have it or not to have it. Because we have multiple, often conflicting desires, each desire confronts us with the question "Do I want to have this desire, or do I want not to have it?" In order to answer this question, we are led to assess the entailments and consequences of our different desires, to identify contradictions between different desires and/or their entailments and consequences, and on this basis to identify which desires we most desire and which actions will be most likely to fulfill these desires. Ultimately, we desire those desires that will bring us the most gratifying recognitions. And the most gratifying recognitions are, as we have seen, recognitions from the real, those that demonstrate that we, through our being or our actions, have fulfilled the desires of other people: namely, helping others realize their deepest desires, seeing these results in actuality, and having others acknowledge our contribution not only through their words and gestures but also—and often most importantly—through actual changes in their state of being. Thus when we recognize care for the other as one of our desires and assess the relative gratification it provides, it tends to become a desire that we desire above all others and thus plays a greater role in directing our behavior.

That pursuing the question of our own desire far enough ultimately leads to our desire for the other's well-being is also entailed by Lacan's statement that analysis, pursued to its logical conclusion, leads the analysand to assume the analyst's desire (*Ethics* 300–301), which Lacan defines as the desire for absolute difference. By the desire for absolute difference Lacan means that the *analyst* desires that the *analysand* desire not the analyst's own (concrete, specific, contingent) first-order desires but rather that the analysand desire to recognize and own his or her *own* first-order desires, which in their concrete specificity may be radically different both from the *analyst's* first-order desires and from the *analysand's* own second-order desires. This desire for absolute difference, which governs the entire analysis and which arises in the analysand at the conclusion of analysis, thus expresses in perhaps the purest form possible that primordial care for the other that is necessary in order for a subject to be produced by the other's desire.

The logic of Lacanian desire thus entails that when one pursues one's *own* desire as far as possible, that desire inverts itself, in Moebius-strip fashion, into a caring for the *other*. And such caring, and the pursuit of our own desire that leads to it, is crucial in directing our teaching in pursuit of social justice, for two reasons. First, without embracing our own care for the other—our own desire for others to realize their desires—we will lack the necessary motivation to carry our academic activity very far toward social change, resting satisfied instead with more superficial recognitions and enactments of more peripheral components of our identities, such as the sorts outlined in chapters 7, 8, and 9. And second, without being in touch with the diverse forms and modes of our other desires—and especially our own subjective destitution and the anxiety, depression, and rage produced in us by crucial failures in the Other's recognition of us—our primal caring for the other will risk being overridden by our fear of our own unacknowledged desires, and we will be unable to understand or even to countenance the desires that are motivating the behaviors of those others that we need to change in order to promote social justice. Only to the extent that we are in touch with our own deepest and most obscure desires (identity needs) and their frustrations can we eschew our more accessible and socially sanctioned impulses to respond to people who are violent or prejudiced by exposing, denouncing, and punishing them, and address instead the particular frustrations and gratifications of their identity needs that are producing their destructive acts—frustrations and gratifications that we understand through the echoes of them that we find in ourselves. Without recognizing these desires/needs in ourselves, we will see no reason for resisting our desire to denounce and punish the others in whom we find these desires—which will also serve to keep our own unacceptable desires externalized and thus hidden from ourselves—and we will be unable to fathom the desires motivating the other's harmful behavior and will thus have difficulty understanding how to intervene effectively and ethically to stop such behavior. A monumental example of such failure is the U.S. response to the September 11 terrorist attacks, with George W. Bush and other politicians, as well as many pundits, expressing genuine bafflement at how anyone could have the thoughts, beliefs, feelings, and behaviors that the terrorists manifested. The consequence of such failure to understand the other's desire/identity needs, which results from a failure to acknowledge our own similar desires/needs, is often the production of more of the very behavior that one wishes to prevent.

That our desire is the desire of the other ultimately means that our deepest desire is for the other's deepest desire to be realized. If an analysand has not yet uncovered and recovered this desire and experienced it as the most profound and primal desire, that fact in and of itself demonstrates that the analysis has not yet reached bedrock, which—contrary to Freud, who thought that the Oedipus complex was the ultimate foundation of the human subject—lies in the primal, preoedipal relation with the (m)Other. Thus, to put things very succinctly, by rigorously pursuing the implications of the Lacanian psychoanalytic ethical principle of not giving ground on one's desire, we are led to a position opposite to that normally assumed to be entailed by Lacan's pronouncements on the ethics of psychoanalysis. Whereas the Lacanian ethic is often taken to entail and legitimize greater and greater self-involvement, it is rather the case that if we pursue our own desire as far as possible, it will lead us not to self-involvement but to a Lévinasian care for the other that is prior to being—a care for the other that we must enact in order to become subjects in the first place. Or, stated somewhat differently, as we recover and metabolise the primal mutuality that is the origin and core of our identity, both the content and the structure of our identity are altered in ways that involve our coming to embrace the other as such as an essential dimension of our identity, such that the maintenance of our own identity requires that we nurture the other.

Erikson: Generativity and the Need to Teach

Erik Erikson makes a similar point about the bedrock of identity in terms that explicitly evoke the activity of teaching. For Erikson, one of the deepest impulses of adult human beings is the impulse of "generativity," by which he means "the instinctual power behind various forms of selfless 'caring' " (Erikson, *Insight* 131). And this "instinctual power" of generativity manifests itself, Erikson says, in the need to teach, or "the teaching passion" (*Insight* 131). This generative impulse—this need to teach, to help others thrive, develop, and flourish—is a fundamental and central component of adult identity: it is "the fulfillment of . . . identity," Erikson says, so central to our identity that it can be said of us that "we are the teaching species" (*Insight* 131, 130).

The generativity impulse in general and the need to teach in particular both have their origins in our earliest experiences with our caregivers, in which we were the recipients of their generative impulse, their need to teach, their need to be needed:

A baby's first responses can be seen as part of an actuality consisting of many details of mutual arousal and response. While the baby initially smiles at a mere configuration resembling the human face, the adult cannot help smiling back, filled with expectations of a "recognition" which he needs to secure from the new being as surely as it needs him. The fact is that the mutuality of adult and baby is the original source of hope, the basic ingredient of all effective as well as ethical human action. As far back as 1895, Freud, in his first outline of a "Psychology for Neurologists," confronts the "helpless" newborn infant with a "help-rich" ("*hilfreich*") adult, and postulates that their mutual understanding is "the primal source of all moral motives." (Erikson, *Insight* 231)

Thus at its deepest level, "the identity of the subject comes," as Emmanuel Lévinas states, "from the impossibility of escaping responsibility, from the taking charge of the other" (Lévinas 14). And if we pursue our identity needs and desires far enough in our self-analysis, we encounter this primal, generative urge, the need to teach, nurture, and take care of others who need such care in order to develop their own (ultimately generative) identities.

Generativity is a function not only of the need to be needed (i. e., recognized by the real), but also the need to enact a more capacious structure of identity in which the other in need is experienced as myself in need. Insofar as our self-analysis enables us to more fully realize and integrate our primal empathic impulses, these impulses will assume a central position in each identity structure: empathy and care for the other will be our guiding impulse, our central imperial project, the core and aim of our interpersonal relationships, the missions of our institutions and systems, and the foundation of our interindividual orientation. And since the generative impulse extends ultimately to all humans (and beyond, to nonhuman forms of life as well), cultivating this impulse in any identity structure will ineluctably lead one to develop more capacious structures, culminating in the interindividual structure.

The more we are able to recognize, own, and integrate 1) our deepest needs for recognition for our identity (which include those others whom we experience as parts of our extended identity) in all their manifestations and 2) our most obscure and profound anger and rage at those who harm or threaten our identity (including its extensions into others), the more our own identity will take on the interindividual structure, in which our common humanity overrides our differences with all others, so that we spontaneously perceive even the most despised others—including murderers, rapists, racists, serial killers, child molesters, terrorists, imperialists, and war-mongers, as well as students who may respond to our teaching with overt hostility, smug indifference, undisguised boredom, chronic laziness, or manipulative flattery—as "us" rather than "them." The reasons are that 1) owning our own depraved and "criminal" impulses obviates the need to externalize them, hence eliminating the need for a "them," and 2) recognizing our own "criminal" impulses brings the realization, "There but for my good fortune am I"—the acknowledgment that the only differences between ourselves and these despised others are genetic differences and environmental differences, neither of which can be credited to ourselves or blamed on the others.

More fully integrating, cultivating, and developing our generative, teaching impulse is thus important not only for our well-being and that of our students but also for the welfare of the world at large, because generativity is the only secure ground of ethics and social justice (see Bauman). Studies of altruists such as those who rescued Jews during the Holocaust have found that what motivated these rescuers to risk their lives to help others was not primarily moral values or religious beliefs but rather an interindividual identity, a sense of self as integrally connected to the welfare of other individuals. Noting that the rescuers she interviewed experienced their decisions to save Jews as reflexive or even instinctual rather than rationally determined, Kristen Monroe reasons that "the prime force behind ethical acts is not conscious choice but rather deep-seated intuitions, predispositions, and habitual patterns of behavior related to our central identity. . . . Ethical political action emanates primarily from one's sense of self in relation to others" (Monroe, *Heart* 218, 217). "Universal moral behavior," Monroe concludes, is rooted "not in religion or reason but in identity and a sense of self" (Monroe, "Explicating" 106). We teachers thus need to integrate, cultivate, and develop our own generative impulse because we need to help others develop it, and we need to cultivate it in others both because they need it individually in order to be fulfilled and also because it is the only secure basis for undermining the various forms of violence that produce human suffering and constitute injustice.

Generativity and the need to teach thus ultimately entail "the responsibility of each individual for the potentialities of all generations and of all generations for each individual" (Erikson, *Insight* 157). When our generative identity—our caring, nurturing, teaching self, which reaches its culmination in Kegan's interindividual identity structure—is dominant, we care about every individual human being that we know, encounter, hear about, or even only imagine, and not only in the present but also indefinitely into the future. Generativity extends beyond our family, beyond our community, beyond our national borders, and beyond our—and our children's—generations. The generative, teaching instinct thus entails a species-wide identity embodying a truly universal ethics, an identity in which one "sees all beings in [one's] own self and [one's] own self in all beings" (*Upanishads*, qtd. in Erikson, *Insight* 221).

Enacting generativity means not only enacting a species-wide identity embodying a universal ethics but helping others to achieve such an identity as well. This is because enacting generativity means helping others develop and enact their identities to the fullest. And their identities reach such a state only to the extent that they, too, realize and enact their own generativity and teaching passion, which entails for them as for us the achievement of a species-wide identity embodying a universal ethics. Thus in addition to saving people from "undernourishment, morbidity, and early mortality," a generative person "cannot evade the problem of assuring ethical vitality to all lives saved" (Erikson, *Insight* 238), which means striving to assure that all others are able to realize and develop their generative impulse, their teaching passion, "the instinctual power behind [the] various forms of selfless 'caring' " that is at the heart of a universal ethics. As Don Browning explains,

> [I]t is the great task of generative [people] to develop the "ethical potential of our older youth"—those who are so close to their own childhood, so close to full adulthood, and so intensively sensitive to the ethical and generational needs of both. Generative [people] in the generative society will compose [themselves] into a chain of interacting and responsible people, all of whom have their age-specific ethical responsibilities and roles, all of which are aimed at giving generative strength to individuals and generative integrity to society as a whole. (Browning 207)

Teaching so as to help our students develop their identities to the fullest thus means helping them develop generative identities. And our enactment of our own (always still developing) generative identity in helping them develop their generative identity is also an enactment of the fundamental ethical act as defined by Erikson: an act that strengthens both parties (*Insight* 233). The paradigm for such action derives, once again, from the primal scene of caregiving:

> A parent dealing with a child will be strengthened in *his* vitality, in *his* sense of identity, and in *his* readiness for ethical action by the very ministrations by means of which he secures to the child vitality, future identity, and eventual readiness for ethical action. . . . Understood in this way, the [Golden] Rule would say that it is best to do another what will strengthen you even as it will strengthen him—that is, what will develop his best potentials even as it develops your own. (*Insight* 233)

Truly ethical teaching is teaching that helps our students learn, grow, and develop their identity to its optimal extent. Such action is a profound identity need of everyone, but one that most people, including most of us teachers, have not realized, integrated, and metabolized into our own identity as fully as we can. By helping us identify, recover, and integrate this deepest of impulses, our self-analysis can bring us to realize, or to realize more fully, that the best way to maintain and enhance our identity is by 1) assisting with the support and development of our students' (ultimately generative) identities and in doing so also 2) helping to reduce suffering and injustice. To the extent that we become more aware of our generative need and capacity and assess the degree to which our various pedagogical aims and teaching practices enact it, ignore it, or even thwart it, we are led to cultivate those aims and practices that enact it most fully and abandon those that enact it only slightly or not at all. As we more fully realize this primal identity need, this caring for the other, we will become more vigorous, rigorous, and hence successful in enacting it through our teaching and our scholarship as well as in our lives generally, thus promoting in the most fundamental way possible not only our own well-being and that of our students, but also social justice, the well-being of everyone.

Part Four
Promoting Students' Identity Development

CHAPTER 12
SUPPORTING PROSOCIAL IDENTITY
CONTENTS

Given the fundamental role played by identity in learning, resistance to learning, social problems, and counterproductive responses to social problems, educators in all roles—from teachers and advisors to administrators and policymakers—should devote themselves to promoting the development of students' identities. Equipped with the understanding of identity laid out in the preceding chapters, and motivated by the generative elements of their own identities, educators can take various steps to promote learning, personal well-being, and social justice by addressing students' identity needs. Such steps include:

1. understanding, recognizing, anticipating, avoiding, and (when necessary) changing or counteracting the numerous ways in which various aspects of education threaten students' identities;
2. providing recognition and enactment opportunities for students' benign, prosocial identity contents, as well as for contents that support intelligence and learning;
3. helping students recode qualities and activities such as knowledge, learning, studying, and intelligence in terms congruent with rather than opposed to their benign identity-bearing signifiers and affective-physiological states;
4. helping students redefine their identity-bearing signifiers (gender, sexual, racial, class, peer group, etc.) to include rather than exclude knowledge, learning, studying, intelligence, and academic success;
5. enabling students to understand the various defenses that interfere with learning, personal well-being, and social justice;
6. helping students become aware of and integrate their anxiety and resistance to learning as well as the various destructive or socially unacceptable characteristics and impulses that they have heretofore repressed and therefore act out, chief among which are hateful, aggressive, and even murderous thoughts, feelings, and desires; and

7. helping students develop more complex and capacious identity structures, thereby enabling integration, reducing the need for primitive defenses, and expanding the boundaries of identity to include an increasingly greater number and diversity of other people.

In elaborating on these points in the following chapters, I will once again focus primarily on my home discipline of literary study, but much of what I have to say about the teaching of literature can be adapted to the teaching of other disciplines as well, especially those in the humanities and social sciences.

Providing Students with Recognition and Enactment Opportunities

The importance of avoiding unmanageable threats to students' identities was explained in chapter 8. Many of our educational practices, however well intentioned, are counterproductive either because they involve identity threats that we are not aware of or because we mistakenly believe that those threats are not harmful. But even apparently mild traumas and identity threats can, when sustained over a period of time, produce serious consequences and should therefore be avoided. The first rule for teachers aiming to promote personal well-being and social justice as well as education is thus to do no harm to students' identities.

The second principle, providing students with recognition of and opportunities to enact key identity contents, is perhaps the most direct means by which teachers can promote students' identity development and the various personal and social benefits that follow from it. Providing such support for academic and prosocial identity contents can be challenging in a society that values such qualities less and less. Opportunities to enact such contents are much harder for students to come by than opportunities to enact nonacademic and non-prosocial contents such as physical attractiveness, sexiness, wealth, social status, athletic prowess, physical dominance, racial or ethnic identity, and sexual orientation. These latter contents can often be enacted and expressed continuously through various aspects of one's physical appearance and bodily movements in the classroom, the hall, and the athletic field or court. There do not exist similar opportunities for students to enact, on an ongoing basis, knowledge, intelligence, reflectiveness, compassion, or altruism. Even in the classroom, opportunities to enact such contents are often hard to come by, and it is therefore incumbent on educators to make a special effort to protect and expand such opportunities where they already exist and to seek to create new ones wherever possible.

The active learning approach in education, together with the emphasis on lifelong learning, has helped to increase opportunities for students to enact their academic identity contents. The assumption of this approach, however, is that the value of student activity lies primarily in its enhancement of memory and its more efficient development of cognitive skills and capacities. What is usually overlooked is the fact that active learning also provides important opportunities for students to enact their academic identity contents, and even, where such skills or capacities have not yet been embraced as part of one's identity, to come, through enacting them, to own them as parts of one's sense of self, or identity. By seeing active learning not just as a memory-enhancing and skill-developing technique but also as an opportunity for students to enact and develop their academic identity contents, teachers can construct and administer active learning activities and opportunities so as to more effectively promote the development of identity in addition to skills and knowledge—for example, through helping students embrace their skills and knowledge not just as tools but as important parts of their selves.

The primary venues for enacting academic and prosocial identity contents include class discussions, class reports, small-group work and discussions, and homework, including writing. Each of these activities, especially when it receives significant recognition of some sort, can provide students with a vibrant, powerful sense of self. As Tingle observes regarding students' engagement in academic discourse,

> One may . . . receive enormous narcissistic gratification [i.e., identity support] by moving into and mastering a particular mode of discourse. At the simplest level, one may experience oneself, for example, as particularly intelligent. Additionally, one may be rewarded by the applause of one's peers . . . and by recognition as a specialist or "expert" knower in a certain area of knowledge construction. (Tingle 111)

As Tingle's comments indicate, when students do manage to enact academic identity contents, it is crucial that these contents be supported and fostered through recognition. It is also important that students receive ongoing recognition for other identity contents that is adequate to sustain their identity and thus save them from the need to seek identity support in ways that are personally or socially harmful. Concerning the importance of recognition in education, Rauno Huttunen and Hannu Heikkinen observe:

> [T]he processes of the dialectic of recognition are at the heart of the process of education (*Bildung*). . . . A teacher's work is a process of receiving and giving recognition. . . . [I]t is [thus] essential to know the mechanisms of recognition. In learning communities, these mechanisms are substantial, because the processes of learning and identity formation are intrinsically connected with the process of recognition . . . ; understanding the mechanisms of recognition helps us to become better teachers and mentors. (164–165)

The mechanisms by which educators can provide recognition to students are many, and virtually all of them are already in operation in literature (and other) classes, though often without teachers' being aware of them. And only rarely are these various forms of recognition employed in a systematic, coordinated manner with the aim of promoting students' identity development. Outside of those relatively few classes that make empowerment of students their central aim, such recognition-providing practices are usually implemented in piecemeal and desultory fashion, and in the service of "getting students to participate" or "getting students to love literature" or another discipline, rather than with the primary aim of facilitating students' identity development. Thus before a more systematic and effective provision of recognition for students can be implemented, we need to fully embrace the reversal of priorities that feminism began in literary studies with its (sometimes explicit, sometimes tacit) insistence that students do not exist to serve literature (by studying it, learning it, appreciating it, enjoying it, loving it, fetishizing it, or increasing its value by devoting their lives to promoting it) but that literature, rather, exists for the purpose of serving students and others, by helping them cope, thrive, and develop into fulfilled individuals and responsible and productive members of society. Students are the ends, literature is but the means.

In providing recognition for students, it is helpful to distinguish three different levels of the self (see Josephs), the recognition of which takes different forms and produces different results. First, there is the public self, which includes those parts of oneself that one acknowledges and freely displays to others in hopes of their being recognized. Then there is the private self, encompassing elements that one acknowledges and yearns to have others recognize and accept but that one hides from others out of fear that they will not approve of these elements. And finally there are the unconscious elements of one's self, those parts of the self that one is unaware of possessing because one has disowned them, excluded them from identity, largely as a result of socializing pressures. For each of these levels there are multiple forms, modes, and channels of recognition available through literary study.

Recognition for Public Aspects of Identity

Interpersonal Recognition

Recognition for the public self is the most common in literature classes as well as generally, and its provision usually produces an immediate boost to identity. Direct expressions of admiration or approval by the teacher or other students for a student's knowledge, understanding, insight, or sensitivity are both immediately energizing and profoundly nourishing for identity. Direct, explicit, second-person modes of address ("You are very perceptive" or "That's an excellent observation") are the most obvious form of such recognition, but silent, respectful listening to a student's comments or questions can also constitute a powerful form of recognition, particularly when accompanied by a respectful gaze, gestures, or facial expressions. Explicit third-person modes of address (e.g., "As Jane noted earlier in our discussion . . .") can have a similar function when made in the presence of the person being recognized. Such statements demonstrate that one has been listened to, understood, and remembered—that one has made a lasting impact on one's listener—such an impact being a form of recognition from the Real.

Literary study also offers powerful forms of implicit recognition, which results from reading, discussing, and writing about aspects of a character or author that are also components of or issues concerning one's own identity. Whenever we read or hear others talk about someone embodying identity attributes that we claim for ourselves as well, those parts of ourselves are being recognized by the mere fact that they have been expressed (and hence noticed) by someone else. Any approbation that may be attached to these attributes provides further recognition for us. A similar recognition is embodied in any mention a teacher may make of books, movies, television shows, and popular songs that are important to students: when someone else acknowledges the importance, or even the existence, of something that is important to me, my own importance is affirmed.

Today literature classes provide greater recognition for the public selves of many groups that were previously marginalized or entirely excluded from literary study, including women; gay, lesbian, and queer individuals; African American, Asian American, and Hispanic people; working class people; and adolescents. Yet crucial components of the public selves of most of our students are still denied recognition in our classrooms. One such component is hypermasculinity, which manifests itself in public consumption of, and professions of enthusiasm for, violent and brutal sports, movies, video games, music lyrics, and pornography. When such components of hypermasculinity are addressed at all in literature classes, the mode of address is usually ridicule, scorn, and condemnation. There is of course a logic to such nonrecognition: one way to change behavior is to starve it by depriving it of the nourishment that comes with recognition. Sometimes this strategy works. But it does so only if all sources of recognition are cut off (which is very difficult to do when some of the sources have been internalized, and impossible when the recognition is cultural rather than interpersonal) and if one is simultaneously provided with an alternative source of recognition that adequately compensates for the loss of the first. In the absence of these conditions, withholding recognition can simply heighten the need for it and intensify its pursuit through precisely that identity content—in this case, violent hypermasculinity—that is being deprived of it. A more effective strategy for literary study is to inquire into and explore these identity contents in ways that manifest respect for the identity needs embodied in them and interest in understanding where these needs come from and what consequences they produce. Such a mode of inclusion offers recognition and respect for the individuals who possess these identity components but does not endorse the behaviors that often follow from them. And it sets the stage for providing potentially transformative recognition for the private and even unconscious elements of the self that underlie this public persona of hypermasculinity, elements that I discuss later in this and in the following chapters.

Structural Recognition

Structural recognition for the public self is found in the tacit acknowledgement of one's importance that is present in the ways in which group activities and relationships are organized. For example, as most literature teachers have understood for some time now, different arrangements of desks in a classroom (e.g., a circle as opposed to columns of desks with all students facing the teacher) accord different degrees of recognition to students. A traditional seating arrangement, with students all facing the teacher, may suggest that it is more valuable for students to pay attention to the teacher and what the teacher says than it is to engage with other students. The same lack of recognition of students is embodied in the lecture structure, whereas teacher-led discussions and small-group discussions or workshops accord greater structural recognition to the students. One of the most powerful forms of structural recognition in education generally is the jigsaw method developed by Elliot Aronson, in which students are formed into small groups with each member of the group being given a specific task that he or she must perform successfully for the successful accomplishment of the group's task. Here the recognition of each student's importance is built into and communicated by the structure, which, in addition, makes it necessary for the other group members to provide express recognition in the form of attentive listening and questioning of each student (Aronson 135ff.). To the extent that such structures can be employed in literary study, it will provide enhanced recognition for students.

We also need to realize how structural recognition and its lack are embodied in our assignments, our grading criteria and procedures, and the relative importance of different factors in determining a student's final grade. Assignments that are rigidly prescriptive—requiring all students to write about the same text or the same topic and/or to employ the same perspective or methodology—can embody (and be experienced as expressing) lack of recognition, and the poor performance that this lack of recognition may help to produce will itself then elicit another lack of recognition. A Procrustean, one-size-fits-all approach to reading and writing assignments, schedules (due-dates), and grading criteria is often experienced as embodying lack of recognition for students in several ways, including not caring about students' needs at all, not recognizing individual differences among students and their respective needs, and not believing or trusting students when they explain why they have not yet completed a certain assignment. While it is probably not possible to avoid all Procrustean features in designing a course, awareness of the recognition implications of such design can motivate us to do so where we can.

Institutional Recognition

Literary study also provides and withholds recognition through various institutional forms. Institutional recognition for one's public self comes in the form of grades, awards (e.g., for the best poem, story, or critical essay), and degrees. Equally important in literature classes, as feminists have been emphasizing for decades, is the institutional recognition accorded by the inclusion of components of one's own identity in the literature deemed canonical. Opening an anthology or reading a syllabus and finding one's own identity groups present in abundance provides significant recognition of one's identity, whereas finding one's own groups absent or underrepresented can be identity-depleting. What is true of anthologies and syllabi is also true of curricula and course schedules: the presence of courses on Chaucer, Shakespeare, Milton, and Hemingway but not on Emily Dickinson, George Eliot, Toni Morrison, or Margaret Atwood offers institutional recognition for some identities and withholds it for others. Considerable progress has been made during the past forty years in enhancing the institutional presence of previously marginalized identities. The expansion of the term "literature" to include popular texts of all sorts has made a significant contribution to the expansion of institutional recognition to previously ignored or marginalized identities.

But as is the case with interpersonal recognition, many students' most important identity components—including the components of hypermasculinity—still receive little or no institutional recognition from literary study, apart from a few sporadic efforts to institute "masculinity studies." It is true, of course, that most literature courses, curricula, and anthologies have been and still primarily are masculinist (and white, and Euro-American), but most hypermasculine boys and men today do not experience this institutional recognition of the masculine as including their form of masculinity. In light of this fact, we might consider instituting courses that more explicitly name, and devote themselves to engaging and exploring, such identity contents. Such possibilities might include the literature (including film) of war, of sports, of gangs, of revenge, and of other types of aggressivity and violence. In addition to providing recognition for hypermasculine individuals, such courses could also set the stage for exploring the private and unconscious dimensions of hypermasculine identity.

Cultural Recognition: Language

Cultural recognition is found wherever the elements or processes of culture acknowledge the existence of a component of one's identity. In literary study cultural recognition is present most obviously in the topics and attributes foregrounded in texts' agents (characters), actions, and objects. Institutional recognition in literary study, as described above, is partly a function of providing students with access to the specific types of cultural recognition embodied in different texts. Perhaps the most fundamental source of cultural recognition is language itself, where the existence of words for certain categories, states of being, and actions recognizes and validates them while the absence of words for other identity components deprives them of recognition. An example is the way in which the absence of the title "Ms" withheld recognition from women as agents in their own right apart from their marital status (designated by "Miss" or "Mrs."). Finding words for one's experience can in and of itself provide profound recognition, for it indicates that somewhere at some time someone else experienced what one is oneself experiencing. Finding no words for one's experience, or at least none that anyone has dared to utter in public, constitutes, in contrast, a significant nonrecognition of one's state of being, as E. M. Forster's novel *Maurice* documents for gay male experience and Jeanette Winterson's *Oranges Are Not the Only Fruit* does for lesbian experience. We literature teachers should thus aim to provide our students with texts that support their identities by giving words to those elements of their selves that the popular culture has marginalized—which means those parts of their selves that are likely to have remained private or even unconscious. Providing recognition for these dimensions of identity will be discussed further below.

Cultural Recognition: Images

Cultural recognition is also distributed through images.[1] The accordance of recognition for certain body images and physical abilities is powerfully evident in television and film. Feminist critics pointed out long ago how the camera's frame, focus, and movement construct the female body as an object for the male gaze, and in doing so, not only gratify and reinforce that gaze but also prompt girls and women to invest their identities in certain body images and physical attributes and reject others. That the same process works to produce and sustain imagistic-perceptual identity components of boys and men can be seen in the extent to which boys (and some men) will go to assume the look (clothes, facial expressions, walk, posture, and gestures) and the moves (in the athletic arena or on the street) of the male entertainers and athletes who are the objects of the camera's admiring gaze. Such efforts can entail not only the risk of severe bodily injury (imitating the stunts of characters in films such as *Jackass* or the smackdown moves of professional wrestling) but also violence and indifference. In some cases, violence is entailed as an instrument for procuring a certain imagistic-perceptual identity, as in those instances in which one man attacks (and sometimes even kills) another for his sneakers or starter jacket. But more often violence is entailed as the means of demonstrating the physical attributes of masculinity, such as the capacity of one's body to overpower other bodies or to withstand brutal assault without collapsing or surrendering.

Textual recognition can also promote a violence-enabling indifference, by interpellating individuals to adopt identity-bearing body images embodying impassivity, affectlessness, stoicism, and "cool" in the face of suffering and to reject body images embodying desolation, anguish, compassion, sympathy, pity, and guilt. Many boys and men have sought recognition by emulating the icy stare of a Clint Eastwood character or the cold glares and sneers with which other action heroes confront danger and suffering. In such action narratives, it is virtually impossible to find a male protagonist weeping, sobbing, or wailing in anguish, and almost as rare to find one expressing compassion, sadness, tenderness, or guilt through facial expressions, postures, gestures, or bodily movements. This toughness is no doubt a reaction formation or counterphobic response to the threats to bodily integrity and masculinity that are central to these same narratives.

The fundamental way literature affects these and other imagistic identity contents is by providing (or withholding) recognition for them. Such recognition comes not only in the form of explicit praise of a character's physical attributes, but also in the form of detailed descriptions of bodies with particular characteristics and the absence of descriptions or even the mention of bodies with other characteristics. One thinks of Pindaric odes describing the triumphant exploits of Greek athletes, Petrarchan sonnets cataloguing and praising bodily features of the beloved mistress, or contemporary young adult literature portraying the athletic prowess of sports heroes. Even an apparently indifferent mention of certain bodily characteristics of a character one admires or identifies with can prompt readers to invest in those characteristics as parts of their own bodily identities. When a narrator describes certain bodily attributes with approbation, readers who possess such attributes experience recognition and validation, and their investment in these attributes as part of their identity is reinforced. Readers who lack the represented and recognized attributes often experience a desire to acquire them as a means of achieving such recognition. I recall as a young boy of about eight hoping that I would grow up to have the tall stature, broad shoulders, and deep voice of the hero of a pioneer novel I read at the time, and that when I got to high school I would be able to play football like the star of the Chip Hilton novels I was reading. What was decisive for me in both cases was the admiration—recognition—that both the narrators and the other characters expressed for these attributes. I also recall the power of the interpellation of physical toughness and violence that I experienced in the narratives I consumed in early adolescence when I felt vaguely inadequate upon realizing a) that I was the only boy (of about a dozen) in my class who had not received a paddling in the principal's office (a deficiency that I soon remedied) and b) that I had never been in a fistfight (a shortcoming that I never overcame) and so was still far short of achieving that ideal of masculinity that I saw embodied in the brawling cowboys that populated my favorite television programs. And I remember absorbing *Readers Digest* narratives in high school vaunting the physical suffering and courage of soldiers in Vietnam whose bodies were blown apart by mines or grenades or riddled with bullets, and feeling that I could not fully respect myself or claim the highest respect from others because my body had not sustained anything close to such horrors.

In addition to providing recognition for certain bodily images and states, literature also enables their virtual enactment, either directly, through portrayals of them, or indirectly, through portrayals of surrogate bodies or descriptions of landscapes and other places that elicit simulations of bodily actions to cope with those represented environments. Representations of bodies and environments that elicit simulations of hypervigilance, struggle, competition, or violence help to construct or reinforce imagistic identity components that are more capable of being enacted through violence than are other imagistic identity components.

Changing Harmful Identity Contents

In addition to supporting identity by providing recognition for various identity contents, literary study can also promote beneficial changes in harmful identity contents—that is, those that oppose learning, undermine personal well-being, or entail violence and other social problems. One way to do so is by decreasing or undermining recognition for such contents while simultaneously increasing recognition for benign and prosocial contents.

Such provision and withholding of recognition can be produced not only through teachers' remarks in class discussions and responses to written assignments but also through the selection of texts and the focusing of discussions and written analyses of those texts. Thus texts that approvingly foreground attributes such as toughness, autonomy, and dominance or describe them in glowing terms and great detail may be eschewed in favor of texts that provide such accounts of empathy, compassion, and tenderness. Alternatively, the recognition of violence-entailing identity contents provided by texts such as the former, or by texts extolling patriotism, group loyalty, or tribalism, can be vitiated by careful analysis and scrutiny of the connections between the recognized identity contents and the suffering they entail.

Another way to promote beneficial changes in students' identity contents is through deconstruction. For example, identity-bearing signifiers such as toughness and dominance, imagistic identity contents such as hypermasculine bodies, and identity-bearing narratives of violent physical actions can be analyzed to reveal the mutually antithetical qualities present in their origins, consequences, and motivational core. Such inquiry into the reasons why men pursue hypermasculine bodies and engage in hypermasculine physical actions will reveal decidedly "unmasculine" characteristics such as fear, shame, and even cowardice to be the motive forces behind the quest for hypermasculine bodies. And pursuit of the consequences of this quest will expose the prematurely decrepit, maimed, and even dead bodies of some of the most successful questors and their opponents, along with significant social and emotional costs. Such connections constitute a profound withdrawal of recognition by the real for hypermasculine identity contents.

Another major strategy for replacing harmful identity contents is to help students experience the benefits of alternative contents. One can provide recognition for—and in some cases even opportunities to enact—alternative, nonviolent identity contents through the texts one chooses, the topics one discusses, and the approbation and disapprobation one bestows on various contents represented in literary texts. Much classroom discussion of literary texts implicitly engages in such provision and withholding of recognition for students' linguistic identity contents—that is, their identity-bearing signifiers, systems of knowledge or belief, and narratives—whether such discussions focus on "the moral of the story," the motives or justifications for characters' actions, or the text's presentation of "human nature" or "the human condition." The traditional function of universal literary education as a means of "broadening students' horizons" also gestures toward the importance of providing students with alternative identity contents, though this traditional mission has rarely if ever been formulated in those terms (or in any very precise terms). Recognizing that these traditional literary pedagogical aims and practices already broach significant ways of promoting students' identity development, literature teachers can reformulate and refine them to explicitly focus on this end and pursue it more systematically and consistently.

Literary study can also support the development of benign body-imagistic and affective identity contents. One activity that is especially effective for some students is the reading of descriptions of landscapes and other natural phenomena. By providing students with literary texts that engage their senses through vibrant imagery, and by helping the students respond to such imagery with vivid sensory imaginings, teachers can provide students with experiences of new or heretofore unacknowledged body states. Insofar as landscapes and other physical settings evoke certain body orientations and responses, helping students to imaginatively immerse themselves in a poetic landscape will automatically evoke a certain body state and image in them. An attentive reading of Keats's "To Autumn," for example, can elicit in the reader a relaxed, contented, androgynous body that is extended into and disseminated among the myriad forms of life populating the lazy autumn afternoon at the end of the harvest—a body image that is poles apart from the hypermasculinized form. Focusing on and identifying with bodies described in literary texts can produce a similar enactment of alternative bodily states and images. Keats's poem provides an example of this principle as well, in the description of the anthropomorphized androgynous Autumn, drowsing in the late afternoon harvest field. As Keats himself indicated, in his account of imaginatively inhabiting the bodies of birds he saw pecking in the ground for food, when we are not distracted by other concerns, we automatically identify with and inhabit other bodies—human, animal, floral, and even inanimate—that we encounter. Thus by having students encounter literary descriptions of gentle rather than violent bodies, and landscapes and situations that elicit gentle rather than violent bodily postures and actions, literature teachers can enable students to divest themselves of some of their harmful imagistic identity contents and invest in more benign, prosocial contents. Such experiences can be facilitated, elaborated, extended, and consolidated in memory through class discussions and writing assignments that focus students' attentions on their sensory—visual, tactile, kinesthetic, olfactory, auditory, gustatory, and visceral—states as they read, reflect on, and write about such texts.

Developing Benign Identity-Bearing Affects

Literary study can also promote the development of benign identity-bearing affective states that are crucial not only for personal well-being but also for social justice. Literature, including movies and television programs, is a powerful means of enacting and receiving recognition for specific identity-bearing affects. Virtually every affect, from sadness and rage to lust and joy, can be aroused by a particular genre of literature, and many people consume particular genres of books, films, or television programs on a regular basis for precisely this reason. It follows that different types of literature can either reinforce, threaten, or alter our affective-physiological identity elements in ways that either increase or diminish our tendencies toward violence and violence-enabling indifference. Stimulus-seeking behavior, for example, includes the consumption of certain genres of literature, especially those that represent and display violence and revenge, whether they be Renaissance revenge tragedies, mid-twentieth-century Westerns, or more recent martial arts movies, television police dramas, and gangsta rap lyrics that evoke anger and hatred for the bad guys. While the consumption of such texts may in some cases help, as some have claimed, to prevent violent behavior by serving as an alternative to it, in the long run such consumption probably serves to reinforce violence by more firmly grounding one's sense of self in the vitality affects associated with violence. By withholding recognition and enactment opportunities for such affects, and deconstructing them—exposing their antithetical, identity-dystonic dimensions (such as tenderness and passivity)—literary study can reduce or even eliminate their identity-bearing capacity.

Literary study can also promote the development of identity-bearing prosocial affects. In recent years, a growing number of moral philosophers have argued that the path to social justice must pass not through rational Kantian or utilitarian principles but through the emotions. Richard Rorty calls for educators to focus not on moral principles or moral philosophy but on what he calls "manipulating sentiments," or "sentimental education" ("Human Rights" 73): the key emotion that needs to be developed is sympathy or compassion. Such tender emotions, however, are not the most highly valued and recognized in our culture, especially in the case of men. American culture offers many opportunities for men to openly feel, express, and even act on hypermasculine emotions such as anger, pride, disdain, and triumph but tightly restricts the expression of sadness, vulnerability, dependency, and depression (emotions that, ironically, underlie most displays of hypermasculine behavior and against which such behavior is often attempting to defend identity). For example, some candidates for public office have seen their support vanish when they expressed such tender emotions in public, or in some cases when they merely confessed to having had them in the past. A culture that affirmed tears and anguish as much as laughter and anger would not have so many people (mainly men) who feel threatened by feelings of sadness, weakness, helplessness, and by desires to submit to and be taken care of by more powerful others, and who thus feel the need to deny such tender feelings by enacting their opposites.

Literary study currently participates in this cultural withholding of recognition for tender emotions through conventions that exclude certain types of emotions and the texts that evoke them from literature courses. Literary study in the university has traditionally avoided all strong affects, engaging students instead in intellectualizing their experiences of the texts. The New Critical notion of the affective fallacy, for instance, tried to outlaw affective experience as such. This same intellectualized orientation to the literary text was present in the structuralist and deconstructive approaches, the successors of New Criticism, and in other highly theorized modes of literary criticism and pedagogy that continue to be prominent in graduate and undergraduate classrooms. However, expressions of anger, disdain, ridicule, and even contempt are not uncommon in literature classes, and when they occur, any discomfort they may evoke is usually relatively mild. It is feelings of tenderness and vulnerability, including sadness, helplessness, and compassion that are particularly excluded from expression in literature classes. Keith Johnstone's experience captures the situation well. "One day, when I was eighteen," he recalls, "I was reading a book and I began to weep. I was astounded. I had no idea that literature could affect me in such a way. If I'd have wept over a poem in class the teacher would have been appalled" (qtd. in Tompkins, *Life* 212). Jane Tompkins testifies to a similar effect from her education. "When I look back at my schooling today," she says, "I see what Johnstone sees—a person who was taught not to feel" (*Life* 212). When tender affects arise, they evoke more discomfort than their opposites—especially if they are accompanied by tears, choking, sobbing, or anguished wailing. The silent prohibition of such emotions in the classroom, and the embarrassment experienced by both the culprit and the witnesses in those rare cases when this taboo is broken, reinforce the more general withholding of cultural recognition from the tender as opposed to the aggressive affects.

In addition to the dominant critical and pedagogical approaches to literature, the very criteria for admission to the literary canon have also denied recognition to tender, prosocial affects by excluding or marginalizing texts that represent and valorize them in characters or evoke them in readers. The most obvious instance of such discrimination has been the refusal of first-rank canonical status to *Uncle Tom's Cabin*, which not only represents and praises powerful tender affects in its characters and evokes them in its readers but also admonishes its readers to cultivate such affects as central components of their identities and guides to moral action. Because such affects have been defined as antithetical to the masculinist identities of impassivity and stoicism on the one hand and violence and rage on the other, texts in which they figure prominently and receive positive notice have been largely excluded from the literary canon and from the study of literature.

Literary study can reverse this tradition and provide significant recognition and enactment opportunities for prosocial, tender affects and reduced recognition and enactment opportunities for affects associated with violence. To the extent that our literature classrooms recognize tears and compassion as much as laughter and derision, or affectless intellectualizing, we will begin to change this culture and thus reduce all the forms of violence it supports. But some identity contents are antithetical to sympathy and/or its attendant affective states, and such contents thus require the repression of these affects. Linguistic-conceptual identity contents such as "manly" or "masculine," for example, can prevent people from feeling sympathy, sadness, fear, and distress: since sympathy and its attendant affective states are coded feminine, people for whom masculinity is an important identity component prevent themselves from having such emotions because to have them would contradict their masculine identity. As Robert Solomon notes, the general disparagement of sentimentalism is inseparable from the assumption that it is "both more common (even 'natural') and more forgivable in women than in men" ("In Defense" 228). To be sentimental—that is to experience intense sympathy and its attendant tender emotions—means that one is not manly. The presence of such linguistic-conceptual identity contents thus confronts sentimental education with the task of either reworking the definitions of such contents, at both the individual and the collective level, so that they no longer exclude sympathy—and perhaps even *include* it—or helping students divest themselves of such identity contents and substitute new, sympathy-entailing contents in their place.

In order that recognition can foster tender identity-bearing affects, then, we must simultaneously either revise or withdraw recognition from those identity contents that are antithetical to such affects—namely, the contents from all three registers that constitute the hypermasculine identity. As a first step in this dual process of revising contents and/or reallocating recognition, we can introduce our students to (and refamiliarize ourselves with) alternative literary and social conventions concerning the tender affects, such as that of the eighteenth-century man of sentiment who openly and proudly (if also, inevitably, sometimes histrionically) shed tears of sadness at the plight of characters on stage, or the tradition of the sentimental novel, which has enjoyed something of a resurgence over the past decade or so.

Another effective strategy is to help students deconstruct the opposition between masculinity and sympathy, by exposing the elements of sympathy that can inevitably be found in even the most masculine persons and behaviors. Such relativizing and deconstruction reduce the amount of recognition that the collective definitions provide for these particular attributes, which in turn lessens their identity-bearing and hence sympathy-resisting power, and at the same time demonstrate that sentimentalism is already implicit in the very identities that attempt to exclude it. Students can also be engaged in reworking their own individual investments in such attributes. One way to promote such reworking is to help students explore their own past experiences for instances of sympathy, which they can then be encouraged to acknowledge and embrace as part of their identities. Most effective may be giving students narratives that are powerful elicitors of sympathy and then helping them recognize, name, and embrace their sympathetic feelings while these feelings are still active. *Uncle Tom's Cabin* is an ideal text of this sort, combining the evocation of strong feelings of pity, sympathy, and compassion with exhortations to readers to cultivate these emotions.

We also need to overcome the resistance to sympathy that is posed by antithetical affective-physiological and imagistic identity contents. Individuals whose primary vitality affects are opposed to or otherwise incompatible with the physiological states associated with sympathy are resistant to experiencing sympathy because such affective states are experienced as loss of identity in the affective-physiological register. Here a sentimental education needs to provide holding environments in which students' other identity components are secure enough for them to begin to entertain some of these unfamiliar and discomfiting affective-physiological states. Such environments include various forms of recognition and opportunities for enactment of key linguistic-conceptual and imagistic-perceptual identity elements, and they might also include models—teachers, public figures, fictional characters—who demonstrate that they can maintain their identities even when in the affective-physiological states of intense sympathy. Students need to be introduced to such states in doses that are of an intensity and duration that they can handle, and then taken through increasingly intense and prolonged experiences of such affective-physiological states, supported by assurances before each experience that they will be able to survive it and by explicit affirmations after each experience that they have indeed survived it.

Such a supportive environment can also help students deal with the repression of sympathy arising from their body-imagistic identity contents. The facial expressions, posture, and body language that accompany sympathy-induced emotions such as sadness, indignation, guilt, or shame are often incongruent with students' ideal, identity-bearing facial and postural images. In particular, the depressive body positions, flaccid muscles, and sagging facial features that accompany sadness are incompatible with the erect, firm, poised bodies that our culture idealizes. And a weeping body, with its contorted face, spasmodic sobbing, and drippings from eyes, nose, and mouth, is not only antithetical to our culture's ideal body but also reintroduces the anxieties of early childhood when control of the body's motions and emissions—and hence a sense of bodily agency and integrity—was still extremely tenuous. A sentimental education thus needs to counter the threats to students' imagistic identity posed by both the deviation from the ideal body image and the loss of bodily control that are entailed by the most intense experiences of sympathy. In general, a holding environment that supports and protects the various forms of bodily softness and passivity helps to foster an identity that includes sympathy and its attendant emotions. More specific interventions can involve visual narratives in which individuals with erect, self-controlled bodies give their bodies over to the condition of sympathetic anguish and helplessness and then demonstrate that their identities, though perhaps changed by the experience, are nonetheless still intact and perhaps even enhanced. Such interventions can also involve relativizing the cultural ideal of the self-contained, self-controlled body by presenting images of bodies from cultures in which the depressive body images were a valued identity content rather than a threat to identity.

Through these sorts of strategic reallocations of recognition and opportunities to enact specific identity contents in each register, literature teachers can help students develop more benign identity contents that are both personally and socially beneficial. But while it is possible to reduce one's investments in harmful identity contents, it is not possible to entirely eliminate such contents from identity. What is needed instead is a way to contain them and limit their sway, rather than repressing them and thus making oneself vulnerable to their unconscious influence, in "the return of the repressed." Such an achievement means integration, which itself requires the development of more complex structures—the respective topics of the final two chapters.

Chapter 13
Promoting Identity Integration

Identity Integration through the Discourse of the Analyst

As we saw in chapter 4, the failure to integrate excluded parts of the self can contribute to various kinds of social problems as well as personal problems, including interferences with the learning process. An identity that simply rejects and excludes shameful elements of the self—such as impulses of aggression, dominance, or greed, or qualities such as fear, weakness, or laziness—will, as we have seen, be victimized by the return of these repressed elements in the form of externalizations, projections, projective identifications, and disguised enactments, which are at the root of many social problems and which also interfere with learning and personal well-being. To be secure and productive, one must therefore integrate rather than exclude the most powerful elements of the self, even those that are harmful when enacted in some contexts.

Literary study can promote integration through some of the same basic strategies that are used in psychoanalytic treatment. As we discussed earlier, psychoanalysis promotes integration of identity components through a strategy that Lacan called the discourse of the analyst. The crucial difference between this discourse and the other three discourses we examined is that in this discourse the analyst's identity is maintained not by recognition from the analysand, in the form of the analysand's adoption, identification with, or rejection of the analyst's identity contents, but by recognition from the real, in the form of the beneficial changes in the analysand's identity. Here it is the analysand, not the analyst, who chooses which components of self—that is, which affects, images, signifiers, knowledge, and narratives—will compose his identity. When an analysand in transference demands of the analyst, "Tell me what my problem is!" or "Tell me who I am!" the analyst attempts not (like most therapists or friends) to provide the analysand with any answers, but rather to help the analysand develop the capacity to provide a satisfactory answer for himself. Knowing that answers from her would often not suffice and might actually be alienating, the analyst seeks to help the analysand detect, identify, and assume ownership of those repressed or projected qualities, impulses, identifications, desires, enjoyments, or anxieties (denoted by the small a) that are antithetical to the analysand's current identity-bearing master signifiers (S_1) that are thus causing the self-division and alienation ($) from which the analysand is suffering (see Bracher, *Lacan* 68–73). An important role of the analyst is to help analysands monitor their own discourse—including all aspects of their speech, their fantasies, and their dreams—as well as their bodily states and behaviors, for indications of these rejected elements (a) of their own being. To this end, the analyst foregrounds in her discourse not her own identity-bearing signifiers (S_1), knowledge/beliefs (S_2), or lack/desire ($), but rather the analysand's rejected elements (a) as they manifest themselves in the analysand's discourse:

$$\text{Analyst} \quad \text{Analysand}$$
$$\frac{a}{S_2} \longrightarrow \frac{\$}{S_1}$$

In thus foregrounding the analysand's rejected elements (a) and allowing them, as it were, to speak, the analyst summons the analysand to recognize and own these elements. Such foregrounding produces an acute experience of self-division ($) in the analysand, because the rejected elements conflict with the analysand's current identity (S_1). The analyst then helps the analysand assume ownership of the rejected elements and work through the conflicts between them and the identity-bearing signifiers (S_1), with the result that the analysand often produces a new identity-bearing signifier (S_1) that incorporates the previously rejected affects and impulses (a) and thus mitigates the severity of self-division, $.

This is precisely what many women helped each other accomplish in the early years of women's liberation. The feminism of the 1960s and 1970s derived to a significant degree from the personal, first-hand recognitions by women that the master signifiers (such as "lady") to which they were subjected excluded significant elements of their being and experience, such as their aggressive impulses and their sexual desires and enjoyments. Many women therefore came to renounce these identity-bearing signifiers and instituted new ones in their place in an attempt to integrate into their identities the excluded qualities, impulses, and affects (the a). And these new master signifiers, including "woman" and "Ms," with which they replaced the old oppressive ones were signifiers that they themselves produced or selected.

We literature teachers can foster a similar identity integration by helping our students encounter their own repressed elements and develop new linguistic identity contents that incorporate these elements into their identities.

The basic strategy of such a pedagogy is to help our students recognize and examine both their identity contents and the rejected impulses and affects (*a*) that conflict with these contents and that are often manifested in the interest in or enjoyment of a particular genre, work, scene, character, or author. Here it is not the literary work itself, or the "truth" or "knowledge" embodied in that work, that is the focus of our interest and hence of discussion and writing, but rather the students' identity contents, defenses, and structures. Such a process of uncovering and examining rejected elements of the self produces a challenge to students' identity contents, but the challenge is from within, from the students' own excluded elements of self, rather than from without, from their teacher, their peers, or any other instance of external authority. The purpose of discussion and writing is to help students work through and integrate these excluded contents.

Exactly what forms such a pedagogy takes must be determined by each teacher who practices it. To prescribe the types of texts that should be taught, the kinds of writing assignments that should be given, or the sorts of classroom activities that should be engaged in would be to institute another University discourse (S_2) for teachers to submit to, whereas the key to a psychoanalytic pedagogy is, as we have seen, the teacher's operating in all such choices from a desire for her students to come to recognize and own previously rejected parts of themselves.

We can, however, identify certain general practices that will in all likelihood follow from such a desire. First, instead of trying to get our students to learn any of the information that we generally bring to literature courses—for example, names and dates of figures and events, certain received interpretations, or certain ways of reading a text—we will attempt to use the literary texts at our disposal to help them encounter and integrate excluded elements of self.

Second, concerning the texts to be studied, if we are trying to help students encounter their excluded elements of self, then we will probably find it more effective to select texts that clearly engage these elements—as manifested by our students' interest in and enjoyment of such texts (for example, their favorite popular fiction, song lyrics, movies, or television programs), rather than selecting texts that *we* find to be particularly enjoyable, meaningful, or profound. Or, to the extent that we have a fairly good understanding of the general sorts of identity issues our students are grappling with in their lives, we might select texts that deal with these issues at an emotional and intellectual developmental level most suitable for our students. In any event, the criterion for selecting works to teach will be the likelihood that a given work will engage students' core identity contents and other, excluded elements of their selves in such a way that they can recognize, own, and integrate these elements.

Third, as we have already indicated, such a pedagogy will focus not on the texts themselves, but rather on the responses of our students to and around the texts. It will be the students' individual and collective identity elements, needs, and maintenance practices that will be the focus of discussion, of writing, and of our interest in general, rather than the literary work itself. Having our students reflect on their own responses to certain texts and textual elements (plot, theme, character, style, tone, and so on) and investigate the identity needs motivating their consumptions of and responses to these elements will be more effective than traditional writing assignments in helping students to recognize and take responsibility for their needs and the behaviors they motivate. When students offer an interpretation or judgment articulating what they think the author, text, character, or teacher means or values, we will direct their attention back onto their own utterances in such a way as to help them become more aware of their own identity elements, needs, conflicts, and maintenance tactics.

More specifically, we will help our students pose the following sorts of questions regarding each of the four identity-formative/transformative elements of language denoted in Lacan's diagrams:

1. What are the structure and contours of my primary systems of knowledge and belief (S_2)? How did I come to have these beliefs or possess this knowledge? What results, for myself and for others, does my adherence to these systems have? What alternative systems are available, and what would their consequences likely be, for myself and for others? Would the alteration or replacement of any of these systems be desirable?

2. What are my primary identity-bearing signifiers, the ideals and values that I cherish and that I want desperately to believe that I embody (S_1)? What are the origins and the consequences (personal and collective) of these identity contents? Are any of the consequences negative, causing suffering for me or for others? Would replacement of any of my master signifiers be desirable?[1]

3. What is my fundamental fantasy, my secret scenario of ultimate bliss, absolute fulfillment? What sublime object or other (a) would, if I could but attain it, make my life complete? What types of stories do I enjoy most, and what can my enjoyment of these tell me about the fantasy involved? What are the consequences of this fantasy, for myself and for others? Would any changes here be desirable?[2]

4. What conflicts or self-division ($) can I detect in myself? What identity components are involved in these conflicts? Are there conflicts between different ideals or values (S_1)? Between different systems of knowledge or belief (S_2)? Different affective states (a)? What makes me most anxious, depressed, ashamed, guilty, or alienated, and what identity elements are at

issue here? What changes in my identity components might reduce the constrictive and destructive aspects of this self-division?[3]

Developing effective integrative practices from this strategy will require effort, ingenuity, perseverance, and, above all, continuous monitoring of our own pedagogical impulses and aims. As long as our discipline is still dominated by the various pedagogies described in earlier chapters, implementing new practices such as those we are discussing will have to negotiate a considerable amount of inertia and resistance on the part of both teachers and students, especially of those who have grown comfortable with and who excel under current pedagogical practices. But the integrative efficacy of the identity-integrating and supporting practices we are discussing, together with the knowledge they provide concerning the nature and consequences of one's own and others' investments in language, have unparalleled personal and social benefits, as well as practical value, and this fact constitutes a compelling reason for pursuing them.

A number of effective techniques for promoting identity integration through literary study have already been implemented. One is to engage students in reading about traumas—experiences of identity dis-integration—together with writing and sharing with the class narratives of their own traumas. This is an approach that Jeffrey Berman has used for thirty years now in many of his college literature and writing classes, and in the four books that he has written on this method, he presents case after case of students who experienced profound healing as a result of the various forms of recognition that the local culture of Berman's classes provides for the repressed feelings and isolated experiences of their original trauma as well as for their ongoing efforts to cope with those experiences. What Berman's pedagogical practices reveal, among other things, is the need of most of his students (and hence of most people, we might assume) for recognition of their private and unconscious elements of self—and in particular their prohibited emotions—as well as their public identity elements. After finishing Berman's classes, many students report that they had never before disclosed their traumas to anyone and that the most beneficial part of the class was the nonjudgmental recognition they experienced from the teacher and the other students when their private autobiographical stories of trauma were read either by Berman alone or aloud (by either Berman or by the students themselves) to the entire class.

The traumas written about by Berman's students are of the dramatic type—being raped, sexually abused, physically abused, psychologically humiliated or shamed, or traumatized by parental discord or divorce. One of the most remarkable of Berman's findings is that a sizable majority of his apparently confident and well-adjusted middle-class students have experienced acute traumas of this sort and as a consequence have identities that are in certain respects quite vulnerable. This fact alone suggests that identity dis-integration has a major presence in literature classes and that there is thus a substantial need to provide students with recognition for those parts of themselves that they have kept hidden as a result of these traumas. And when we add to this the virtually universal trauma of socialization and its excision of parts of the self, we must acknowledge that virtually all our students suffer from the nonrecognition, and hence dis-integration, of key private and unconscious elements of their selves. To the extent that literary study can provide such recognition, it can help students integrate these private and unconscious elements of self and thus reduce their need both to keep these elements at bay through harmful defenses and to seek identity support in one or another form of harmful and perhaps socially destructive behavior.

In addition to writing about one's personal traumas, integration of disowned impulses and qualities can be facilitated by helping students understand how American men (the primary perpetrators of interpersonal physical violence) in general have been coerced by socialization to exclude both their tender and their bloodthirsty elements from their identities, how women have been coerced to eliminate all but their tender elements, what the psychological and social consequences of these exclusions are, how these rejected parts can be reclaimed, and what the benefits of such reclamations are. One of the best ways to help students understand these processes of rejection and the return of the repressed is to have them study novels, sto-ries, plays, poems, films, songs, and television shows in which the processes can be discerned. Identifying, exploring, discussing, and writing about characters' unconscious elements and the dynamics of their relation to the public and private elements will familiarize students with such elements and processes, which will in turn prime them to recognize, own, and integrate their own rejected elements.

Such literary attention also constitutes a kind of categorical recognition for any rejected qualities of self and their attendant processes. And the pres-ence of such recognition can begin to render the rejection of these elements unnecessary. When students realize that it is safe within the classroom to have, say, tender feelings or bloodthirsty impulses (though it is not accept-able to act on the latter), they will no longer guard so vigilantly against hav-ing or recognizing such impulses and as a result may sooner or later begin to acknowledge and own them. Recognition provided by a text, a teacher, classmates, culture at large, or an institution for elements of one's self that one has disowned can further enable ownership of such elements because such owning brings with it the recognition accruing to these elements, which can compensate for the loss of (cultural, institutional, structural, or now internal) recognition for other qualities that owning these elements also entails. Thus providing all sorts of recognition for parts of the self that socialization forces one to disown can help repair the traumas of socialization and aid in the development of a secure identity that has less need of behavioral, institutional, structural, or cultural violence to maintain itself.

This process can be enhanced by encouraging students to use their understanding and explorations of characters as a basis for inquiring into, exploring, and writing about the rejected parts of their own socially traumatized selves—in the same manner as Berman's students use reading about dramatic traumas as a basis for exploring and writing about their dramatically traumatized private selves, and with similar beneficial results. Reader-response analysis can be used to good effect here. For example, by presenting students with texts or films in which villains are punished, made to suffer, and even savaged and then asking students to recall and describe their responses to the violent acts of vengeance, teachers can help students recognize their own desire for and enjoyment of violence and hence the murderous impulses that they, like everyone else, harbor (see Strean and Freeman). Ingmar Bergman's film *The Virgin Spring* produced the dawning of such a realization in me when I first saw it as an undergraduate. In the film, set in rural medieval Sweden, an adolescent girl is brutally robbed, raped, and murdered by a band of brothers who that night are given shelter from a storm by the girl's family. As the brothers lie sleeping, the girl's father spots his daughter's cross among their possessions and surmises why she has not returned home. After methodically purifying himself, he proceeds to kill the brothers one at a time. Having killed the adult brothers, he turns toward the youngest, a boy of about six who had nothing to do with the girl's rape and murder and who is cowering in terror. Still enraged by what the older brothers have done, the father kills the boy as well. No sooner has he done so than he stares in horror at his hands, in anguished realization that he himself embodies, and has enacted, the same brutality that has killed his innocent daughter. At this point I realized that insofar as I had been exulting in the father's bloodthirsty vengeance, which had extended to the innocent boy, I possessed the same bloodthirsty impulses as not only the father but also the brutal killers themselves.

Dramatic reading or viewing experiences of this sort, in which students become aware of parts of themselves of which they had been ignorant, can help them begin to own and integrate unconscious and dissociated parts of themselves that drive them in various ways to engage in various sorts of counterproductive and harmful ways of being. Such reading experiences will not by themselves produce a more integrated identity, but they can serve as a basis for further exploration of the self via writing (stimulated by further reading) in search of other subjective manifestations of such rejected parts of the self, as well as of the causes of the rejection and the behavioral consequences of the unintegrated presence of these parts.

Objections to Such Integrative Practices

Some may worry that such practices may have the ethically questionable consequences of 1) coercing or seducing students into highly personal revelations, 2) turning education into therapy, and 3) perverting the true function of literary study. The first possible consequence, coercing students into self-revelations that they do not want to make, is certainly to be avoided, and it *can* be avoided, as Jeffery Berman has demonstrated (*Diaries* 2), by making certain that students have at all times the opportunity of discontinuing (or not embarking on) a particular line of self-investigation without being penalized.

Concerning the second possible consequence, such a practice would indeed involve a kind of therapy, if "therapy" is understood in a broad sense as a practice that benefits people and contributes to their well-being. But how could anyone legitimately object to such a use of literature? Certainly not with the assertion that helping people is unethical!

Nor with the third objection's claim that such therapy is a perversion of the "true" or "natural" function of literature. To refute this claim, one has only to recall Aristotle's *Poetics* to recognize that therapy in this broad sense has as much claim as anything else to being the "true" or "natural" function of literature. Recent developments in cognitive science, moreover, support the idea that promoting identity integration is itself a "true" and "natural" function of literature. Literary study "naturally" promotes integration between registers by providing linguistic formulation of previously unarticulated affective and imagistic experiences. As Wilma Bucci observes, the symbolizing of affective-physiological experience that is at the heart of psychoanalytic treatment, and that most of us find very difficult, is what poetry excels in. Poets, she says, construct metaphors in order to capture emotion in a manner similar to the ways that wine writers utilize images from diverse areas of experience to describe the precise taste and smell of a particular wine (216). "In the expression of emotion," she explains, "metaphors may be understood precisely as concrete and discrete symbols for unnamed, subsymbolic feeling states" (216). Such metaphors can take the form of not only individual images but also entire narratives: "Narratives about other people, in relation to one's self, may be seen precisely as metaphors of the emotion schemas" (218).

Literary narratives and poetic images, moreover, are precisely those metaphors that are most effective in evoking in readers a subsymbolic, affective-physiological response and integrating these affects into linguistic-conceptual meaning and identity:

> When the metaphor is transmitted to a listener or reader, it may serve to evoke the emotional experience with some of its subsymbolic components, permitting one to reconstitute elements of the experience that could be only partially represented in words. Poets use images whose emotional meanings are likely to be widely shared. The poets who speak to us most directly are those whose symbols activate our own subsymbolic, representational worlds. (Bucci 215)

Simply reading literature, then, can, like psychoanalytic treatment, produce an activation of subsymbolic, affective-physiological codes, and—also like psychoanalytic treatment—it can establish new linkages of these codes to words and images. These processes of translation between registers can be extended and intensified by discussion and writing about the texts that elaborate on one's affective and imagistic memories, fantasies, and associations to the images and events in the text.

Since literature is thus "naturally therapeutic," it is hard to object to using it as therapy in this broad sense. And if, on the other hand, one conceives of therapy in the narrower, more technical sense, as a mode of treatment distinct from psychoanalysis, then the integrative pedagogy being described here would, rather than *turning* literary study *into* therapy, actually *reclaim* literary study *from* therapy. For most current forms of literary pedagogy, insofar as they provide any significant benefits to students, are nonpsychoanalytic forms of therapy: as we saw in earlier chapters, most pedagogies operate with transference in such a way as to inculcate specific beliefs, values, and ideals, which is precisely how many nonpsychoanalytic modes of therapy operate. Much therapy, that is, uses transference to encourage patients to vent (the discourse of the Hysteric), to provide them with moral support and encouragement (the discourse of the University), or to get them to accept the therapist's advice, diagnosis, or prescription (the discourse of the Master). Psychoanalysis, in contrast, operates with transference in such a way as to help analysands encounter and integrate excluded elements of self.

Even so, some will insist, literature teachers are trained in language and literature, and our job is to teach our students about language and literature. Perhaps it is. But what kind of knowledge about language and literature should we be teaching our students? What kind of knowledge is most valuable to them? I maintain that the most beneficial knowledge is an understanding of how the various elements of language function to construct, deconstruct, and restructure both our individual and our collective identities. Such a knowledge is more valuable than the knowledge usually cultivated in literature courses because it increases the ability of students "to intervene in the construction of their own subjectivities," as Giroux and Simon put it (189; see also McLaren 214).

Such a knowledge of language is precisely what the psychoanalytically informed process of integration can help students to attain. The four aspects of language highlighted by Lacan in his discourse formulas—S_1, S_2, a, and $\$$—refer to four aspects of language that play crucial roles in both the construction and the transformation both of individual subjects and of groups and societies. Each of the four formative/transformative elements of language identified by Lacan is currently a concern (under a different rubric) of one or more branches of literary study. Moreover, our literature courses often aim, implicitly or explicitly, to produce changes in one or more of these elements—that is, changes in knowledge (S_2), values or ideals (S_1), or desire or enjoyment (a). And even when such changes are not our aim, they are often the result of our current pedagogical practices. As Marshall Alcorn notes, "As a result of textual identifications, people come to fantasize about themselves differently, to define themselves differently, to act differently" (Alcorn, *Narcissism* 21). For example, at one time or another, many of our students, especially our majors, probably alter their identifications and embrace new master signifiers (S_1) when they read literature, much in the way that the Greeks, according to Shelley, identified with the qualities of Homer's heroes. A similar effect operates with regard to the S_2: our teaching frequently alters the systems of knowledge or belief, as well as the life narratives, that our students inhabit. In fact, alteration of knowledge is the basic aim (and effect) of education in general. Our teaching produces such alteration in various ways, including the production of formalist and historicist systems of knowledge in literary study, and the construction of tragic, comic, or ironic views of life through reading certain types of literature, as well as the more general initiation into academic discourse that our students undergo. A similar change occurs regarding the form of our students' relation to the rejected parts of their being, which represent the lost enjoyment that they are searching for. The particular form taken by the object a manifests itself in our fantasies (see Zizek, *Sublime*), and the nature and intensity of fantasies can change, we know, through literary study. And finally, reading and studying literature can alter the mode in which students live their self-division, $\$$, whether by bringing words to previously foreclosed elements, or by bringing repressed contents into awareness, or by giving license to speak what had hitherto remained anxiously or shamefully silenced (see Berman, *Diaries*).

The changes that current modes of pedagogy promote in each of these orders, however, are frequently unobserved by students and often by their teachers as well, because these changes have not been identified as the aim of our teaching and the object of our knowledge. And even more important, these changes, as we have seen, are currently being produced in a way that is ethically problematic. If, however, we make the formative/transformative forces of language, as they are currently operating on our students, in class and outside of class, objects of our students' inquiry, we produce much broader and deeper benefits for our students in a way that is ethically more defensible, because, unlike current literary pedagogies, we are not inculcating a specific S_1 or S_2.[4]

Diachronic Integration and Prosocial Emotions

Literary study also "naturally" promotes diachronic integration of identity, which is often crucial for experiencing compassion and guilt. Reading novels and plays that take them by the hand and lead them step by step along the multiple chains of cause and effect that link a character's present personality and actions to past experiences can help students internalize integrative structures that constitute both the capacity and the inclination to view and experience the present in terms of both the past and the future. Indeed, since, as Wolfgang Iser pointed out, the very act of reading both requires and exercises these capacities of retention and protension, any reading of narrative may be deemed to foster such an inclination "naturally." And in developing students' capacities for greater temporal integration in the form of retention and protension, literary study also further supports their experience and integration of compassion and guilt. Compassion and guilt, like all emotions, are the result of emotion-specific cognitive appraisals of the causes of particular actions, events, or states of affairs (see Lazarus). In order to experience compassion, for example, we must reach the judgments that a) another person is suffering, b) the person cannot easily or quickly end the suffering, and c) the person is not responsible for the conditions that are producing the suffering. Research and everyday observation show that many people resist concluding that sufferers are not responsible for the conditions that produce their suffering—an instance of the "fundamental attribution error" that is widely recognized in the phenomenon of blaming the victim. One hypothesis that has been advanced to explain this phenomenon is the "just world hypothesis," which maintains that people have a need to believe that the world is basically fair, and that individuals ultimately get their just deserts. Such a belief constitutes an important component of the linguistic-conceptual identity not only of Job's comforters but also of many people living today, and hence, like Job's comforters, many people resist concluding that sufferers are not ultimately themselves responsible for their suffering. In American culture, the ideology of the American Dream has reinforced this resistance with its identity values of independence, autonomy, and unlimited freedom and opportunity, all summed up in the Great Lie, still repeated to our children, that in America you can be whatever you want to be. This ideology further predisposes us to see people's predicaments as their own fault, and such an appraisal makes sympathy impossible.

Reading narratives, by developing the capacity for greater diachronic integration, undermines the tendency toward such exclusion of the past and thus reduces the likelihood of the sort of faulty, truncated view of causation and responsibility that produces the fundamental attribution error and precludes compassion and guilt. Narratives dealing with poverty, unemployment, and homelessness are particularly rich resources for such development, insofar as they detail how the current state of a particular individual or group is the result of temporally and logistically distant forces beyond the control of the agent in question. In some cases, close attention to people's material conditions and the historical circumstances that brought them about is sufficient to provide compelling evidence that the people heretofore blamed for their own suffering are not responsible for it. Such is the case of *The Grapes of Wrath*'s account of the massive and precipitous ruin of farmers as a result of drought and the collapse of their markets, of depositors by the failures of banks, and of workers by the absence of jobs—an account that compels readers to recognize the blamelessness of these victims.

A similar integration can be pursued through the painstaking deconstruction and reconstruction, either by literary texts or by critical analysis of them, of appraisals of responsibility regarding victims in all sorts of circumstances. Such an operation involves starting from a condition, such as poverty, for which the victims themselves are widely presumed to be responsible, and then tracing the causes of this condition step by step back to the point at which the victims' responsibility dissolves. At that point, one's appraisal of responsibility is reversed, dissolving hatred and contempt and replacing these emotions with sympathy and compassion.

If such temporal integration is thorough and extensive, it eventually implicates all well-to-do individuals in the suffering of the less fortunate, through the dawning realization that if those who suffer in the world are not solely responsible for their own suffering, then the responsibility must lie with others—and ultimately, if not immediately, with those who are responsible for creating or maintaining a society or a world in which such suffering is allowed to persist. Full integration of temporal and logical elements thus ultimately implicates us and many of our students, the middle- and upper-class members of the richest and most powerful nation ever to exist. And here a new set of massive resistances is encountered, resistances to accepting responsibility not only for the economic and political conditions that produce the suffering of so many people but also for failing to alleviate or even to reduce most of the suffering in the world. The reason for the resistance to such assumption of responsibility is that it produces powerful feelings of guilt, which is itself quite threatening to the identities of most Americans. And this refusal of guilt is one of the greatest obstacles we face on the path to social justice. As Walter Davis has argued, it is our national repression of guilt for atrocities we have perpetrated—such as the holocausts of Hiroshima and Nagasaki—that is motivating many of our current international policies, which are heavy on blaming and punishing victims of our own previous policies and light on providing humanitarian aid to these victims. What we desperately need, Davis argues, is acceptance of responsibility for terrible realities to which one's actions have contributed, even if one may have never intended these consequences or may have even sought to avoid them.

To be able to experience such guilt, we must be able to endure the identity threats it entails in each register. The challenge for education is to, on the one hand, provide enough identity support so that the threats can be borne, while on the other hand helping students recognize and integrate the alien, guilt-entailed affects, body images, signifiers, knowledge, and narratives that are already part of their self but that have not been owned and metabolized as part of their identity. The basic strategy here is the same as that of psychoanalytic treatment: activate the disowned elements and then provide a holding environment sufficiently supportive and protective of identity to allow it to accommodate these elements.

To the extent that education helps students integrate guilt as part of their identities in each register, it makes a contribution to social justice, for it removes a major motive for denying their own responsibility and blaming the victims. It reduces the psychological need for arguments such as, "I don't own slaves, and none of my ancestors ever did, so why should I sacrifice financially or professionally for the benefit of black people?" And it may also help reduce our collective psychological need for current U.S. foreign policies that, no longer able to deny the overwhelming historical and contemporary evidence of American responsibility for many of the current horrors in the world (see Honderich), seek to avoid guilt by interpreting American responsibility as one of policing and punishing its victims rather than making reparations to them. In this case, while the assumption of guilt may threaten our identities, our failure to assume our guilt threatens our very existence, and that of everyone else on the planet. By providing supportive recognition for students' unconscious guilt in this regard, and thus helping them to own it, literary study can contribute to the alleviation of this problem.

CHAPTER 14
DEVELOPING IDENTITY STRUCTURES

The integration of temporally dispersed elements also contributes to the development of the more complex identity structures described by Kegan, structures that the reading and study of fiction seems particularly well suited to promote. Culture, as Kegan has pointed out, performs three key functions necessary for the development of more complex and inclusive identity structures: offering adequate support for identity as it is currently structured, confronting individuals with experiences of the inadequacy of this structure, and providing bridging experiences whereby the currently structured identity can incrementally enact and transform itself into a more complex and inclusive structure. Teachers who are aware of these cultural functions can do a number of things to help students develop more complex structures, each of which provides one or more forms of recognition for the students' current identity structure and/or their struggle to transform that structure into a larger, more adequate one.

Literature teachers, for example, can choose literature texts that provide optimal degrees of support, challenge, and bridging for the particular students we are teaching. Such support, challenge, and bridging are found in the plots, characters, and themes of texts, each of which can be seen to enact a particular identity structure, thereby supporting students operating substantially within this structure as well as challenging students operating with less complex structures and/or providing a bridging experience for such students to a more complex structure. In addition, we can direct our students' attention to both the fulfillments offered by the structure at issue and the frustrations and harmful consequences it produces, as represented by the events of the text. And we can help our students see how a more complexly structured identity can avoid the negative consequences produced by the simpler structure, and how it offers new gratifications of its own. Ideally, we will find texts that themselves engage students, through identification or empathy with characters or through another means, in experiencing, desiring, and/or enacting the identity structure and moment of development that is at issue. To this end, we can also provide our students with opportunities and encouragement to identify and experience the operation of both the simpler and the more complex structure in their own individual and collective identities, including history, current events, and popular culture, and particularly to explore their own investment, and the consequences thereof, in those structures that most characterize their own current identities. To flesh out these tactics, consider briefly some forms they might take with each of the identity structures.

Impulsive Structure

For students with a strong impulsive dimension, who are still struggling to attain or sustain a sense of themselves as ongoing (imperial) forces in the world, texts with impulsive characters, episodic plots, and themes of pleasure (e.g., oral, anal, or phallic gratification) will clearly be the most engaging and hence the most effective in facilitating their consolidation of an imperial identity structure. Kindergartners are obvious examples, but older children, adolescents, and even some "adults" still operate, in some domains of their lives, out of an impulsive identity structure. Whatever their age, such students will identify most easily with the impulsive characters, episodic plots, and pleasure themes of genres such as fairy tales, fables, cartoons, action movies, and pornography. Popular music is also rife with celebrations of impulsivity, from the unfettered libido of many rock songs to the raw aggression of gangsta rap. To support our students' impulsive identities, we can empathize with these characters and with our students' empathy and identification with them, enjoying and affirming the characters' pleasure and our students' pleasure in the characters' pleasure and sympathizing with the characters' and students' displeasure. A basic classroom activity at this point is simply expression of pleasure and pain, gratification and frustration, an activity that enacts impulsive identity contents in a setting that offers them recognition.

As our students are enacting their impulsive identities, we can help them recognize the inadequacies of the impulsive structure. In many cases this can be done simply by directing a class's attention and discussion to the text's own representations of this inadequacy. Many fables, for example, demonstrate quite clearly and even brutally the grief that the impulsive structure produces. In the tale of the tortoise and the hare, the hare's impulsive approach to the race—running fast when he feels like it and stopping when he feels like it—produces the physical pleasures of movement and rest and the narcissistic pleasures of showing how much faster he is than the tortoise, but it also ultimately produces the narcissistic wound of losing the race to a much slower opponent. And in the fable of the grasshopper and the ant, the grasshopper's impulsive identity and its resulting *carpe diem* attitude leads ultimately to starvation and death, while the ant's imperial identity and future-oriented action produce survival and comfort during the winter. Emphasizing the causal relation between two moments in time or two states of being—and especially directing students' attention to this outcome while they themselves are enacting the impulsive structure—operates like insight in psychoanalysis and works to extend the impulsive individual beyond the isolated moment of present pleasure that has (momentarily, at least) constituted his or her sense of self. Such insight can also be promoted by engaging students in critiquing narratives, characters, and the actions of real people who indulge in or celebrate impulsivity without recognizing its destructive consequences, and especially by enlisting students in examining their own individual and collective impulsive behaviors, such as lashing out impulsively against evil others (e.g., violent criminals, terrorists, Saddam Hussein) or indulging in pleasure without foresight (e.g., consuming junk food, binge drinking, drug use, or having unprotected sex). When they are able to catch themselves thinking, feeling, or acting from—that is, *being*— the impulsive identity structure, and then connect this impulsivity with the undermining or demise of their identity, they will have taken a significant step beyond impulsivity and into the imperial identity structure.

The experience that foregoing pleasure in the present moment can actually produce a greater sum of pleasure overall constitutes a bridge, whereby individuals enact features of a more complex structure of identity because they experience such actions as means of supporting their currently structured identity. In this case, they see deferral of gratification as a means to increase the gratification of their impulses. As Freud put it, the reality principle comes into play as a means of sustaining the pleasure principle. We can reinforce this bridging by emphasizing that the surest way of procuring pleasure is to be circumspect and operate with foresight, and we can engage students in searching their experiences and observations for other instances of this principle, as well as in scrutinizing how they themselves are already similar to the imperial ant and tortoise as opposed to the impulsive grasshopper and hare.

Imperial Structure

To support and help our students consolidate their imperial identity structure, we can assign literary texts in which the plots integrate behaviors and occurrences into extended actions and overarching events, the protagonists are defined in terms of their sustained actions or intentions, and the themes involve perseverance, endurance, commitment, duty, steadfastness, cause-effect relations, progress, and so on. Horatio Alger novels are perhaps the purest instances of such texts, showing that with hard work, perseverance, and self-sacrifice, poor boys can become men of wealth, status, and power. Tales of military heroism, sports fame, and entertainment celebrity, along with detective novels, *Bildungsromanen*, biographies, and countless examples in children's and young adult literature, provide similar support of imperial identities. Many popular songs also celebrate this form of identity, including Frank Sinatra's anthem, "My Way." We can provide support for our students' imperial identities by encouraging their consumption of such texts and providing opportunities for them to describe their heroes and explain what they admire and identify with in them. Further support can be provided by engaging our students in noticing, discussing, celebrating, and writing about perseverance and identity continuity in their favorite songs, television and movie characters, and celebrities, as well as in their own behavior. We can reinforce such support by ourselves expressing admiration for the hardworking, persevering protagonists of the texts as well as emphasizing, affirming, and explaining the benefits of perseverance both in the texts and in real life.

We can also support the imperial identity structure by engaging our students in modes of literary analysis, interpretation, and criticism that enact imperialist processes of perception and judgment. Whereas the mode of criticism corresponding to the impulsive structure is expressivist and impressionistic commentary on various random features of a text, the appropriate mode for an imperial identity is an extended linear analysis, such as the tracing of a theme (perseverance, for example) through multiple events and/or characters of a text.

To challenge imperial identities to transform into the more inclusive interpersonal structure, we can assign texts that demonstrate one or more of the many inadequacies of the imperial structure, such as texts representing the loneliness of imperial characters, the impossibility of absolute independence or self-reliance, the failure of mere perseverance to sustain identity, the fact that each individual life inevitably affects and is affected by the lives of others, and the fact that imperial characters and people often do significant harm to others. We can also help our students to recognize the suffering and even the demise of imperial identities that can result from their failure to take account of other people and their needs, deficiencies, and intentions. Novels such as Hemingway's *The Sun Also Rises*, Fitzgerald's *The Great Gatsby*, and Camus's *The Stranger* provide rich resources for such realization in the form of their alienated protagonists. We can encourage our students not only to recognize imperial characters' vulnerability and frustration but also to feel it and share it, and we can have them identify and provide accounts of such instances in their own experience and observation. Popular music—such as the Eagles' song "Desperado"—can be effective in not only articulating the principle but also in evoking the corresponding feelings of the inadequacy of the imperial identity. We can also engage our students in literary critical activities that stymie imperialist identities, such as reading the differing interpretations produced by critics or listening to their classmates' differing readings of a text. Such encounters will confront students with perspectives, textual evidence, and arguments that cannot be assimilated by their own monolithic, imperialist interpretations of the text and its characters and thus demonstrate the inadequacy both of such an approach and of the one-dimensional, celebratory response to imperialist characters.

Such realization, together with feelings of loneliness and other types of sadness produced by the imperial mode of operation, can be useful in helping students bridge to the interpersonal structure when experienced in conjunction with texts that demonstrate that relationships can be an integral and even essential component of the imperial identity. Wordsworth's Lucy poems, for example, can help students experience how imperial identities often depend on interpersonal relationships without realizing it until it is too late. Texts that show the necessity of others for achieving one's goals, portray the need for relationships, thematize cooperation and collaboration as essential for completing a task or realizing the goal of a quest, or portray characters who achieve gratification from sharing goals and labors with others can also contribute to this end. Tennyson's "Ulysses" provides a good example, in its title character's dependence upon his comrades to provide both the physical and the psychological support necessary for his imperial adventures.

In addition to promoting identification with the interpersonal needs of such characters, we can engage our students in enacting various classroom roles for which relationships with others are an integral part. Such roles include being an interlocutor with us and with other students, being a partner in a research project, and being a reporter to the class (e.g., concerning how relationships can enable one to achieve one's goals). We can then engage our students in reflecting on and describing the gratifications of such roles as well as other relationships in their lives. Through such enactment and reflection, our students can come to experience and recognize more clearly the gratifications of relationships, which will then become less ancillary and more integral to their sense of self, or identity.

Interpersonal Structure

Literary support for interpersonal identities can be found in numerous genres, including fairy tales (*Sleeping Beauty, Snow White*), Shakespeare's romantic comedies, romantic movies, Harlequin romance novels, love poetry, love songs (e.g., the Beatles' "All You Need is Love"), and buddy movies. In particular, texts that evoke the feelings of fulfillment produced by interpersonal relationships, the yearning for romance or friendship, or the mourning of their loss can help students not only to grasp their importance intellectually but also to experience it affectively and, in doing so, to essentially enact the interpersonal identity structure. In addition, we can direct our students' attention to the relationships they and others form with literary characters (including television and movie characters and celebrities) and help them reflect on the role played by these relationships in defining, enacting, and maintaining their identities. Having our students read, discuss, analyze, and write about the fulfillment brought by these various relationships of love, friendship, and even rivalry and opposition offers enhanced internal and external recognition for their own interpersonally structured identity-components and thus helps to consolidate this dimension of their identities.

Experiences of the limitations of the interpersonal form of identity can be provided by literary texts demonstrating that, unfortunately, love is not all you need and that love and friendship—and sometimes even life itself—are themselves in jeopardy if one defines oneself exclusively through such a relationship. Particularly effective in this regard are texts that depict characters experiencing debilitating jealousy (Browning's "Porphyria's Lover" and "My Last Duchess"); conflicting loyalties—between family and friends, between friends and lovers, between two or more lovers, between one's spouse or parents and one's children, or between two different children (*Sophie's Choice*); or deprivation and even death as the result of devotion to a relationship (*Romeo and Juliet, Elvira Madigan*). Also effective are texts portraying the destruction of relationships of all sorts by military, economic, and political forces, such as Oliver Goldsmith's "The Deserted Village," Wordsworth's "The Ruined Cottage," Upton Sinclair's *The Jungle*, and Toni Morrison's *Beloved*. In addition to having our students read such texts and focus their discussion on these points, we can engage them in imagining, discussing, and writing about problems that might arise for other characters and persons—including themselves—who operate with interpersonal identities but who have not (yet) come to grief as a result.

Bridging to an institutional/systemic identity structure is facilitated by literary texts that represent characters in fulfilling relationships—with parents, lovers, children, friends, coworkers, and so on—that are supported and nurtured by institutions or systems of various kinds, or characters who are striving to institutionalize their relationships in order to protect them and allow them to flourish. Texts, such as Shakespeare's comedies, that portray marriage as the consummation of a personal relationship and/or represent the struggle of a (straight or gay) couple to become married provide this sort of bridge. Sympathetic characters who strive to attain a social position in order to establish or solidify a relationship engage readers in identifying with the enactment of an interpersonal identity by means of assuming identity within a system, the first step of identifying with the system or institution prior to assuming an institutional/systemic identity structure. This transition can be further facilitated by asking our students to search for textual (and extratextual) evidence of the supportive function of society and its institutions with regard to relationships and having them analyze, discuss, and write about the various ways social/institutional support is essential for maintaining any identity-bearing relationship.

Institutional/Systemic Structure

Helping students attain and maintain a substantial institutional/systemic identity structure is a major challenge for college teachers. For literature teachers, the key resources in this effort are texts that emphasize, and protagonists that enact, the principle of working for the good of the group or society as a whole. Most effective are texts that engage readers in experiencing the fulfillment of uniting with others in working to improve the lot of everyone. An excellent example is Upton Sinclair's *The Jungle*, in which the immigrant laborer Jurgis Rudkus finally achieves a modicum of peace and fulfillment after joining the socialist movement. Themes of patriotism and nationalism and narratives of nation building or institution building also enlist identity investment in systems and institutions, and readers can also be prompted to identify with a system by a text's exposition of a particular system of knowledge or belief, such as the account of socialism Sinclair provides in *The Jungle*. Such expositions engage readers in, and habituate them to, the perceptual, analytic, and judgmental processes through which systemic identities enact themselves.

The consolidation of systemic awareness, perception, and judgment can also be promoted by getting students to employ critical methodologies such as New Criticism, structuralism, and deconstruction, which require grasping each element of a text in terms of its function within the whole. Such activities must be practiced interminably, because as we have seen in earlier chapters, various dissociative defenses as well as enactments of certain identity components continually short-circuit the systemic perspective that underwrites the systemic identity structure by cutting off awareness of distal causes and effects.

There are, however, some domains in which a form of systemic identity is fairly stable and widespread. Ironically, these are the domains of national, ethnic, racial, gender, sexual, and class identities, which often do great harm to individuals not included within their boundaries. It is thus crucial that while we pursue the interminable task of engaging our students (and ourselves) in enacting systemic identities, we simultaneously provide them (and ourselves) with demonstrations of the ultimate inadequacy of systemic identities. The simplest way to experience this inadequacy is by encountering a conflict between two systems. Thus texts portraying conflicts between characters with different systems of values or beliefs can be used to demonstrate the need for something besides a system as a basis for identity, for if a system is the ultimate arbiter, on what grounds is one to choose which system to identify with? When two groups are at war because each believes its religion is true and good and the other group's religion is false and evil, how can the bloodshed be stopped before one group is exterminated? Such challenges can be brought by texts representing the conflicts, sometimes leading to bloodshed, between opposing systems, such as different religious beliefs or political ideologies, thus demonstrating the need for an identity foundation or standpoint that subtends or transcends such systems. Satires such as *Gulliver's Travels* and *Candide* are effective texts for making this point, with their demonstration of the triviality of the differences of belief that set groups against each other. Students can be encouraged to extend these texts' demonstrations of the inadequacy of system-based identities to the operation of system-based identities in the world today, including in our own country, where such system-based identities often drive both foreign and domestic policies to disaster. And from here, students can be prompted to examine the operations of their own identity-bearing systems: how these systems—including beliefs about the causes and potential cures of the various forms of violence—lead them to do violence, in one form or another, to other people.

The dilemma of a systemic identity becomes even more acute when the conflict is between two identity-bearing systems of the same person. When one subscribes to both Science, with its valorization of evidence and reason, and Religion, with its insistence on supernaturalism and the sacrifice of reason, on what grounds does one invest one's identity in one and not the other? Thus we can also help our students realize the need for an identity anchor beyond any system by presenting them with texts portraying such intracharacter conflicts between identity-bearing systems, and by enabling them to explore the same or similar conflicts in themselves.

Deconstruction, or internal critique, is another very effective way to undermine investment in identity-bearing systems. Novels such as *Uncle Tom's Cabin, Native Son,* and *Invisible Man* implicitly deconstruct white racist ideology by presenting black protagonists who embody more of the supposedly white virtues than the white people themselves do. By showing Tom to be more of a humble, loving Christian and less of a savage than many Christian white people, and George Harris to be more like America's founding patriots than are the slaveholders and slave catchers, *Uncle Tom's Cabin* effectively distances readers from the system of white supremacy. *Native Son* and *Invisible Man* do much the same by showing their respective protagonists, Bigger Thomas and Jack the Bear (the narrator), to be ultimately more insightful and humane than the white people who use, abuse, and (in Bigger's case) kill them. By training our students in the basic techniques of internal critique—seeking various forms of contradiction within systems of belief and between such systems and the actions (including institutions and policies) they entail—we can enable them to experience the incapacity of their systems—including "the American Dream," "Christianity," and the American economic, legal, penal, and education systems—to function as the ultimate and absolute basis for their sense of self. And this realization, in turn, will make the violence-entailing "we're good, they're evil" position more difficult to maintain.

One of the most effective means of helping students experience the inadequacy of systems as the basis for identity are texts that demonstrate the terrible suffering and injustice perpetrated by individuals and groups rabidly enacting their system-based identities, including racism, nationalism, homophobia, sexism, and classism. Texts that get readers to empathize and identify with victims of such oppressive systems are particularly effective in helping readers divest themselves of such identities. *Uncle Tom's Cabin* is here again exemplary, engaging and admonishing readers to feel what the slaves feel when they are separated forever from their children, parents, or siblings, when they are beaten mercilessly or brutally killed for taking food because they are starving, and when they are continuously denied any semblance of freedom or dignity. *Native Son* and *Invisible Man* elicit a similar empathy for the victims of Jim Crow racism, by presenting in Bigger Thomas and Jack the Bear not only the physical trauma but also the psychological trauma and consequent psychopathology it causes.

Interindividual/ Trans-Systemic Structure

In addition to demonstrating the moral untenability of identities based on oppressive systems, such texts also serve as bridges to the interindividual identity structure. They do so in their activation of empathy, which is the basis of interindividual identity and the ultimate arbiter for judging the fitness of particular systems to be (partial) bearers of identity. For as Zygmunt Bauman has observed, it is the individual's ethical impulse—that is, empathy—that is ultimately the only safeguard against oppressive systems. We can reinforce this bridging by engaging our students in perspective-taking and role-taking concerning characters and actual people, training them in perceiving others empathically by asking them to focus on, vividly imagine, discuss, and write about what it would be like to be in another's situation with the other's vulnerabilities and limited capacities and thus to suffer as the other is suffering. In thus enacting empathy, our students enact the core process of the interindividual identity structure.

The interindividual identity is essentially an integration of each of the previous structures into a sense of self or mode of being that simultaneously enacts all the simpler structures. This simultaneous, integrated enactment is possible because all the structures have the same core content, empathy, which, as we saw in our discussion of generativity in chapter eleven, is the most primal of human impulses. Interindividual identities experience empathy as their primary impulse, as their central project, as the basic form of all interpersonal relationships, and as the core principle and guiding force of all their systems of knowledge and belief. Development and consolidation of the interindividual identity structure is thus most effectively promoted by helping students experience the empathic impulse and the gratifications of its enactment; recognize its nature and its importance for both individual fulfillment and social justice; and understand, by observing models and coming themselves to enact, the behaviors, challenges, and gratifications entailed by empathy enacted as the life project of an imperial identity, as the fundamental role or mode of relatedness of an interpersonal identity, and as the litmus test for the legitimacy of any social or ideological institution or system they might embrace.

Cultivation of the empathic, ethical impulse constructs a bridge to the interindividual structure not from the systemic but rather from the impulsive identity. Bridging can also occur from an imperial identity composed of empathy and love. When *Uncle Tom's Cabin*, for example, urges its readers to be true Christians—that is, loving and compassionate—it is attempting to enlist their imperial identity structure (the project of being a Christian) in the construction and enactment of an interindividual identity. Some texts also use Christianity to construct bridges from interpersonal or systemic structures to the interindividual structure. *Uncle Tom's Cabin* and *The Grapes of Wrath*, for instance, admonish certain characters (and the reader) to transfer their interpersonal love for one (Christ-like) character (Little Eva and Uncle Tom in the former, Jim Casy and Tom Joad in the latter) into an interindividual devotion to all humans. *Uncle Tom's Cabin* quotes a key text from the Bible in which Jesus, by asserting an equivalence between people's interindividual relation to others and their interpersonal relation to him, summons his followers to execute such a transference:

> Then shall the king say unto them on his left hand, Depart from me, ye cursed, into everlasting fire: for I was an hungered, and ye gave me no meat: I was thirsty, and ye gave me no drink: I was a stranger, and ye took me not

in: naked, and ye clothed me not: I was sick, and in prison, and ye visited me not. Then shall they answer unto Him, Lord when saw we thee an hungered, or athirst, or a stranger, or naked, or sick, or in prison, and did not minister unto thee? Then shall he say unto them, In as much as ye did it not to one of the least of these my brethren, ye did it not to me. (Matthew 25. 31–45; qtd. in Stowe 270)

Another bridge to the interindividual identity structure is provided by metasystems of various sorts that transcend all identity-bearing systems and incorporate them into structures including all humanity or life in general. To provide this bridge for our students, we need to help them extend their systemic perception and understanding indefinitely to the point where they recognize, and metabolize their recognition of, the interconnection of all humans (and everything else as well) in an all-encompassing ecological system, a vast network, web, or fabric of cause and effect relationships in which, as Alfred North Whitehead put it, everything is in a sense everywhere at all times, since everything ultimately participates in everything else as either a (direct or indirect) cause or effect. Most systems, and the identities composed of them, truncate chains of cause and effect after just a few links. Current American nationalism, for example, identifies the Islamic terrorists' hatred of America as the cause of the 9/11 attacks, but refuses to inquire into the causes of that hatred, especially those involving American ignorance of, disdain and contempt for, and exploitation of Arabic and Islamic peoples. And the American Dream ideology explains professional, social, or economic success and failure as the result of an individual's (sufficient or insufficient) effort and that effort as the result of the individual's (sound or flawed) character, but refuses to acknowledge the factors other than character that determine effort, or the forces that have caused the individual's character to be what it is. A fully developed interindividual identity structure includes a trans-systemic perspective whereby one can recognize, and respond appropriately to, the causal role played by one's own identity-bearing impulses, actions, relations, and systems in those of other individuals, and vice versa.

Literary texts can be invaluable in providing such a totalizing, trans-systemic perspective. Some texts produce in readers trans-systemic, totalizing visions that can provide a kind of epiphanic adumbration of an interindividual identity. Many British Romantic poems do this in one way or another. Poems such as Keats's "To Autumn," Shelley's "Ode to the West Wind," Coleridge's "Frost at Midnight," Wordsworth's "Tintern Abbey," and Blake's *Milton* engage readers in affectively, imagistically, and conceptually experiencing their identities as extending temporally and spatially beyond their individual existence and participating in the existences of other humans, animals, and inanimate objects—and this not only in the present but also into the proximal and distal past and future.

Realistic and naturalistic novels offer excellent tutorials in extending the causal chain far beyond the boundaries of most current systemic identities. *The Jungle* and *The Grapes of Wrath*, for example, follow characters (and thus lead readers) through a gradual uncovering of further and further links in the chain of causality responsible for the suffering and injustice that victimizes them. In *The Jungle*, Jurgis initially disdains men who cannot find work and workers who complain about their jobs, assuming along with the American Dream that such individuals have only themselves to blame for their failure and unhappiness. Before long, however, as Jurgis and the reader witness even the most robust and enthusiastic of workers being worn down and destroyed by their labor through no fault of their own, it becomes evident that the causes of their demise lie outside themselves. The immediate causes are found in ruthless bosses, rapacious supervisors, cold calculating businessmen, and corrupt police and city officials. But rather than simply denouncing such individuals as evil, the novel brings Jurgis and the reader to realize that eliminating these evil individuals would not solve the problem, for other individuals would simply take their place and become just like them. The novel reveals the ultimate cause of both the workers' suffering and the corruption of those in power to lie in the laissez-faire system of capitalism that institutes a struggle of each against all and that thus victimizes even the supremely rapacious, filthy-rich capitalists themselves, as seen in the person of Freddie Jones, the wealthy and pampered but dysfunctional and miserable son of the owner of the meat-packing plant where Jurgis had once worked. The novel thus elicits empathy not only for Jurgis and the other members of his desperate family, but also, through this extension of the network of causality, for their victimizers as well. And from this empathic position, readers are summoned to divest themselves of the nationalistic and capitalistic systems of belief—ideologies—that constitute part of their systemic identities and to operate from an interindividual identity instead.

The Grapes of Wrath operates in a similar fashion to help readers develop an interindividual identity structure. First, it evicts readers from the comfortable position of blaming the poor and homeless for their plight, showing their poverty to be caused by the inexorable forces of nature in the form of drought and dust storms and their homelessness to be the inescapable consequence of the bank's foreclosure on their property due to their inability to repay the mortgages that they had been forced into by the drought. Nor does the novel allow blame to be placed on the officers of the dispossessing banks or their agents, the hired men who bulldoze the farmers' houses, for they are both simply doing what they have to do in order to survive and feed their families. The novel locates the evil here not in the individual perpetrators but rather in the institutions (large banking conglomerates) and systems (capitalism) in which they are caught up. This point is made repeatedly throughout the novel regarding the various merchants, clerks, landowners, and law enforcement officers who demean, exploit, attack, demonize, and dehumanize the Joads and other homeless Okies: the victimizers do what they do and are what they are because they are themselves caught up in a system that extorts such behavior as the price of survival.

Reading and analyzing narratives such as these incorporates more lines of cause and effect, and hence more others, into one's identity. The totalizing systemic perspective, extending one's grasp of the network of causation, unites with the empathic impulse to enact an interindividual perspective, a sense of oneself as both an effect and a cause of others' actions and states of being, and thus as both dependent on and responsible for their wellbeing. It produces the realization that all harm done to another is ultimately harm to oneself. As the Okies on a number of occasions tell those who attack them, "You don't know what you're doing. We're the same as you. You're one of us."

Helping readers enact the interindividual structure, through their identification with a protagonist's experience of the profound connectedness, sameness, and participation with the core being of even those individuals who are most different from and hostile to oneself, is the culminating and most important effect of *The Grapes of Wrath* and other protest novels as well, such as *Native Son, Invisible Man,* and *To Kill a Mockingbird. Native Son* provides one of the most poignant instances, when Bigger Thomas, the young black protagonist sentenced to death for killing (and, it is mistakenly assumed, raping) a young white woman and demonized by the racist prosecutor as a vicious wild beast, recognizes that not only his own violent criminal activities but also the violence of the prosecutor, the mob that wants to lynch him, and the entire racist system that has formed and deformed him are the result of the same fundamental need of all individuals: the need to live, to survive psychologically. As Bigger sits in his cell with his white attorney Mr. Max just hours before his execution, he is comforted by the sense "that at bottom all men lived as he lived and felt as he felt" (Wright 422), and he seeks to solidify this newfound interindividual identity as he goes to his death by eliciting recognition of it from Mr. Max:

> "I'm going to die. Well, that's all right now. But really I never wanted to hurt nobody. That's the truth, Mr. Max. I hurt folks 'cause I felt I had to; that's all. They was crowding me too close; they wouldn't give me no room. . . . Mr. Max, I didn't mean to do what I did. I was trying to do something else. But it seems like I never could. I was always wanting something and I was feeling that nobody would let me have it. So I fought 'em. . . . Mr. Max, I know the folks who sent me here to die hated me; I know that. B-b-but you reckon th-they was like m-me, trying to g-get something like I was, and when

I'm dead and gone they'll be saying like I'm saying now that they didn't mean to hurt nobody . . . th-that they was t-trying to get something, too . . . ?" (Wright 425)

Mr. Max, operating within a systemic identity structured on Marxist principles, gives a multifaceted response laden with ambiguity and irony that finally affirms Bigger's basic premise, though in the more limited terms of his Marxist-systemic identity:

> "Bigger, the people who hate you feel just as you feel, only they're on the other side of the fence. . . . They want the things of life, just as you did, and they're not particular about how they get them. . . . They do like you did, Bigger, when you refused to feel sorry for Mary. But on both sides men want to live; men are fighting for life." (Wright 429)

With this (partial) recognition from Mr. Max, Bigger is able to recognize and empathize with his own murderous self:

> "When I think about what you say I kind of feel what I wanted. It makes me feel I was kind of right. . . . I ain't trying to forgive nobody and I ain't asking for nobody to forgive me. I ain't going to cry. They wouldn't let me live and I killed. Maybe it ain't fair to kill, and I reckon I really didn't want to kill. But when I think of why all the killing was, I begin to feel what I wanted, what I am. . . . I didn't want to kill!" Bigger shouted. "But what I killed for, I *am*! . . . What I killed for must've been good!" (Wright 429)

Max responds to this final insight of Bigger's with despair, terror, and finally tears, indicating that this insight and the interindividual identity from which it springs exceed the capacity of Max's systemic identity and/or that Max, and through him the attentive reader, realizes the supreme irony and tragedy of the fact that here, minutes before he is to be put to death for bestial behavior, Bigger has attained the deepest insight and fullest humanity of any of the characters in the novel, including Max.

Scenes such as this offer rich and multiple forms of challenge and support that we literature teachers can make use of in our efforts to facilitate our students' (and our own) apprehension and consolidation of their (and our) own (always at least partly nascent) interindividual identity structures and compassionate contents. By helping our students to clarify and elaborate on interindividual identities such as Bigger's and to identify and explore their thoughts, feelings, and judgments about the utterances, actions, and reactions of both characters, we can help them develop and extend the sway of their own interindividual identity components. The basic interindividual faculties of empathy and extended causal awareness can be further practiced and developed by asking our students to apply the novel's final (interindividual) picture of Bigger to contemporary violent, animalistic criminals, and to apply Bigger's final (interindividual) perspective on the white racists to contemporary racists, genocides, and chauvinistic and punitive national leaders.

To the extent that we can formulate pedagogical practices that help our students develop more capacious and complex identity structures, integrate more of the rejected components of their selves, and experience their sense of self more through benign identity contents and less through malignant ones, we will contribute significantly not only to our students' psychological development and educational achievement but also to social justice and the reduction of human misery in the world at large. This should be our constant and ultimate goal, both as teachers and simply as human beings. It is an imperative that is not only ethical but also developmental, directing us toward the culmination of our own identity development in a generativity in which our personal sense of self is a function of our helping others to develop their own generativity and interindividual identity structure to the fullest.

Notes

Chapter 1   Identity, Motivation, and Recognition

1. Damasio describes this identity-bearing relationship of the three registers as follows: "Autobiographical memory is architecturally connected, neurally and cognitively speaking, to the nonconscious proto-self and to the emergent and conscious core self of each lived instant. This connection forms a bridge between the ongoing process of core consciousness, condemned to syssyphal transiency, and a progressively larger array of established, rock-solid memories pertaining to unique historical facts and consistent characteristics of an individual. In other words, the body-based, dynamic-range stability of the non-conscious proto-self, which is reconstructed live at each instant, and the conscious core self, which emerges from it in the second-order non-verbal account when an object modifies it, are enriched by the accompanying display of memorized and invariant facts—for instance, where you were born, and to whom; critical events in your autobiography; what you like and dislike; your name; and so on" (173).

Chapter 2   Linguistic Identity

1. In an experiment, one group of students was told that they had scored well on a test and another group that they had scored poorly. Those who believed their scores were good were not very interested in seeing the tests of other students. Those who believed their scores were bad desired, in contrast, to see other students' scores, but only when they believed those scores were low (Hoyle et al. 104–105).

Chapter 4   Identity Integration and Defenses

1. For an account of how such defenses interfere with writing, see "The Psychopathology of Everyday Prose" in Bracher, *The Writing Cure.*

Chapter 5   Identity Structure

1. Kegan refers to these structures as forms of self and "orders of consciousness."
2. While Kegan describes the movement from one stage to the next as a relatively global and irreversible progression of the entire self, other theorists (such as Greenspan and Noam), as well as everyday experience and observation, indicate that individuals progress unevenly in different domains of life and also regress

under stress to earlier, simpler structures. Here, however, we will be concerned mainly with the *progression* from the simpler to the more complex structures and what this progression means both for identity and for learning and intelligence.

Chapter 6   Teachers' Identities as Obstacles to Radical Pedagogy

1. As demonstrated by the 1995 conference, The Role of Advocacy in the Classroom, proceedings from which are published in the volume *Advocacy in the Classroom* (Spacks).
2. On transference in teaching, see Felman; Penley, "Teaching"; Frank; and Simon, "Face."
3. For more detailed accounts of transference, see Silvèstre; Porge; Cottet; and Safouan.
4. As Constance Penley notes, "The student can always sense the hidden demands of the teacher or parent. The student, like the child with the parent, is almost *clairvoyant* when it comes to understanding the desire of the Other and how best narcissistically to mirror what the Other desires" (Penley, "Teaching" 133).

Chapter 7   Authoritarian and Establishment Pedagogies

1. For a characterization and condemnation of the narcissism inherent in this mode of teaching, see Amirault 70.
2. For a condemnation of this aim, see Strickland 129.

Chapter 9   Historicism as Impediment to Radical Pedagogy

1. See Zizek, *For They Know not* 101–102; Bracher, *Lacan* 5–7; Copjec 1–14, 68, 126; Dean; and Evans.
2. Scholarly demonstrations of the historical specificity of, for example, Freud's nineteenth-century scientism, his position as a Viennese Jew, and the particularity of his patient population (turn-of-the-century bourgeois Viennese) have been quite valuable, rescuing psychoanalysis from certain essentializing and universalizing elements of its theory.
3. See pp. 14–15 for Steele's account of the destructiveness of this identification with victimization. Steele's quite astute psychodynamic insights must be distinguished from his social policy recommendations (e.g., his advocacy of the elimination of affirmative action).
4. For similar views, see Cox and Reynolds 9, 15, and 25; Ohmann 178; Belsey 166; and Thomas, *New Historicism* 161–162, 166, and 211.
5. Marjorie Levinson also emphasizes the parallel between history and psychoanalysis, noting "the cleavages opened between conscious and unconscious *within* the historian/analyst and his subject/patient; and also, *between* the unconsciousness of the analyst and patient, critic and poet, present and past" ("Introduction" 14).

6. The question of how a nation's brutality in the past affects the nation's present subjects needs to be investigated systematically in its own right, with special attention given to the manner in which the lies and secrets of one generation get transmitted to succeeding generations, who, like the Rat Man (as Lacan points out), are often confronted with a demand for payment of the symbolic debt incurred by their forbears.

7. See also Kristeva and Young-Bruehl.

8. See Pommier for a contrast between historicizing and nonhistoricizing modes of psychoanalysis.

9. For a fuller account of the Lacanian view of transference, see Silvèstre; Safouan; and Cottet.

10. This fantasy of the Other's omnipotence is perhaps most striking when it takes the form of a fantasy of the primal scene, the scene of production, procreation, and full jouissance. Greenblatt expresses this fantasy as follows: "If one longs as I do to reconstruct . . . the negotiations through which works of art obtain and amplify such powerful [social] energy . . . , one dreams of finding an originary moment, a moment in which the master hand shapes the concentrated social energy into the sublime aesthetic object" (7). Once again, Greenblatt realizes the unrealistic nature of this fantasy. "The quest is fruitless," he says, "for there is no originary moment, no pure act of untrammeled creation" (7). But as in fetishistic disavowal, that fantasy operates even though it is recognized as an illusion. Greenblatt continues: "In place of a blazing genesis, one begins to glimpse something that seems at first far less spectacular: a subtle, elusive set of exchanges, a network of trades and trade-offs, a jostling of competing representations, a negotiation between joint-stock companies. . . . Gradually, these complex, ceaseless borrowings and lendings have come to seem to me more important, more poignant even, than the epiphany for which I had hoped" (7). Although Greenblatt recognizes the impossibility of "finding an originary moment," the fantasy of recovering lost jouissance, of being beyond contingency, is alive and well, operating in a more subtle and sublimated form as the animating principle of the New Historicist project. What Greenblatt refers to as the "subtle, elusive set of exchanges," the "jostling . . . between joint-stock companies," which constitutes the focus of New Historicist investigations, is perhaps a subtle version of that primal intercourse that produced the "blazing genesis" where the uncastrated, omnipotent father of unlimited jouissance engendered life that continues to animate the New Historicist in the present.

11. The author, Foucault explains, "allows a limitation of the cancerous and dangerous proliferation of significations within a world where one is thrifty not only with one's resources and riches, but also with one's discourses and their significations. The author is the principle of thrift in the proliferation of meaning. . . . He is a certain functional principle by which, in our culture, one limits, excludes, and chooses: in short, by which one impedes the free circulation, the free manipulation, the free composition, decomposition, and recomposition of fiction. . . . It does not seem necessary that the author function remain constant in form, complexity, and even in existence. I think that, as our society changes, . . . the author function will disappear. . . . All discourses . . . would then develop in the anonymity of a murmur" (274–275).

Chapter 12   Supporting Prosocial
Identity Contents

1. Underlying and in part defining identity categories (such as "woman" and "man") are prototypical (largely visual) images of particular physical features, actions, and personal attributes (see Johnson). These images, in addition to providing and withholding recognition themselves, also limit the application of the categories (and hence the recognition the categories confer) to a subset of the entire category. Thus to the extent that words such as "professor," "doctor," "judge," and "colonel" are associated with the prototypical image of a man, women who hold these positions are denied their due cultural recognition. And insofar as the category "man" is associated with images of big, muscular, tough, hard bodies engaging in strenuous, dangerous, and/or violent activities, men who do not possess these attributes will feel themselves deprived of recognition as men, and all men will tend either to suppress (keep private, refrain from expressing) or to repress (render unconscious and thus disown) parts of themselves that fail to conform to those images.

Chapter 13   Promoting Identity Integration

1. For some innovative assignments that can help students identify and work through their master signifiers, see DiBernard and Reiter.
2. For two excellent examples of investigating one's own individual and collective *a* (fantasies, desires, enjoyments, and disgusts), see Kipnis, and Penley, "Feminism." For the importance of investigating one's affective investments, see Giroux 137.
3. For "a useful strategy for illuminating differences within each student," see Berry and Patraka 140ff. On helping students "experience the contradictions of their various discursive selves through reading and discussing texts," see Clifford 110. See also Reagan 54.
4. For a discussion of some of the personal and social benefits of investigating one's own language use, see Bleich 184–185, 210, and 216.

WORKS CITED

Alcorn, Marshall W., Jr. *Narcissism and the Literary Libido*. New York: New York University Press, 1994.

———. *Changing the Subject in English Class*. Carbondale, IL: Southern Illinois University Press, 2003.

Altieri, Charles. "Can We Be Historical Ever? Some Hopes for a Dialectical Model of Historical Self-Consciousness." *Modern Language Quarterly* 54, 1 (March 1993): 41–52.

Amirault, Chris. "The Good Teacher, the Good Student: Identifications of a Student Teacher." In *Pedagogy: The Question of Impersonation*, ed. Jane Gallop. Bloomington, IN: Indiana University Press, 1995. 64–78.

Anderson, Kevin. "Erich Fromm and the Frankfurt School Critique of Criminal Justice." In *Erich Fromm and Critical Criminology: Beyond the Punitive Society*, ed. Kevin Anderson and Richard Quinney. Urbana: University of Illinois Press, 2000. 83–119.

Aronson, Elliot. *Nobody Left to Hate: Teaching Compassion after Columbine*. New York: W. H. Freeman, 2000.

Atwood, Joan, ed. *Family Scripts*. Washington: Taylor and Francis, 1996.

Baumeister, Roy F. "Ego Depletion and the Self's Executive Function." In *Psychological Perspectives on Self and Identity*, ed. Abraham Tesser, Richard B. Felson, and Jerry M. Suls. Washington, DC: American Psychological Association, 2000. 9–33.

Belsey, Catherine. "Towards Cultural History—In Theory and Practice." *Textual Practice* 3, 2 (1989): 159–172.

Berman, Jeffrey. *Diaries to an English Professor*. Amherst, MA: University of Massachusetts Press, 1994.

———. *Empathic Teaching*. Amherst, MA: University of Massachusetts Press, 2004.

———. *Risky Writing*. Amherst, MA: University of Massachusetts Press, 2001.

———. *Surviving Literary Suicide*. Amherst, MA: University of Massachusetts Press, 1999.

Bernstein, H. E. "The Courage to Try—Self-Esteem and Learning." In *Learning and Education: Psychoanalytic Perspectives*, ed. Kay Field, Bertram J. Cohler, and Glorye Wool. Madison, CT: International Universities Press, 1989. 143–157.

Berry, Ellen, and Vivian Patraka. "Local Struggles/Partial Explanations: Producing Feminist Theory in the Classroom," 122–148 in *Changing Classroom Practices: Resources for Literary and Cultural Studies*, ed. David B. Downing. Urbana, IL: NCTE, 1994. 122–148.

Blanchard, Phyllis. "Psychoanalytic Contributions to the Problems of Reading Disabilities." *Psychoanalytic Study of the Child* 2 (1946): 163–187.

Bleich, David. *The Double Perspective: Language, Literacy & Social Relations.* New York: Oxford University Press, 1988.

Bloom, Sandra L., and Michael Reichert. *Bearing Witness: Violence and Collective Responsibility.* New York: Haworth Press, 1998.

Bracher, Mark. "Healing Trauma, Preventing Violence: A Radical Agenda for Literary Study." *JAC* 24, 3 (2004): 515–561.

———. *Lacan, Discourse, and Social Change: A Psychoanalytic Cultural Criticism.* Ithaca: Cornell University Press, 1993.

———. *The Writing Cure: Psychoanalysis, Composition, and the Aims of Education.* Carbondale, IL: Southern Illinois University Press, 1999.

Britzman, Deborah P. *After-Education: Anna Freud, Melanie Klein, and Psychoanalytic Histories of Learning.* Albany: SUNY Press, 2003.

Browning, Don. *Generative Man.* Philadelphia: Westminster Press, 1973.

Bucci, Wilma. *Psychoanalysis and Cognitive Science: A Multiple Code Theory.* New York: Guilford, 1997.

Burton, John. *Violence Explained.* New York: Manchester University Press, 1997.

Certeau, Michel de. *Heterologies: Discourse on the Other.* Trans. Brian Massumi. Minneapolis: University of Minnesota Press, 1986.

Chickering, Arthur W., and Linda Reisser. *Education and Identity*, 2nd ed. San Francisco: Jossey-Bass, 1993.

Clifford, John. "The Reader and the Text: Ideologies in Dialogue." In *Practicing Theory in Introductory College Literature Courses*, ed. James M. Cahalan and David B. Downing. Urbana, IL: NCTE, 1991. 101–111.

Cohen, Geoffrey L., Joshua Aronson, and Claude M. Steele. "When Beliefs Yield to Evidence: Reducing Biased Evaluation by Affirming the Self." *Personality and Social Psychology Bulletin* 26, 9 (2000): 1151–1164.

Cohler, Bertram J. "Psychoanalysis and Education: Motive, Meaning, and Self. *Learning and Education: Psychoanalytic Perspectives*, ed. Kay Field, Bertram J. Cohler, and Glorye Wool. Madison, CT: International Universities Press, 1989. 11–83.

Cohler, Bertram J., and Robert M. Galatzer-Levy. "Psychoanalysis and the Classroom." In *Educating the Emotions: Bruno Bettelheim and Psychoanalytic Development*, ed. Nathan M. Szajnberg. New York: Plenum, 1992.

Copjec, Joan. *Read My Desire: Lacan against the Historicists.* Cambridge, MA: MIT Press, 1994.

Coté, James E., and Charles G. Levine. *Identity Formation, Agency, and Culture.* Mahwah, NJ: Lawrence Erlbaum Associates, 2002.

Cottet, Serge. *Freud et le désir du psychanalyste.* Paris: Navarin, 1982.

Cottle, Thomas J. *A Sense of Self: The Work of Affirmation.* Amherst, MA: University of Massachusetts Press, 2003.

Cox, Jeffrey N., and Larry J. Reynolds. "Introduction: The Historicist Enterprise." In *New Historical Literary Study*, ed. Cox and Reynolds. Princeton: Princeton University Press, 1993. 3–37.

Currie, Elliott. *Crime and Punishment in America.* New York: Henry Holt, 1998.

Damasio, Antonio. *The Feeling of What Happens.* New York: Harcourt, 2000.

Dash, Leon. *When Children Want Children.* New York: William Morrow, 1989.

Dean, Tim. Review of *Read My Desire.* *JPCS* 1, 1 (1996): 149–156.

DiBernard, Barbara, and Sheila Reiter. "Two Women on the Verge of a Contextual Breakthrough: Using *A Feminist Dictionary* in the Literature Classroom." In *Changing Classroom Practices: Resources for Literary and Cultural Studies*, ed. David B. Downing. Urbana, IL: NCTE, 1994. 104–121.

Dunn, Robert G. *Identity Crises: A Social Critique of Postmodernity*. Minneapolis: University of Minnesota Press, 1998.

Eagleton, Terry. *The Idea of Culture*. Malden, MA: Blackwell, 2000.

Erikson, Erik H. *Identity: Youth and Crisis*. New York: Norton, 1968.

———. *Insight and Responsibility*. New York: Norton, 1964.

Evans, Dylan. "The Lure of the Already There and the Lure of the Before: Psychoanalytic Theory and Historiography." *JPCS* 2, 1 (1997).

Faludi, Susan. *Stiffed: The Betrayal of the American Man*. New York: Morrow, 1999.

Fein, Steven, and Steven J. Spencer. "Prejudice as Self-Image Maintenance: Affirming the Self Through Derogating Others." *Journal of Personality and Social Psychology* 73, 1 (1997): 31–44.

Felman, Shoshana. "Psychoanalysis and Education: Teaching Terminable and Interminable." *Yale French Studies* 63 (1982): 21–44.

Fetterley, Judith. *The Resisting Reader*. Bloomington: Indiana University Press, 1978.

Fonagy, Peter, George S. Moran, and Mary Target. "Aggression and the Psychological Self." *International Journal of Psycho-Analysis* 74 (1993): 471–485.

Foucault, Michel. "What Is An Author?" In *Contemporary Literary Criticism: Literary and Cultural Studies*, ed. Robert Con Davis and Ronald Schleifer. New York: Longman, 1989. 262–275.

Fox, Tom. "Basic Writing as Cultural Conflict." *Journal of Education* 172 (1990): 65–83.

Frank, Arthur W. "Lecturing and Transference: The Undercover Work of Pedagogy." In *Pedagogy: The Question of Impersonation*, ed. Jane Gallop. Bloomington: Indiana University Press, 1995. 28–35.

Freud, Sigmund. *Inhibitions, Symptoms and Anxiety*. Trans. Alix Strachey. New York: Norton, 1959.

———. *Introductory Lectures on Psychoanalysis*. Trans. James Strachey. New York: Norton, 1966.

Garbarino, James. *Lost Boys: Why our Sons Turn Violent and How We Can Save Them*. New York: Free Press, 1999.

———. *Raising Children in a Socially Toxic Environment*. San Francisco: Jossey-Bass, 1995.

Gardiner, Lion F. *Redesigning Higher Education: Producing Dramatic Gains in Student Learning*. ASHE-ERIC Higher Education Reports. Vol. 23, No. 7. Washington, DC: George Washington University, n.d.

Gates, Henry Louis, Jr. "Beyond the Culture Wars: Identities in Dialogue." *Profession* 93 (1993).

Gendlin, Eugene. *Experiencing and the Creation of Meaning*. Evanston, IL: Northwestern University Press, 1997.

———. *Focusing-Oriented Psychotherapy*. New York: Guilford, 1996.

Gilligan, James. *Violence: Reflections on a National Epidemic*. New York: Random House, 1996.

———. *Preventing Violence*. New York: Thames & Hudson, 2001.

Giroux, Henry. "Living Dangerously: Identity Politics and the New Cultural Racism." In *Between Borders: Pedagogy and the Politics of Cultural Studies*, ed. Henry A. Giroux and Peter McLaren. New York: Routledge, 1994. 29–55.

Giroux, Henry, and Roger Simon. "Popular Culture as a Pedagogy of Pleasure and Meaning: Decolonizing the Body." In *Border Crossings: Cultural Workers and the Politics of Education*, ed. Henry Giroux. New York: Routledge, 1992. 180–206.

Glassner, Barry. *The Culture of Fear: Why Americans Are Afraid of the Wrong Things*. New York: Basic, 1999.

Goleman, Daniel. *Emotional Intelligence*. New York: Bantam, 1995.

Graff, Gerald. *Beyond the Culture Wars*. New York: Norton, 1992.

Grand, Sue. *The Reproduction of Evil: A Clinical and Cultural Perspective*. Hillsdale, NJ: Analytic Press, 2000.

Greenblatt, Stephen. *Shakespearean Negotiations: The Circulation of Social Energy in Renaissance England*. Berkeley: University of California Press, 1988.

Greenspan, Stanley I. *The Growth of the Mind and the Endangered Origins of Intelligence*. New York: Addison Wesley, 1997.

Grossberg, Lawrence. "Introduction: Bringin' It All Back Home—Pedagogy and Cultural Studies." In *Between Borders: Pedagogy and the Politics of Cultural Studies*, ed. Henry A. Giroux and Peter McLaren. New York: Routledge, 1994. 1–25.

Hedges, Chris. *War is a Force that Gives Us Meaning*. New York: Public Affairs, 2002.

Herman, Judith. *Trauma and Recovery*. New York: Basic, 1997.

Holland, Norman N. *The I*. New Haven: Yale University Press, 1985.

Honderich, Ted. *After the Terror*. Edinburgh: Edinburgh University Press, 2002.

Honneth, Axel. *The Struggle for Recognition*. Cambridge, MA: MIT Press, 1995.

hooks, bell. *Teaching to Transgress: Education as the Practice of Freedom*. New York: Routledge, 1994.

———. "Toward a Revolutionary Feminist Pedagogy." In *Falling into Theory*, ed. David H. Richter. Boston: St. Martin's, 1994. 79–84.

Hoover, Kenneth. *The Power of Identity*. Chatham, NJ: Chatham House, 1997.

Horowitz, Mardi J., Constance Milbrath, and Charles H. Stinson. "Signs of Defensive Control Locate Conflicted Topics in Discourse." *Archives of General Psychiatry* 52 (December 1995): 1040–1047.

Horowitz, Mardi J., Constance Milbrath, Steven Reidboc, and Charles Stinson. "Elaboration and Dyselaboration: Measures of Expression and Defense in Discourse." *Psychotherapy Research* 3, 4 (1993): 278–293.

Hoyle, Rick H., Michael H. Kernis, Mark R. Leary, and Mark W. Baldwin. *Selfhood*. Boulder, CO: Westview Press, 1999.

Huttunen, Rauno, and Hannu L. T. Heikkinen. "Teaching and the Dialectic of Recognition." *Pedagogy, Culture and Society* 12, 2 (2004): 163–173.

Jameson, Fredric. *The Political Unconscious: Narrative as a Socially Symbolic Act*. Ithaca: Cornell University Press, 1981.

JanMohamed, Abdul R. "Some Implications of Paolo Freire's Border Pedagogy." In *Between Borders: Pedagogy and the Politics of Cultural Studies*, ed. Henry A. Giroux and Peter McLaren. New York: Routledge, 1994. 225–241.

Jaynes, Julian. *The Origin of Consciousness in the Breakdown of the Bicameral Mind*. Boston: Houghton Mifflin, 1976.

Johnson, Mark. *Moral Imagination*. Chicago: University of Chicago Press, 1993.

Jones, James M. *Prejudice and Racism*. New York: McGraw-Hill, 1997.

Jones, Richard M. *An Experiment in Psychoanalytic Education*. Chicago: Charles C. Thomas, 1961

———. *Fantasy and Feeling in Education*. New York: New York University Press, 1968.

Josephs, Lawrence. *Balancing Empathy and Interpretation*. Northvale, NJ: Aronson, 1995.

Judges, Donald Philip. "Scared to Death: Capital Punishment as Authoritarian Terror Management." *Dissertation Abstracts International* 60 (March 2000): 4228.

Katz, Jack. *Seductions of Crime: Moral and Sensual Attractions in Doing Evil*. New York: Basic, 1988.

Kegan, Robert. *The Evolving Self: Problem and Process in Human Development*. Cambridge, MA: Harvard University Press, 1982.

——. *In Over Our Heads: The Mental Demands of Modern Life*. Cambridge, MA: Harvard University Press, 1994.

Khantzian, Edward J. *Treating Addiction as a Human Process*. Northvale, NJ: Jason Aronson, 1999.

Kipnis, Laura. "(Male) Desire and (Female) Disgust: Reading *Hustler*." In *Cultural Studies*, ed. Lawrence Grossberg, et al. New York: Routledge, 1992. 373–391.

Klein, Emanuel. "Psychoanalytic Aspects of School Problems." *Psychoanalytic Study of the Child* 3/4 (1949): 369–390.

Kristeva, Julia. *Strangers to Ourselves*. Trans. Leon S. Roudiez. New York: Columbia University Press, 1991.

Krystal, Henry. "Self- and Object-Representation in Alcoholism and Other Drug-Dependence: Implications for Therapy." In *The Dynamics and Treatment of Alcoholism: Essential Papers*, ed. Jerome D. Levin and Ronna H. Weiss. Northvale, NJ: Jason Aronson, 1994. 300–309.

——. "Self Representation and the Capacity for Self Care." In *Essential Papers on Addiction*, ed. Daniel L. Yalisove. New York: New York University Press, 1997. 109–146.

Krystal, Henry, and Herbert A. Raskin. *Drug Dependence: Aspects of Ego Function*. Detroit: Wayne State University Press, 1970.

Kunda, Ziva. "The Case for Motivated Reasoning." *Psychological Bulletin* 108, 3 (1990): 480–498.

Lacan, Jacques. *Ecrits: A Selection*. Trans. Alan Sheridan. New York: Norton, 1977.

——. *The Ethics of Psychoanalysis*. The Seminar of Jacques Lacan, Book VII, ed. Jacques-Alain Miller. Trans. Dennis Porter. New York: Norton, 1992.

——. *The Four Fundamental Concepts of Psychoanalysis*. Trans. Alan Sheridan. New York: Norton, 1977.

——. *Le séminaire, livre XVII: L'envers de la psychanalyse*, ed. Jacques-Alain Miller. Paris: Seuil, 1991.

Lazarus, Richard. "Progress on a Cognitive-Motivational-Relational Theory of Emotion." *American Psychologist* 46, 8 (1991): 819–834.

Lee, Harper. *To Kill a Mockingbird*. 1960. New York: Warner, 1982.

Levin, Jerome D. *Primer for Treating Substance Abusers*. Northvale, NJ: Jason Aronson, 1999.

Levinas, Emmanuel. *Otherwise than Being: Or beyond Essence*. Trans. Alfonso Lingis. Pittsburgh: Duquesne University Press, 1998.

Levinson, Marjorie. "Introduction." In *Rethinking Historicism: Critical Readings in Romantic History*, ed. Marjorie Levinson, Marilyn Butler, Jerome McGann, and Paul Hamilton. London: Basil Blackwell, 1989. 1–17.

——. "The New Historicism: Back to the Future." In *Rethinking Historicism: Critical Readings in Romantic Ideology*, ed. Marjorie Levinson, Marilyn

Butler, Jerome McGann, and Paul Hamilton. London: Blackwell, 1989. 18–63.

Lichtenstein, Heinz. *The Dilemma of Human Identity.* New York: Aronson, 1977.

Lingis, Alfonso. "Translator's Introduction." In Emmanuel Levinas. *Otherwise than Being: Or beyond Essence.* Trans. Alfonso Lingis. Pittsburgh: Duquesne University Press, 1998. xvii–xlviii.

Liu, Alan. "Local Transcendence: Cultural Criticism, Postmodernism, and the Romanticism of Detail." *Representations* 32 (Fall 1990): 75–113.

Liu, Thomas J., and Claude M. Steele. "Attributional Analysis as Self-Affirmation." *Journal of Personality and Social Psychology* 51, 3 (1986): 531–540.

Lockley, Paul. *Counseling Heroin and Other Drug Users.* London: Free Association, 1995.

Loth, R. "The Silber Agenda." *Boston Globe Magazine* (December 14, 1986): 22–24, 33–37, 49–56, 59.

Mannoni, Octave. "Je sais bien, mais quand même." *Clefs pour l'Imaginaire.* Paris: Seuil, 1969. 9–33.

Markus, Hazel Rose, and Shinobu Kitayama. "Culture and the Self: Implications for Cognition, Emotion, and Motivation." *Psychological Review* 92, 2 (1991): 224–253.

McGann, Jerome. *The Romantic Ideology: A Critical Investigation.* Chicago: University of Chicago Press, 1983.

———. "The Third World of Criticism." In *Rethinking Historicism: Critical Readings in Romantic History,* ed. Marjorie Levinson, Marilyn Butler, Jerome McGann, and Paul Hamilton. London: Basil Blackwell, 1989. 85–107.

McGregor, Holly A., Jeff Greenberg, Jamie Arndt, Joel D. Lieberman, Sheldon Solomon, and Linda Simon. "Terror Management and Aggression: Evidence that Mortality Salience Motivates Aggression Against Worldview-Threatening Others." *Journal of Personality and Social Psychology* 74, 3 (1998): 590–605.

McLaren, Peter. "Multiculturalism and the Postmodern Critique: Toward a Pedagogy of Resistance and Transformation." In *Between Borders: Pedagogy and the Politics of Cultural Studies,* ed. Henry Giroux and Peter McLaren. New York: Routledge, 1994. 192–224.

Menand, Louis. "The Demise of Disciplinary Authority." In *Falling into Theory: Conflicting Views on Reading Literature,* ed. David H. Richter. 2nd ed. New York: Bedford, 2000. 103–110.

Michaels, Walter Benn. "The Victims of New Historicism." *Modern Language Quarterly* 54, 1 (March 1993): 111–120.

Miller, Jacques-Alain. "*Extimité.*" *Prose Studies* 11 (1988): 121–130.

Monroe, Kristen Renwick. "Explicating Altruism." In *Altruism and Altruism Love: Science, Philosophy, and Religion in Dialogue,* ed. Stephen G. Post, Lynn G. Underwood, Jeffrey P. Schloss, and William B. Hurlbut. New York: Oxford University Press, 2002. 106–122.

———. *The Heart of Altruism: Perceptions of a Common Humanity.* Princeton: Princeton University Press, 1996.

Musick, Judith S. *Young, Poor, and Pregnant: The Psychology of Teenage Motherhood.* New Haven: Yale University Press, 1993.

Nietzsche, Friedrich. *The Use and Abuse of History.* Trans. Adrian Collins. New York: Bobbs Merrill, 1957.

Noam, Gil G. " 'Normative Vulnerabilities' of Self and Their Transformation in Moral Action." In *The Moral Self*, ed. Gil G. Noam and Thomas E. Wren. Cambridge, MA: MIT Press, 1993. 209–238.

Ohmann, Richard. "Teaching Historically." In *Pedagogy Is Politics: Literary Theory and Critical Teaching*. Ed. Regina-Maria Kecht. Urbana: University of Illinois Press, 1992. 173–189.

Oliner, Pearl M., and Samuel P. Oliner. *Toward a Caring Society: Ideas into Action*. Westport, CT: Praeger, 1995.

Palmer, Parker. *The Courage to Teach*. San Francisco: Jossey-Bass, 1998.

Pearson, Gerald H. J. *Psychoanalysis and the Education of the Child*. New York: Norton, 1954.

Penley, Constance. "Feminism, Psychoanalysis, and the Study of Popular Culture." In *Cultural Studies*, ed. Lawrence Grossberg, et al. New York: Routledge, 1992. 479–500.

———. "Teaching in Your Sleep: Feminism and Psychoanalysis." In *Theory in the Classroom*, ed. Cary Nelson. Urbana, IL: University of Illinois Press, 1986. 129–148.

Perkins, David. *Is Literary History Possible?* Baltimore: Johns Hopkins University Press, 1992.

Pommier, Gerard. *Le dénouement d'une analyse*. Paris: Point Hors Ligne, 1987.

Porge, Erik. 1978. "Sur le désir de l'analyste." *Ornicar?* 14: 35–39.

Pyszczynski, Tom, Jeff Greenberg, and Sheldon Solomon. "A Dual-Process Model of Defense against Conscious and Unconscious Death-Related Thoughts: An Extension of Terror Management Theory." *Psychological Review* 106, 4 (1999): 835–845.

———. "Why Do We Need What We Need? A Terror Management perspective on the Roots of Human Social Motivation." *Psychological Inquiry* 8, 1 (1997): 1–20.

Qualley, Donna J. "Being Two Places at Once: Feminism and the Development of 'Both/And' Perspectives." In *Pedagogy in the Age of Politics*, ed. Patricia A. Sullivan and Donna J. Qualley. Urbana, IL: NCTE, 1994. 25–42.

Reagan, Daniel. "Naming Harlem: Teaching the Dynamics of Diversity." In *Pedagogy in the Age of Politics*, ed. Patricia A. Sullivan and Donna J. Qualley. Urbana, IL: NCTE, 1994. 43–55.

Richter, David H. "What We Read." In *Falling into Theory: Conflicting Views on Reading Literature*, ed. David H. Richter. 2nd ed. New York: Bedford, 2000.

Rorty, Richard. "Ethics Without Principles." *Philosophy and Social Hope*. New York: Penguin, 1999. 72–90.

———. "Human Rights, Rationality and Sentimentality." In *The Politics of Human Rights*, ed. Obrad Savic. New York: Verso, 1999. 67–83.

———. "Justice as a Larger Loyalty." In *Justice and Democracy*, ed. Ron Bontekoe and Marietta Stepaniants. Honolulu: University of Hawaii Press, 1997.

Safouan, Moustapha. *Le transfert et le désir de l'analyste*. Paris: Seuil. 1988.

Samuels, Robert. *Between Philosophy and Psychoanalysis: Lacan's Reconstruction of Freud*. New York: Routledge, 1993.

Scheuer, Jeffrey. *The Sound Bite Society: Television and the American Mind*. New York: Four Walls Eight Windows, 1999.

Schimel, Jeff, Linda Simon, Jeff Greenberg, Sheldon Solomon, Tom Pyszczynski, Jeanette Waxmonsky, and Jamie Arndt. "Stereotypes and Terror

Management: Evidence that Mortality Salience Enhances Stereotypic Thinking and Preferences." *Journal of Personality and Social Psychology* 77, 5 (1999): 905–926.

Scholes, Robert. "Toward a Curriculum in Textual Studies." In *Reorientations: Critical Theories and Pedagogies,* ed. Bruce Henricksen and Thaïs E. Morgan. Urbana, IL: University of Illinois Press, 1990. 95–112.

Schwartz, Donald D. "Implications of the Infantile Neurosis for Learning Problems in Childhood." In *Learning and Education: Psychoanalytic* Perspectives, ed. Kay Field, Bertram J. Cohler, and Glorye Wool. Madison, CT: International Universities Press, 1989. 539–598.

Schwartz, Fred. "Psychoanalytic Research in Attention and Learning: Some Findings and the Question of Clinical Relevance." *The Annual of Psychoanalysis* 1 (1973): 199–215.

Showalter, Elaine. "Feminist Criticism in the Wilderness." In *The New Feminist Criticism,* ed. Elaine Showalter. New York: Pantheon, 1985. 243–270.

Siegel, Daniel J. *The Developing Mind: Toward a Neurobiology of Interpersonal Experience.* New York: Guilford, 1999.

Silvèstre, Michel. "Le transfert dans la direction de la cure." *Ornicar?* 30 (1984): 11–45.

Simon, Roger. "Face to Face with Alterity: Postmodern Jewish Identity and the Eros of Pedagogy." In *Pedagogy: The Question of Impersonation,* ed. Jane Gallop. Bloomington: Indiana University Press, 1995. 90–105.

———. *Teaching Against the Grain.* New York: Bergin and Garvey, 1992.

Sinclair, Upton. *The Jungle.* 1906, ed. Claire Virginia Eby. New York: Norton, 2003.

Smith, Eliot R., and Michael A. Zárate. "Exemplar-Based Model of Social Judgment." *Psychological Review* 99, 1 (1992): 3–21.

Snell, Bruno. *The Discovery of the Mind.* Trans. T. G. Rosenmeyer. Cambridge: Harvard University Press, 1953.

Solomon, Robert. "In Defense of Sentimentality." In *Emotion and the Arts,* ed. Mette Hjort and Sue Laver. New York: Oxford University Press, 1997. 225–245.

Southgate, Beverley. *History: What and Why?* New York: Routledge, 1996.

Spacks, Patricia Meyer, ed. *Advocacy in the Classroom: Problems and Possibilities.* New York: St. Martin's Press, 1996.

Staub, Ervin. *The Roots of Evil.* New York: Cambridge University Press, 1989.

Steele, Claude M. "The Psychology of Self-Affirmation: Sustaining the Integrity of the Self." In *The Self in Social Psychology,* ed. Roy F. Baumeister. Philadelphia: Psychology Press, 1999. 372–390.

Steele, Claude M., Steven J. Spencer, and Michael Lynch. "Self-Image Resilience and Dissonance: The Role of Affirmational Resources." *Journal of Personality and Social Psychology* 64, 6 (1993): 885–896.

Steele, Shelby. *The Content of Our Character: A New Vision of Race in America.* New York: HarperCollins, 1991.

Steinbeck, John. *The Grapes of Wrath.* 1939, ed. Peter Lisca with Kevin Hearle. New York, Penguin, 1997.

Stern, Daniel N. *The Interpersonal World of the Infant: A View from Psychoanalysis and Developmental Psychology.* New York: Basic, 1985.

Stowe, Harriet Beecher. *Uncle Tom's Cabin*, ed. Elizabeth Ammons. New York: Norton, 1994.

Strean, Herbert, and Lucy Freeman. *Our Wish to Kill: The Murder in All Our Hearts.* New York: St. Martin's Press, 1991.

Strickland, Ronald. "Confrontational Pedagogy and the Introductory Literature Course." In *Practicing Theory in Introductory College Literature Courses*, ed. James M. Cahalan and David B. Downing. Urbana, IL: NCTE, 1991. 115–130.

Swann, W. B., Jr., A. Stein-Seroussi, and R. B. Giesler. "Why People Self-Verify." *Journal of Personality and Social Psychology* 62 (1992): 392–401.

Taylor, Charles. *The Ethics of Authenticity*. Cambridge, MA: Harvard University Press, 1991.

Thomas, Brook. "The Historical Necessity for—and Difficulties with—New Historical Analysis in Introductory Literature Courses." In *Practicing Theory in Introductory College Literature Courses*, ed. James M. Cahalan and David B. Downing. Urbana: NCTE, 1991. 85–100.

———. *The New Historicism and Other Old Fashioned Topics*. Princeton: Princeton University Press, 1991.

Tingle, Nick. *Self-Development and College Writing*. Carbondale, IL: Southern Illinois University Press, 2004.

Tobin, Lad. *Writing Relationships: What Really Happens in the Composition Class.* Portsmouth, NH: Boynton/Cook, 1993.

Todorov, Tzvetan. *Life in Common*. Tr. Katherine Golsan and Lucy Golsan. Lincoln, NE: University of Nebraska Press, 2001.

Tompkins, Jane. "Pedagogy of the Distressed." In *Changing Classroom Practices: Resources for Literary and Cultural Studies*, ed. David B. Downing. Urbana, IL: NCTE, 1994. 169–178.

Treichler, Paula. "A Room of Whose Own? Lessons from Feminist Classroom Narratives." In *Changing Classroom Practices: Resources for Literary and Cultural Studies*, ed. David B. Downing. Urbana, IL: NCTE, 1994. 75–103.

Trzebinski, Jerzy. "Narrative Self, Understanding, and Action." In *The Self in European and North American Culture: Development and Processes*, ed. Annerieke Oosterwegel and Robert A. Wicklund. Boston: Kluwer, 1995.

Vendler, Helen. "What We Have Loved, Others will Love." In *Falling into Theory: Conflicting Views on Reading Literature*, ed. David H. Richter. 2nd ed. New York: Bedford, 2000. 31–40.

Vignoles, Vivian L., Xenia Chryssochoou, and Glynis M. Breakwell. "Evaluating Models of Identity Motivation: Self-Esteem is Not the Whole Story." *Self and Identity.* 1 (2002): 201–218.

Volkan, Vamik. *The Need to Have Enemies and Allies: From Clinical Practice to International Relationships*. Northvale, NJ: Jason Aronson, 1988.

Wallace, Michele. "Negative Images: Towards a Black Feminist Cultural Criticism." In *Cultural Studies*, ed. Lawrence Grossberg, Cary Nelson, and Paula Treichler. New York: Routledge, 1992. 654–671.

Waxman, Barbara Frey. "Feminist Theory, Literary Canons, and the Construction of Textual Meanings." In *Practicing Theory in Introductory College Literature Courses*, ed. James M. Cahalan and David B. Downing. Urbana, IL: NCTE, 1991. 149–160.

White, Hayden. *Tropics of Discourse: Essays in Cultural Criticism*. Baltimore: Johns Hopkins University Press, 1978.

Wolf, Ernest S. "The Psychoanalytic Self Psychologist Looks at Learning." In *Learning and Education: Psychoanalytic* Perspectives, ed. Kay Field, Bertram J. Cohler, and Glorye Wool. Madison, CT: International Universities Press, 1989. 377–393.

Wright, Richard. *Native Son*. 1940. New York: Harper, 1998.

Wurmser, Leon. *The Hidden Dimension: Psychodynamics of Drug Use*. Northvale, NJ: Jason Aronson, 1995.

Young-Bruehl, Elisabeth. *The Anatomy of Prejudices*. Harvard University Press, 1996.

Zárate, Michael A., and Azenett A. Garza. "In-Group Distinctiveness and Self-Affirmation as Dual Components of Prejudice Reduction." *Self and Identity* 1 (2002): 235–249.

Zinberg, Norman E. "Addiction and Ego Function." In *Essential Papers on Addiction*, ed. Daniel L. Yalisove. New York: New York University Press, 1997. 147–165.

Zizek, Slavoj. *For They know not What They Do: Enjoyment as a Political Factor*. New York: Verso, 1991.

——. *The Sublime Object of Ideology*. New York: Verso, 1989.

——. *Tarrying with the Negative: Kant, Hegel, and the Critique of Ideology*. Durham, NC: Duke University Press, 1993.

Zuwerink, Julia R., and Patricia Devine. "Attitude Importance and Resistance to Persuasion: It's Not Just the Thought that Counts." *Journal of Personality and Social Psychology* 70, 5 (1996): 931–944.

INDEX

Printed in the United States
134967LV00001B/94/A